MW00911180

The Last Aloha

The Last Aloha

CLEO FELLERS KOCOL

Copyright © 2015 Cleo Fellers Kocol
All rights reserved.

ISBN: 1514121697
ISBN 13: 9781514121696

Author's Forward

In forty-three years I met and interacted with many people, some I considered good friends. Not all of them are mentioned in my memoir, not because they are in any way lesser than those mentioned, but because their interactions with me did not fit the events that carry this story forward. If I had written everything that happened during those years, it would have taken at least a thousand pages and would have taken years to complete. Of the people mentioned, the following have given me permission to use their names: Dick and Sue Alvord, Barbara Dority, Dorothy Cysewski, Mary Dessein, Betty File, Margaret and Deems Okamoto, Mynga Futrell, Steven Hall for himself and his late wife, Rhonda, Peggy Rozek for her and her late husband Al, Fran Solomon for her and her husband Tyler Folsom, and my writing buddies Louise Crawford and Naida West. It was difficult looking again at another writing buddy's website as Jay MacLarty is no longer alive.

It was also hard to learn while writing this memoir that Karen Beard, my fellow activist in the women's movement, had died. Her family said she remained proud of her activism to her last days. Other women, in the 70's and 80's, so important in the movement to help women, are still involved in bettering society in various ways including Dejah Sherman-Petersen and Joan Schrammack. Others mentioned in the memoir were or are people whose names are recognizable in the public arena, like Gloria Steinem, Sonia Johnson, or Jerzy and Anna Feiner of Poland and the late Issac Asimov and Carl Sagan.

Some people I was not able to contact. I have given them fictional names. I have also given the fictional names of Amy and Paul who have pre-deceased Hank. They remained our friends throughout their lives, Amy outliving Paul. Others, like the people we met in the Soviet Union remain anonymous. I have used fictional names for them, as well as for residents of mainland China. The Americans we encountered on safari in Africa have been disguised and given fictional names, although the events happened as I wrote them. Other names are mentioned throughout the memoir, in, I believe, non-controversial ways. I firmly believe these people would not object to my naming them.

It was emotionally difficult writing this book, but I hope the effort will prove of worth. It is the story of a life made richer through national non-theism, Hank and I becoming part of the growing movement of NONES. I, like Karen, am proud of my actions to improve the lot of all society by improving women's lives. Also, for any religious people who might read this, I must reiterate, I am not against their right to believe, but I am against any attempt to put religion into government. We must maintain separation of church and state. The adventures, the fascinating travel, the accomplishments Hank and I shared gave us a richer life, including his death with dignity. My legal name is Cleo Kocol, but for many years I have chosen to add my maiden name as a tribute to my parents. Thus I am for writing purposes, Cleo Fellers Kocol.

One

*It is pure illusion to think that an opinion that
passes down from century to century, from generation
to generation, may not be entirely false.*

PIERRE BAYLE (1607-1706)

"When I can no longer follow my intellectual pursuits, when I can no longer drive legally, when I start blaming you for my own inabilities, I'll kill myself. That's it."

We were standing on our lanai, twenty-six stories above Honolulu, Hank half-turned to me. He paused, long enough for me to see the remains of our meal on the round table, the chairs we'd pushed back. "I've decided," he said adamantly

Had I heard right? Traffic rushed by below. The trade winds set the palm trees swaying, fronds rattling. That's it? I stared at Hank, but he had looked away. I tried to still my rapidly beating heart and assimilate what he said. He was my husband, my helpmate, my lover, the man I admired more than any other. His unassuming ways hid an intelligence that sparkled. But his memory had deteriorated incrementally, more apparent here away from home. He had forgotten *The Bus* routes, the bus we depended upon during our winter months on the island. He'd gotten lost, and acted in ways that would have been completely incomprehensible if I hadn't known he suffered from dementia. Coming to a reluctant grip with his declaration, I knew this would be our last Aloha. No more would we see Oahu's turquoise seas from the plane as we arrived and left. No more would we set our clocks to the sun's rise and fall. No more could I pretend his dementia would remain static, manageable. My darling was dying, but he'd aged well, his blonde hair a dark sandy shade, his face relatively free of wrinkles, only a sprinkling of gray in his mustache. This winter's hiatus had been two months of worry, not the wondrous winters that had been ours for twelve years. I wanted to beat my breasts like the professional mourners of ancient Egypt, wail and cry, but that wasn't the way of the western world or me.

Below me, people loaded with beach paraphernalia were hurrying toward Waikiki's sandy shores, happy faced, undoubtedly light-hearted. They had made it to the fabled isles, a place I'd never even dreamed of seeing as a child. During the Great Depression, California had been the fantasy location. A real treat, I'd had oranges in my Christmas stocking, and oranges grew like weeds in California.

"How?" I finally asked Hank, bringing myself forcibly to the present, to the man who looked so determined. People I knew didn't take their own lives; it just wasn't done, but he'd just told me he was.

He turned to me, the line between his blue eyes deepening. "How? I'll work it out."

While I was denying Hank's words, memorizing other details as if such a task was necessary, I glanced toward the table where we had eaten vegetables from the local farmer's market, mahi mahi from the sea.

"I'm glad we stayed at the Pavilions again," he said, adding a smile. It was clear he wanted to change the subject. During the past we'd never considered

2

he'd get dementia although his father, grandmother, and uncle all had suffered from it. At that time everyone said it was a part of aging. A few years before Hank's first signs appeared, I had broached the subject with friends, and they had said, "Oh, Hank's too intelligent for that." Few people had real knowledge of the disease. It was a topic no one discussed. I had been only marginally more informed than they. I conceded they had a point.

"I'm glad we stayed here, too." Located on the corner of Kalakaua and Ala Moana, the Pavilions was the first place we'd wintered after Hank retired, quit working for the state of California. We'd rented the condo sight unseen and had been afraid it would have dinky windows and gray walls. But it had been properly tropical – white wicker furniture, sea-foam colored cushions – and best of all, floor-to-ceiling glass windows and a lanai (balcony) framing views of Waikiki. Now, winter weather invaded my mind. Ice, slick and slippery splintered, cracked in a night holding only darkness. He'd said, End it. That meant suicide. That meant final. I tightened my hold on the railing and let in thoughts seldom contemplated.

During my growing up years, suicide had been linked with words like cancer…never spoken above a whisper. Something naughty or forbidden clung to the murmured expressions. Images of suicidal people being wrestled into life filled me with fear. No! There had to be something else, some other way. Surely some medical miracle could stop or arrest this descent Hank was making into ever more frightening senility. Since the first signs, I'd read the literature, talked to people. By now, I wasn't completely illiterate about the subject, I knew even the most intelligent were afflicted, that the brain developed plaques and tangles, that the synapses that had worked for years, were no longer capable. But he had injected a new element into the existing mix, and I didn't know how to deal with it.

Was religion adding to my confusion? Was that why police worked so hard to keep prisoners from slinging a rope over whatever they could and hanging themselves? For years I had accepted that suicide was a terrible thing. Too many times it was an irrational action founded on an emotional problem of the moment. I never asked why society frowned on suicide. But thinking about it now, I wondered why people with mental or physical problems that caused horrendous hurt were denied release. We shot horses that were injured and were suffering and would die in horrible pain otherwise. We put down favorite dogs and cats. But we let people suffer. And yet, as a people, we were not routinely cruel. What was behind such horrendous thinking? It had to be religion. It had permeated our culture until prohibiting suicide had become tradition. No one questioned, few thought beyond what society had said for years.

I glanced toward the ocean, lifted my face to the Trade Winds, and then looked at Hank again. He wore a deep tan, his hair had bleached in the sun; he looked very healthy. He walked, moved, spoke and appeared fine. Below me, cars were stopping for the light at Kalakaua, but little of the scene registered. We had been married thirty-five years. He was as much a part of my life as anything or anyone. I not only enjoyed our life together, I depended upon him. How could I get along without him? I hadn't balanced a checkbook in all that time. He saw that our car was running perfectly. He backed me on whatever I did, complimented me, laughed with me, and only occasionally got angry at me. He was my partner, my companion, my love. The first time we'd come to Hawaii had been on a honeymoon. There had been empty lots between the hotels on Waikiki. Don Ho was in his prime. My mind whirled so rapidly I found myself back in memory to when Hank and I met.

It was 1970 in the glittery, glitzy neon glow of Las Vegas, each of us single after marriages that had gone sour. Although Vegas lived off visitors, high rollers, gamblers and vacationers, residents lived in the sprawling suburbs surrounded by schools, churches, shopping centers, and the university. Most people seldom went to The Strip unless they had out-of- town visitors. But like everyone, I was very much aware of it.

Before I knew Hank Kocol existed, Las Vegas rocked to the sounds of Frank Sinatra and the Rat Pack. I read about Frank and his entourage's shenanigans in the paper, heard about them on radio and television. Glamour

4

and excitement hung in the air, like a gauze curtain, we could see through dimly. We could know so much and no more. Everyone knew when Robert Goulet headlined a show, when Shirley MacLaine cane to town, or whether Shecky Greene's or Mort Sahl's humor was 'knocking them dead.'

Although never part of it, I felt it each day as I drove the back roads toward the psychiatrist's office where I was girl Friday, jack-of-all-trades. A strong urge to do something more than work and stay home inundated me. Beautiful women and handsome men filled the casinos and show rooms. Word was that an unidentified person scanned all visitors when they arrived at McCarran Field. Only the most attractive were let in.

My first marriage had fallen apart when my husband slammed a plate of spaghetti against the wall. A six-pack under his belt and his eyes blinking in a way I had come to hate, I often asked myself why I had held on so long. Always the answer came immediately. Divorce was never the first option. No matter that the kid was being traumatized by his mother's or father's actions, parents had to preserve the family. A child needed both parents. In the home. I was holding on for Steve, my beautiful, intelligent son. It took me a long time to realize holding on could also be insane. I didn't need to sacrifice myself. I had been wedded, not only to Bill, but to what society and family tradition said was appropriate.

Being a single parent was wonderfully freeing, but it wasn't easy keeping food on the table and the mortgage paid. Bill had gone home to California to his natal family, Steve and I lived in the house we had purchased with a boat and a travel trailer as down payment. After Bill stormed out, and I was alone, not part of a couple, my social life was nil. Evenings, sixteen-year-old Steve watched TV, kept the phone busy, or holed up in his room with a school chum. The thought of making a life for myself sent ripples of trepidation up my spine. I'd walked in double harness too long. When a woman friend persuaded me to attend a Glen Campbell concert with her, I almost backed out. She worked at one of the clubs and knew her way around back-stage. After the show at the Fremont Hotel, I felt like Alice in Wonderland following her past a green room, dressing rooms and clusters of almost-famous stars. Although intimidating, getting Campbell's autograph gave me the impetus for more than listening to eight-track tapes and watching television. Cabin fever was overtaking me. When someone addressed me unexpectedly, I jumped. I had to do something to put myself back on an even keel. After twenty-plus years of marriage, I didn't know how to act outside the confines of couplehood.

An advertisement in the Las Vegas Sun stirred my imagination. The idea of meeting other Parents Without Partners propelled me into action. A national organization, PWP had branches in many cities. Heart racing, I drove across town to the next meeting.

Before getting out of my white Ford with the red leather seats, I told myself humans were stupid living in places where one hundred degree weather was the norm. Nervously, I dabbed at the perspiration on my forehead and leaking from under my arms, and walked into that hall. I had to force myself to look at the few people who spoke to me. They all wore casual clothes, and seemed very much at ease chatting to one another. My outfit, which I had stewed over for days, was too dressy. I practically sneaked to a seat in the back of the room. Fifty or so men and women were seated in the hall, and a few members ran the meeting, speaking as if they had done it all their lives, rattling off secretarial notes, treasury figures and introducing the speaker. I felt like a real dud.

A pediatrician explained how to recognize various children's illnesses. I didn't need such advice. Steve was old enough to know when he was ill. But I was too timid to leave early, fearing to attract attention to myself, if my dress and jewelry hadn't already done it. At home again and breathing easier, I read the schedule of the next week's events. Pizza parties, hiking trips, outings to Warm Springs and Red Rock Canyon were scheduled for parents and children. Once a month an outside speaker addressed parental concerns, but discussion groups for parents only were listed. Dancing parties also took place at the Silver Slipper, the Mint, or the Sands.

The next day, before I could think twice, I asked my psychiatrist boss to speak to the group. He agreed, and I called the club's president. When he heard the name, he sounded impressed and scheduled the doctor immediately. No matter that it was like the hot breath of hell outside my swamp-cooled house, I began to feel as if I were living again.

A week later, no longer dressed for a cocktail party and feeling more self-assured, I entered a Coffee & Conversation group. Hank was the first person I saw, and he took my breath away. Not because he was either handsome or ugly, but because his even features, blue eyes, sandy blonde hair, and deep tan held me for he was looking at me with eyes that said he was extremely interested. I needed that. During my marriage to Bill, I'd received scant praise. I had never been a flirt, or let my imagination fix on other men while I was married. Now, I let my imagination soar. I saw instantly that Hank wouldn't tower over me, being of average height. I had always preferred men who appeared less intimidating. I could see Hank and I together. While the group exchanged information about schools and derided, deplored, or applauded the educational system in America, I continued my analysis of him, concluding he was so damn smooth-faced, he had to be out of bounds, far too young for me. Twenty-five at the most. My age echoed like a boxing bell, and he was in the wrong corner. I was forty-three. For the first time I admitted to myself that I wanted a man in my life, but it certainly would not be someone I had to be responsible for, a kid.

Forced by the conversation to look his way, I made my face blank. My family had never said, "You're pretty," and for years I hadn't realized I was. Since Bill and I broke up, I had been aware of glances coming my way, of admiration from men, of sometimes envy from women. Now, I couldn't shut off my hearing. My biological family had always discussed far-flung topics, making me enjoy more than cocktail chitchat. My son, whose genes were dubious, (he'd been adopted) was a quick study, his IQ higher than most people's. I admired intellect. Hank didn't speak a lot, but when he did, his comments made more sense than anyone else's. Everyone listened, including me. Even so, I put him out of my mind.

A month later, I arrived late at a Wine and Wit evening and was forced to sit at the opposite ends of a sofa from Hank. In an attempt to distance myself further, I argued every point he made. The topic about the universe and the universality of people, no matter where they lived, intrigued me, and holding my own against a man who apparently knew what he was talking about gave me a good feeling. People jumped in on all sides of the subject, but soon it was just the two of us. I attempted to make his point of view look juvenile, silly. I couldn't. His intellect soaring, his eyes told me he was enjoying himself and that he enjoyed looking at me. It was heady stuff. I had never met anyone so intellectually stimulating.

When the evening ended, more than a little confused, I rushed out without speaking to him. Away from the neon of the Las Vegas Strip, the sky put on a marvelous display of twinkling stars. The air was soft as velvet, the night a comfortable eighty degrees, no hint of moisture in the air.

I was starting my car when Hank appeared at my open window; no need for air conditioning after dark.

"You made some good points in there," he said leaning his forearms on the window frame. "We really should expand upon them."

He was very persuasive, his words, his tone, his manner of speaking hypnotic. "Anyway, I've been wanting to talk to you ever since you brought the speaker to the monthly meeting. I'd just returned from a camping trip to Canada with my son. He's seven. I was the guy in the doorway who spoke to you when you left the hall."

I didn't remember, but I recalculated his age. With a probable college degree and a seven-year-old son, he was at least late twenties.

"So coffee and a bite to eat?"

I hesitated briefly. The Big Dipper glowed; Orion's Belt showed clearly. How could a sandwich hurt? No matter how young he was, we could be friendly. I certainly didn't want anything more with a man who had a kid, no matter how intelligent the man appeared.

We drove separately to the Showboat Hotel, casino and bowling alley that hosted the nation's top bowlers. People were everywhere, feeding the slots, bowling, eating. While I munched on a bacon, lettuce, and tomato sandwich, Hank told me his seven-year-old boy was home with a sitter. I blurted out Steve's age. "Obviously, he doesn't need a baby-sitter." I waited for a reaction, but Hank didn't bat an eye. Just talked about his work as a physicist. His office was in town, but he was involved with the nuclear test site. He'd grown up in Chicago.

Good heavens, this guy could be as old as thirty. "I grew up in Chagrin Falls, Ohio, a small town. A river runs through the center. A dam on one side of the street, a natural falls on the other…and a triangle with a gazebo smack in the middle of the town."

"Sounds like a Disney movie.'

"Almost. In summer a band played and my extended family came for concerts. They were always with us for holidays, too."

"Our house was the center of family celebrations, too."

I had to smile. "Did you have a kids' table?"

He grinned. "Par for the course." He said it as if it were a bond.

I had dated other men in the club, but none had taken my fancy. They were either hooked on the "wife who got away," the one who died, or were struggling with how to raise four kids. Some were unknowingly misogynistic. They got nowhere near me, for although I didn't understand the word then, I knew when I was being put down. I was reading light feminist magazine literature, and although some of the men I had dated were nice, they were dull. Others were looking for more than I wanted to give. But, darn it, Hank was too young.

One Saturday, my confidence growing weekly, I went to a club in North Las Vegas that other women in PWP called a 'fun place.' For the price of a beer, you could dance to a band, go alone, be sure of dancing partners and go home alone. I loved it. I'd always felt rhythmic, eager to dance my feet off, but Bill had been no dancer. With the '60's, do-your-own thing, I found my-self gliding around the floor like I had taken lessons. Letting the music fill me, I went with it. The spangles on my new dress, fifteen dollars on a sales rack, caught the light and sent shafts sparkling across the floor. Cinderella for sure.

As I danced around the floor, I could hardly believe how a whole new life had evolved, had taken a turn I liked. I had made it happen. For the first time in my life, I was thinking in a different way, too. I wrote about it to my mother who was living out her final months, much sicker than I realized, having termi-nal cancer, a word she never shared. I told her about the man with four kids, about the other guy who got angry when I insisted on going home after an expensive dinner in the sky-room of the Landmark Hotel. She advised me not to get serious about any man who had so many kids and definitely not one who showed his anger on a date. Enjoy yourself, but use common sense, she advised. "And beware of a man who says, God Bless You." She'd grown up without reli-gion and had passed on most of her non church-going attitudes to me.

On the dance floor, but ready to go home before anyone propositioned me, I lingered when Hank showed up, his smile warmer than anyone else's compliments. All evening I'd seldom left the floor, one man after the other helping elevate my confidence. I felt magical, different, younger. Now Hank sent my confidence soaring by taking all the remaining dances. I accused him of paying the other men to back off. Laughing, he said something witty. He adored puns, and until I knew him better, some of them flew over my head. Nimble vocally, he was not really limber on the polished oak. But he knew the steps, and when I went on a tangent of beer-induced extroversion, he stiff-legged along, although strictly in time with the music. Too soon, the band played a Burt Bacharach song with the new beat that trailed off. It was time to leave.

Under a full moon, my white car had a bluish tint, giving it an other-worldly look that seemed perfect. With Hank in lock step with me, the soft air felt even softer. I got behind the wheel, and he leaned his arms on my open window and asked for my telephone number. I wasn't listed, and seldom gave it out. Now the number seemed to rush from my lips.

"Thanks." He straightened.

I'd expected him to whip out a pen, repeat aloud the digits, and record the number, on his sleeve if necessary. "Aren't you going to write it down?"

He laughed. "I'll remember. Numbers are easy. They're my friends."

"Not for me," I admitted. Would I really hear from him? My suspicions, easily aroused, I looked for the worst. But the next day, while I was fixing another cheap hot-dog, macaroni and cheese dinner, he called. Would I go to dinner with him midweek? We could meet at a Chinese place that served more than Chop Suey. He named a neighborhood restaurant away from The Strip. I considered. I wouldn't be fueled by beer and admiration as I swirled around a dance floor, and I'd be in my own car and could leave after dinner. I agreed to meet him.

As soon as I entered the restaurant with its Chinese lanterns and calligraphy on the walls, I spotted Hank. He sat in a red, pseudo-leather booth to the right of the door, and a little boy was with him. His son was blonde and small and wiggly, not sure, I surmised, of this woman who took the seat opposite him. I figured Hank was trying the two of us out, seeing if we got along. My admiration for him rose.

The following Sunday PWP had an outing to Rhyolite, the ghost town 120 miles northwest of Vegas. Nevadans never thought anything of driving hundreds of miles in one day. It was easy to be a lead foot on the semi-deserted highways. In its 1906 hey-day, Rhyolite had fifty saloons and several gambling halls. Hank suggested I car pool with him.

That day little Henry sat between us, sharing my seatbelt and appearing to enjoy the intimacy. I liked it, too. The wiggly little boy I'd first seen hardly moved. By this time Steve had celebrated his seventeenth birthday, and the thought of being Mama's chaperone held no charms, although he was wise enough not to say so. He had gone to Lake Mead with his friends, the lake that backs up Boulder Dam a favorite place for water sports, swimming, fishing, boating and camping.

But now we were surrounded by desert. Still, crumbling sidewalks and masonry couldn't hide Rhyolits's past. Tramping around the perimeter of the ghost town, my imagination populated it with people. A bonus was seeing a house made almost entirely from beer bottles. Enjoying myself, I blurted, "There must have been a hot time in the old town every night."

Hank laughed as if I'd said something clever. He was always at my side, making jokes, explaining history. He laughed with evident amusement as his son tapped a tarantula on the path ahead of us with a stick until it entered a mason jar. Quickly, the little boy slammed the lid. Watching, I shivered but had to laugh. The furry-legged creature could hardly escape.

With other PWP members we picnicked off a tablecloth I'd brought. Hank added my deviled eggs and spice cake to his salami sandwiches, apples, potato chips, and lemonade. As the others spread out their food, he handed me a plate and hovered over me in a way no one could mistake.

Pretending not to notice, I looked off to where the rubble and half walls ended in a sprinkling of sagebrush. If we continued west we'd end in the white hot heat of Death Valley. I swallowed and wanted to say Hank presumed. But had he? I had almost quit thinking of his age. Back in Vegas I didn't object when he kissed me at my front door. Still, I hardly slept that night. What did this man/woman thing really mean, where was it leading?

As the sun hit my bedroom windows, I'd almost come to a decision. Women were moving away from old roles, doing things they'd never done before. Hadn't I been aware of that when I'd said enough and divorced Bill? The attorney said I'd been deserted, and in one way that was true. That Bill also left me with bills I was struggling to pay, his family most likely didn't know. That they didn't bother to contact me, hear my side of whatever Bill was saying, hurt. It was time I had some fun. It didn't have to be until death do you part. That I still needed to suppress society's pressure, its do's and don'ts eluded me, but I had no sticky religious beliefs holding me back, so I determined to find out Hank's thinking. He certainly wasn't running off to church on Sundays.

Starting that day, Hank and I "talked up a storm," addressing some subjects I'd never thought of before. He didn't hold the Jews responsible for Christ's death, as many Catholics with his upbringing did. I'd never thought of it before. No he didn't care if the Adventists called Saturday Sunday or whatever. I was learning a lot about him, but not all. His parents had been political opposites. As a consequence he tended to call himself an Independent and made me examine my often knee jerk reactions. I liked that very much.

We ate in the swankiest restaurants on the Strip and danced at the top of the Landmark, the Mint, and the Dunes, the city a sparkling fairyland below us, toy cars seemingly navigating the Strip or Fremont Street, the myriad lights turning night into day. With the boys in tow, we went to the all-you-can-eat champagne brunches at the Sahara, the Frontier, and Caesar's Palace. I loved relaxing while sipping champagne and dipping strawberries in chocolate while

Steve filled his plate with eggs benedict and ham and Hank's son went for blintzes and said they were almost as good as "Daddy's." Hank declared he had the makings of a diplomat. The good feelings generated held me the rest of the day and into the following week. Soon, no other man in PWP asked me out. Hank and I had become a recognized couple.

My feelings for him went from like, to like very much. By Halloween I was debating in my mind the word, 'love.' While kids ran door-to-door trick or treating, Hank dropped Henry off at the Hilton Hotel nursery. He'd pick him up in the morning. "Henry will have a ball. They put on quite a party for the kids." He looked at me. "And we can celebrate Nevada Admissions Day."

"What?"

"The day in 1865 when Nevada quit being a territory and became a state."

I had to smile. He was the only person I knew who dropped innuendo into a conversation with history as its marker. I was positively intrigued.

Hank mentioned Nevada Admissions Day several times that night as we danced to a Glen Miller style band, drank Rum Manhattans, and sat side by side in between dances, The Strip glittering below us. When we saw a couple we knew, we said we were celebrating.

"You celebrating Halloween? It hardly seems your style," the man said looking down from his superior height. He had acted bored the one time we had all been at a PWP discussion group where Hank had again been the most knowledgeable.

"No, Nevada Admissions Day," we both said, and Hank added that Lincoln had needed another state on his side for reelection. And as a president fighting a war, he didn't mind adding a state that was knee deep in silver, the Comstock Lode adding millions of dollars to the economy.

"Shit, I've lived here my whole life, and I never heard that," our acquaintance said, almost wrinkling his nose. "You some kind of walking encyclopedia?"

Hank shrugged as if shrugging it off. If it had been Bill the two men would have been exchanging verbal insults if not blows. I was impressed.

After the two left the sky room, Hank said, "When I'm with you, it's always a celebration."

He was laying it on thick, but Bill had been exceedingly spare with compliments, and Hank had me feeling lovely and loved, even if neither of us had used the word.

After we left the hotel, I said, "No matter that our friend was a jerk, you really are well informed."

"So I fooled you, too." He winked at me.

We both laughed. The car radio was purring the Carpenters' "We've only just begun" as I watched familiar streets blur by. When he turned onto a street I didn't recognize, I asked, "Where are we?" Dim light shone from California bungalows, all looking alike in the dark.

"I live in the next block. I got a smaller place after my wife and I split."

I said nothing.

"Unless you prefer I drive you home now." He glanced at me.

We had been moving toward this night from the first, and I knew it. I shook my head.

We walked arm in arm from his driveway into the house. Neon light oozed from The Strip, the neighbors were playing their television loud, but nothing existed except the two of us, and we were passing through rooms to the master suite. Subdued light shone in from the high window over the bed, and contributed to the romance of the night, Hank's sweet words, our passion, the giving and taking that soared up and up to a place that left us both with perpetual smiles.

The air conditioner hummed background music as we talked feverishly between bouts of sensuous pleasure. Tripping over one another's words, we laughed often, presenting our lives in chunks to be assimilated later.

He talked about his parents, his sisters, his upbringing.

By now I knew he wasn't a practicing Catholic, but I knew few details of his religious life. As the moon disappeared from view, he showed me his family album,   and I heard about his Polish/Catholic formative years. Catholic schools, Catholic customs. The words hung around me like dark symbols knotting my stomach temporarily

Daylight was touching rooftops when I repeated my church summer-school experience, my closest brush with religion as a child. Sundays in my family had always been a day of rest, of family fun, encompassing big dinners and day-long games. No church. Religion was a word I never heard. Atheist was a word I never heard either.

The summer after I finished first grade, my best friend, Betty, was going to a summer Bible school. I wasn't quite sure what that was, but I wanted to be with her. My parents relented after I begged and begged. For two weeks, at the church school I munched cookies and other goodies, and gazed at photographs of poor Mexican children, their clothing ragged, their faces sober, their homes no better than shacks. I related.

My first four years I had been a little princess, pampered, having everything, including dolls as big as me. Today, the big house where we lived remains shadowy in my mind, but the stairs that swept in an arc to the second floor, stays the same. My brother and I used to play on them, building houses with blocks and cards. And then we moved, and all that had been so embracing dissolved in a twinkling.

The new house had no grand staircase. The floors canted, and the rooms were smaller than anything I had ever seen. Worst of all, my parents had little time for me. I grew subdued, my bubbly nature in remission. As I got older, I realized we'd been victims of the stock market crash of '29, In 1931 we moved from an upscale address, to Chagrin Falls, a picture-pretty village with normal-sized houses and a few smaller ones. Dad had held on as long as possible

The house that everyone wanted to forget later on, came rent-free because Dad did odd jobs for the owner, a friend who used to go with him to the race tracks. It was a come down for Dad as well as mother who had never lived without. We endured that place with the spidery basement a year before Dad scratched together enough money to move us into a solidly middle-class house.

At the summer school, religion certainly must have been mentioned, but it never got my attention, just flew right over my head. But going from privileged to poor to middle class, I was primed to help the Mexican children. My sympathy knew no bounds. The last day of school we'd entertain parents and staff, and bring pennies to send to the Mexican boys and girls. I had nine pennies and hoped to get another so I could take ten.

The day of the party, Mother brought out my very best dress and was ready to pop the crepe de chine creation over my head when I cried out, "We're supposed to be Mexican kids." Although I loved the ribbons and pleats

17

of the pink dress, I knew it wasn't what Mexican kids wore. I'd seen the photographs.

Mother said, "Believe me, every girl will be wearing her best."

"I don't care," I insisted, shaking my head until my wavy blonde hair danced from side to side. I took my plainest cotton, unadorned dress from the closet.

Mother said nothing more. I ran ahead of her to the party and came to a halt when I entered the recreation room at the church. All the other girls wore their frilliest best.

Miserable, but too shy to say anything, I sat quietly, my mind seething, glad mother sat nearby. How come I hadn't realized the other kids wouldn't follow directions? Was it because they used words *like hunky, polock, spic*, and *nigger*, and I never did? When we were still in the big house I had a doll with a black head on one end and a white head on the other, and I'd loved them both. I also loved books, that took me to far places.

The day of the church school party, the other kids were thanking God that they were able to help the Mexican children. I knew God had nothing to do with my crepe de chine dress. Did this God help certain kids and not others? I asked Mother about him. She said some people believed there was one, some didn't. The believers went to church.

After summer bible school, Betty tried to get me to go to Sunday school with her. I declined. I loved our family Sundays. The next week when I went to her house to play, her mother told me Betty couldn't play. Later I saw her with her new "best friend." In the meantime, Mother's friend and neighbor added to the mystery. When I asked her about God, she said, "I never gave the old guy any thought." She and her family stayed home on Sundays, too.

Hank seemed to understand what I was saying about my childhood experiences. His family had never achieved affluence; his father was a cook, his mother, like mine, was a homemaker. My father died a few years before I met Hank, but my family and Hank's were so average it made us both smile. We'd grown up – he in Illinois, me in Ohio – experiencing the wind whipping off the Great Lakes, rainstorms in the summer, snow and sleet in the winter. We were so much in love that we counted our Midwest backgrounds as another one of the things drawing us together.

But in bright sun morning, the present pushed in hard. With a full sun battering the windows, guilt rode me like a horse set to buck me off. Morning sprinklers were no longer hissing, the wet grass was steaming, baking, neighbors were bringing in newspapers. Last night when Hank and I were declaring our love, had Steve knocked on my bedroom door, discovered I wasn't home? Been alarmed? Tried to call someone, or maybe the police? My mind made wild circuits. "I need to go home," I said flatly.

Hank frowned. "What is it, what's wrong?"

I sat at the kitchen table like a queen to be waited on. He was getting down flour, pulling eggs from the refrigerator, preparing a Polish version of French crepes. He stopped long enough to look at me.

I told him my fears. "Steve. How can I explain staying out all night?"

He smiled. "He's seventeen?" He started mixing the batter.

"Yes."

Again he paused to look at me, his smile a bit broader. "He was probably out late and tiptoed in so he didn't wake you." He grinned.

I sighed. "You're probably right." It did seem as if he were growing up too fast. Still getting out of Hank's car in broad daylight and sneaking into the house wasn't something I looked forward to doing. "But what if you're wrong? I can hardly say, your mother was out all night."

This time he met my gaze straight on. "Tell him we're getting married."

I gasped. His blue eyes were shining brighter than the neon on The Strip. If this was a proposal of marriage, was that what I wanted? I had known him one summer and fall. Winter, when heaters were turned on, was approaching.

"I want to marry you, Cleo." No smile; eyes entreating, he was dead serious.

I looked away. I needed time to think. Was compatibility in bed and friendship and admiration a rock upon which to plan a marriage? Once I'd been told a woman's future was tied to a man. But I'd had that, and it hadn't worked. "I need time."

He said he understood about apprehensions. He'd been married three years, been a single dad for four. He'd not taken any of those actions lightly. After breakfast, he drove me home.

None of the neighbors were in their yards when I entered the house through the back door, and Steve was still sleeping.

For a week I mulled the future. Hank stopped calling when I asked him to. "But you have to promise to meet me at the end of the week."

I promised. No matter what I decided, I owed him that.

Seven days later, Hank was waiting in the dimly lit, almost empty bar I'd chosen for the meeting. I needed anonymity. I needed a place where no one could see me turn red or see tears in my eyes. I needed a place where we'd never been before.

For a while we talked about the day. He was planning to write a peer review article about the tritium samples that he was radiating. By now I knew he had been to Loyola and Purdue. I said I had been busy typing a report that the doctor was submitting in a murder trial where he would be appearing as an expert witness. He nodded rather superficially, I thought. I could see Hank was as nervous as I was. All the previous week he'd called to say goodnight, nothing more, his voice as beguiling as it had been when he'd said he loved me.

He ordered a Manhattan; I decided on a cream sherry. The bartender put the glasses m in front of us. I sipped before blurting out, "I have something to show you." I may have been free of religion, but society's dictates were still strong. I opened my purse, and began to go through it looking for my leather wallet bought in Tijuana years ago. It was the only time I'd been out of the country. It was tooled elaborately and I had used it ever since I had talked the seller down to three dollars. The damned thing seemed to have disappeared. With Hank watching silently, I pulled out comb and compact, lipstick and odds and ends of tissues, plus a small book of telephone numbers. I put them and my keys and the keys for the doctor's office on the table and not hiding my disgust at even this simple task suddenly giving me problems, I finally located my wallet.

Hank said nothing.

Sighing, I handed the wallet across the table to him, open to my driver's license. Back ground music was shivering up my spine, something about a little bird flying away. That's how I felt.

"You want me to look at your driver's license?" His tone was even.

Damn it, show some passion! This isn't easy. "I want you to know my age."

"I think I do."

"Without looking?" My voice sounded foreign to me.

"I don't need to look. I did the math from all the things you've said." He leaned across the table. "Incidentally, I'm thirty-three." He was smiling, not only with his mouth. His eyes were shedding light hotter than the temperature outside.

I refused to be seduced. "And I'm ten years older." There I had said it. Every woman I knew was younger than her husband. Two years, five years, ten. It was like an unwritten law. My kid was probably buying condoms, making out in the back seat of a car. Hank's son was telling me stories about recess and the kids he liked and didn't like. He looked at me in a way that said his father had talked to him about me. He called me Mrs. Hall.

"So?" Hank's voice was like silk. I wanted to wrap myself in it, forget all talk.

"So, in seven years I'll be fifty." It had a horrible ring. Fifty was the entrance to old lady-hood. I glanced over at the bar, my mouth a straight line, my teeth locked together. Was anyone listening? The bartender appeared to be deep into polishing glasses, glancing up at the television screen now and then. No one else was in the place. I looked back at Hank.

"So in seven years I'll be forty." Hank smiled and held my gaze.

Even in the grayish light, with the winking red of the beer sign behind the bar, I could see he was amused, but in a gentle way that impressed me. "Okay, I'm being slightly idiotic, but I know how some people can react." All the people I know.

"So what? Don't you know you don't look a day older than me? You're beautiful."

My mouth fell open. Bill had never called me beautiful. During those last years, I'd come home from work determined to make Bill notice me. "Here she is, Mrs. America," I'd cry coming in the door. He'd be in his re-cliner, a beer can in hand and seldom replied. The last time I tried it, he said, "What have you got to be so god-damned happy about?" I never tried that tack again. Now my face was breaking into a smile and I pulled myself into the present. "You look twenty-five." Some of the cool I had slowly been acquiring took hold. I added a half grin.

"So do you." He winked.

We both had to laugh.

He reached across and took my hand. "Anyway, why does any of that matter? What matters is you and me. How we feel about each other. You know I love you, and I think you love me."

I could not say he was wrong. I wanted to throw myself into his arms, but the table stood between us, and I was too 'shook' to jump up and go sit next to him. I was still concerned with what other people thought. At that moment it was the bartender.

Slowly Hank began laying out the life we would have. First a short hon-eymoon in San Diego and then later when his schedule allowed it, we'd go to

Hawaii for a real honeymoon. "Travel's always been a priority for me, starting on a driving trip from Chicago to the west coast with my parents when I was thirteen. How about you?"

I told him I'd been enamored with the west, ever since I'd read western novels as a kid. California and the gold rush had fascinated me especially. Oh, yes, I wanted to travel, but did I want to chance marriage again? With Bill I had been drawn in, not by his intellect, but by his appearance. His Marlboro man look personified "old west." I'd barely arrived on the West Coast and thought I was marrying the man of my dreams when I married him. Now, I looked across the table to Hank. "I met the old west face first with Bill and got taken in. I don't want to repeat my first travel adventure"

"I'm hardly a carbon copy of your first husband."

I had to lower my gaze. "Sorry." Bill had chased me from the first, his soft, polite, words intoxicating. He called all women ma'am. He drove fast and flew his father's plane, buzzing my family's house.

To my Midwestern eyes, Bill's father's ranch seemed like a small village, and his father treated me like a piece of rare china. He looked like a Hollywood star, scarf tucked into the neck of his shirts. That was heady stuff. I finally agreed to Bill's proposal of marriage, and scales fell from my eyes, beginning with the honeymoon, although I buried the knowledge deep.

High in the Sierra Nevada mountains, the crackle of a campfire, the crack of footsteps broke the silence of that long ago night. I looked past the Sugar Pines silhouetted in the dark. Two of Bill's buddies had stumbled into our camp, and Bill spent the evening swapping hunting exploits with them, never mentioning our wedding the day before. As the coals began to burn down, I blurted out, "We're on our honeymoon." The men left immediately, but the romantic evening I'd fantasized never happened. But that was over twenty years ago and had nothing to do with Hank.

We agreed on a small wedding, just the boys and witnesses. But where? I wanted nothing to do with the chapels that had sprung up in Nevada for quickie weddings, sometimes after a quickie six-week divorce. Neither did I like the thought of having a justice of the peace or a county clerk marrying us. In my family, that was tantamount to elopement, which had a ring seldom sanctioned. But Hank had gone to Catholic schools, been an altar boy. I had trouble contemplating a wedding officiated by a Roman Catholic priest. In my teen years, when I'd encountered forms, I'd just written protestant.

But were my family and I protestant? If so, wouldn't we have gone to church sometime? At one point years ago my mother explained our town was almost 100% Anglo-Saxon, protestant. Even though religion was never mentioned at home, I needed to play it safe, say I was protestant, too, if asked. Only Aunt Kate attended church, but she went in order to socialize with the social elites. My older sisters used to go on Easter so they could show-off their new clothes.

I was uneasy even thinking about a priest presiding. My father's German Catholic background had soured me. He'd left the church at age eleven. At a parish hall card game, he and a grown man had tied for first place. The priest had them cut cards to determine the winner. My father drew an ace, the man a lesser card. The priest declared the ace was the lowest card in the deck and Dad lost. He told himself the priest was a hypocrite, not really following the Christianity he preached. He began thinking through all religion at that time. I told Hank, "I hope some portion of your former religious beliefs hasn't stuck to you and you want a Catholic wedding."

He shook his head, amusement glittering his eyes.. "No problem. Have you forgotten, I went to college with the Jesuits? And I don't send Henry to church either. "

"What does that mean?" I frowned, not ready for guessing games.

"The Jesuits made me think. I just went one step beyond them."

I took a deep breath, my eyes opening wide. "You mean you're completely free of Catholicism?"

"Have you seen me going to mass?"

"No."

"Have you heard me say I was religious?"

"No."

"You have your answer. Once I started to think, I thought myself right out of the Catholic Church and religion of all kinds. It's all based on a belief system thought up by men and kept alive by their need for power and money. Science begins with questions. Religion begins with major premises that have be accepted." He paused and then said, his mouth in a slight smile. "I'm a scientist who at this time is questioning you."

It was enough for me.

A Methodist minister advertised non-denominational ceremonies in a small chapel. There would be no sermon, no scripture, and Jesus Christ was to be mentioned once only. We discussed what we read and came to the conclusion it would be a good compromise. Even my parents had been married by a religiously nominal minister whose wife had invited them to dinner after the brief ceremony. The minister and his wife were so poor, no organized church wanting him to preach, that Mother and Dad had to share a knife.

I relaxed. As a child I'd asked mother about Jesus and she'd said as far as she knew he was just a good man. The resurrection and all those miracles were made up in order to make him seem more important than he was. That probably someone named Jesus lived, but maybe not. I told my assumptions to Hank and he said if Jesus Christ had existed, he had probably been a hippie type, not really condoned by the main stream. It was a popular thought at the time. People were living in communes, women wearing granny dresses, men sporting beards.

We reserved a ten AM slot with the minister for January 8, 1971. Hank would tell his parents after the fact; otherwise his mother would want a big wedding. I would have liked my mother to be present, but her illness had progressed. She couldn't leave home. But her letters were uplifting, telling me that she was happy for me, that Hank sounded fine, and my life should be a good one. "Anyone who sees through faith-based thinking has more than one thing going for him, I'm sure." I had never heard her say anything so to the point about religion before.

That night I told Steve I was getting married. He was nearing the end of his high school years, dating a girl he seemed besotted with. After I finished talking, throwing out detail after detail in my enthusiasm, I noticed he wasn't smiling but actually frowning. I paused. "What?" The neighbor's dog was barking. "Up, up and Away," purred from my 8-track player.

"What 'what'?" His head was high, his eyes unreadable.

"You seem so…." I searched for the right word, "disinterested."

"Mom, it's your life, not mine."

"Well, yes." Maybe he had a point. Why should he be ecstatic about our planned champagne breakfast? Or that in San Diego we'd be staying in a hotel that had chandeliers in the elevators? I told him the date and time of the ceremony, told him to wear a shirt, tie, and sport jacket.

Steve nodded and said he'd be late for work if he didn't leave soon. I imagined him suppressing the words, "Mom, I know how to dress."

We didn't talk again except superficially until the day before the wedding. I had the day off and was going through old papers, kitchen supplies, and bedding, sorting and discarding, packing things for storage when Steve came home from school.

"So what's going on?" With one hand on the doorframe to the hall, he struck a jaunty pose. I could see why he was popular with the girls at school. He was at that slim-hipped, broad-shouldered stage that some high-school boys achieve, and as always his eyes sparkled.

I told him after the wedding we'd all live at Hank's because his house was larger. I didn't add that I wanted to get away from the place where Bill and I had split, where the very walls contained unpleasant memories.

He straightened. "What about our house?" During those rocky final days with Bill, Steve had helped do things Bill should have. I'd bought the house trailer we'd used purchasing the Las Vegas house, with money I'd saved, fifty cents here, a dollar there. The inside had smelled of fried food and smelly socks. The walls were grimy. Steve and I had cleaned it, painted it and made it useable. He had helped me often.

"I plan to sell the house." The money would pay off many of the debts Bill had left behind when he stormed out of the house and out of our lives.

For a while Steve said nothing. Someone shouted at the barking dog. I glanced out to the back yard where the inflatable swimming pool had helped soothe my growing unhappiness. Two old nectarine trees gave ample shade. The clothes line was testament to how I'd pinched pennies as Bill let dollars fly through his fingers. I'd never owned a clothes dryer.

"You putting the furniture in storage, too?" Steve's face was sober, no ghost of a smile, no on purpose jauntiness like I'd seen at Thanksgiving when Hank and I had entertained several members of PWP. One of the women, having more money than sense, had hit on Steve. I'd had to tell her his age.

"I'll sell some of it. We'll keep the sectional sofa, of course." When I'd bought it, before his father left, Steve had been so happy with the purchase, he'd moved the pieces around, joking about it until we were both satisfied with its placement in the living room. Now Steve wasn't even smiling.

Abruptly he said, "Can I have Dad's recliner?"

His confrontational tone startled me. "What do you mean?"

"I want to give it to him."

"If he had wanted it, he could have taken it with him."

"Maybe not."

"What?" He didn't know a thing about that last night or the following morning. He'd been in school when I woke Bill and handed him a suitcase packed with his clothes. Bill had left with little argument. I thought he was ashamed at how he'd acted the night before. Later, I learned he'd embezzled money from his boss. It was a small amount, but they wanted it back. His mother paid the bill for him. Now, it seemed as if Steve sided with his father. I said. "I guess I should have told you."

"Mom, leave it alone. Anyway, I have a ride to California tomorrow. I'm going down to see Dad and taking the chair with me."

I stared at him blankly. "You won't be at the wedding." The flat statement was encased in ice. For all of the twelve years he'd been my son, I'd adored him. I'd wanted to share my new-found happiness, but had I neglected him during the last few months? The thought sent a stitch racing through my chest. I wanted to blurt out, I'm sorry, I'm sorry. But for what? It hardly mattered for Steve was already out the door.

The wedding and wedding breakfast went by too fast, the best part being when little Henry asked, "Are you sure the wedding's legal, I didn't get to speak?" Astounded, I said, 'What would you have said?"

"That I wanted Mrs. Hall to live with us."

His interest helped lessen the pain of Steve's apparent disapproval, and I could enjoy the eggs benedict, champagne brunch at the Copper Cart on the Strip. Hank and I packed four days of memorable moments in San Diego before returning to Vegas.

Steve was already back. He said nothing about his father, and I didn't ask, not wanting to upset the uneasy balance we were achieving. Steve was almost his old self again as we settled in at Hank's house. I watched proudly as Steve played ball with Henry and helped him with homework. I loved the feel of family I thought was emerging. Without saying anything to me, Hank put Steve on his health insurance plan. During the years Steve had suffered from tonsillitis, and now we had his tonsils removed, and once again I had the chance to baby him, feeding him ice cream and hovering over him.

My beloved mother died nine days after Hank and I married. I'd adored her and felt bereft, caught between two conflicting emotions, happiness with Hank and an overwhelming sense of loss. I'd been existing on a plane slightly above the earth. Suddenly I hit bottom. Without Hank, I would have had a hard time handling it. I asked my brother and sisters not to make any plans about mother's burial until I arrived in San Jose, California, where she and dad had spent their last years. My siblings promised to wait.

When we pulled up in front of the California rambler where I'd visited Mom and Dad through the years, it appeared little changed. For a few seconds I felt as if I could go in and find them both there, Dad ready to show me his vegetable garden, the gazebo he'd built, the little touches that made his yard unique, Mother in the kitchen taking a pie from the oven. But they were both gone, and my brother and sisters were waiting in the front room. Through the years they had seen non-believing relatives buried by Christian ministers. It was the accepted way of doing, getting the nearest local theologian who was protestant. They were all set to hire one. I said mother would not have wanted a Christian burial. I was adamant as well as erudite. I recalled for them the various talks Mother and I had had through the years.

"So we have nothing," someone said.

"I suppose," I said, knowing only Mother would not like a Christian ceremony.

"If we don't have a funeral, that's what we'll get. I don't think Mother would want that," my younger sister said.

Probably, she was right on that point. Like so many women her age, except for not going to church, Mother had gone along with tradition, whether she believed in it or not.

During that week disposing of her belongings, I couldn't understand why none of the extended family came by except for my brother's daughter, Melanie. Now, I realize people didn't know how to react. Some sort of gathering is needed when non-theists die. Family and friends need a mutual grieving process, people should have time to laud the deceased, show photos, recall happy times and know that others were thinking similar things about the deceased. Mother would have liked that part. (Through the years I learned to know and love Melanie, who eventually became part of my family.)

It was hard dismantling the house, but we were grateful we had no papers to sort. Mother, who had a sense of personal privacy as well as a desire not to burden anyone with something she could do, had done everything possible before she died. My brother, Leon, Melanie's father, took care of the rest.

Back in Las Vegas, I grieved alone although Hank helped by being extremely understanding. I dropped out of the Spanish class I was taking. I had enough to deal with. I didn't need to learn Spanish grammar. Because he got home from work before me, when I arrived Hank had grilled steaks, baked potatoes and a vegetable going. I slapped together a salad, and dinner was ready. Steve ate with us more often than not. In a short time, I regained my equilibrium.

In March, Hank announced we'd go to Hawaii in April. Steve agreed to look after Henry as we honeymooned in the islands. I arranged for time off from work and went to the local Polynesian shop. The designer's idea of an island wardrobe did not resemble missionary style Hawaiian gowns. Figure flattering, long or mini length, the new dresses were decidedly tropical in flavor and extremely flattering. I left Las Vegas in a cloud of euphoria.

My Cinderella feeling expanded our first night on Kauai. I felt as if my life had been touched with a magic wand as I watched a young man in a loin cloth run along the beach, lighting tiki torches as he passed. A recorded voice told the story of King Kamehameha and transported me completely. I could hardly wait to show Steve and Henry the pictures we'd taken as we toured all the islands, finding something thrilling, educational, and mind-boggling on each. I was walking on rarefied air.

And then we were home, and I was suddenly speechless. Steve had had the use of my white Ford while we were gone. Now the car sat on the side of a highway and needed to be towed in. The mechanic Hank consulted cited multiple problems. "Was me, I'd junk it."

I was stunned.

Hank agreed there was no use pouring money into it.

That night, at home, before Hank could ask the question that un-doubtedly was nagging him, I asked Steve quietly, my heart racing, my cheeks hot. "Where was Henry while you were running around in my car?"

A hurt expression crossed Steve's face and he got up from his chair. Hank and I were already standing. "He was with me, of course. I wouldn't leave him home alone."

"But you could take him with you while you wrecked your Mom's car. A blessing no one got hurt." Hank glanced toward Henry. "So you went riding around with Steve."

Henry, the only one seated, looked as if he'd rather take a licking than speak. His eyes darted from his father to Steve and back.

"So? I asked you a question."

Henry nodded. "I was with Steve and his friends. They smoked cigarettes and drank beer."

"And drank beer," Hank repeated. "Were they smoking real cigarettes or pot?"

"Real cigarettes," Henry said. "I saw the packs."

When Steve didn't deny any of it, Hank turned to him. "While you are under my roof, you follow my rules. Right now you're grounded. Later when you show you're sorry for what you did, I want you home at midnight." He turned to me. "You agree?"

"Yes."

Steve muttered he was sorry. Said, he agreed. But as the weeks flew by, I felt an uneasy truce was in play, .

Spring moved into summer, Hank and other members of PWP who had married, organized PWP Alumnae. We all got together for social events. It was a good time, one I could see going on forever. One day I was marinating steaks for a cookout with the bunch when Hank told me he was wanted back in Washington. We would move to D.C.

The idea of living in or near the nation's capital intrigued me. Henry was visiting his mother and grandparents in Chicago, Steve seemed to have settled in with us when Hank explained we would take a house-hunting trip to Washington

Dressed in our finest – everyone dressed to the nines for airline flights in those days – we flew first to Chicago. Hank's mother, father, sisters, two brothers-in-law and two children greeted us at O'Hare airport. I was really impressed; I'd expected only his parents. His father an older version of Hank, his mother a petite blonde, his sisters also petite and blonde, some of it bottle, some real, all had smiles of welcome.

For the first time I was not the shortest person around. I was at least two inches taller than any of the women, and best of all, they treated me as if I were special. That meant more than anything else. Loss had taken hold deep in my mind. With Mother and Dad dead, the center of my natal family gone, I seldom heard from my siblings. In Chicago, observing the laughter, the jokes, the rapid-fire exchanges between Hank and his sisters, the respect accorded his parents, I felt as if I was gaining a new family.

In Washington, Hank took me on a tour of the nation's capital, me high on new beginnings. "They took me right in," I repeated several times, referring to his family. Hank explained about Polish traditions. He said accepting a new member was the Polish way. My high stayed as we ran starry-eyed around Washington, D.C., Hank snapping my picture at least a hundred times. All the time a realtor had been working for us. In the Virginia suburbs, we located a three bedroom, two bath house, signed papers, put down a down payment, and returned to Las Vegas in a perpetual glow.

I turned in my resignation at work and began to plan for the future. Now that high school was over, Steve was working full time as a bus boy at the Sahara Hotel. In Virginia, he could go to college, become an engineer like Bill and I had advised, or whatever he wished. The day before we left, the moving van with Hank's and my combined household belongings already on its way, Steve told me he wasn't going.

Astounded, I blurted, "Why, not?" A sprinkler hissed over the small lawn, the air conditioner hummed, Ravel's Bolero boomed from the record player Hank had put together in college. I could see Steve doing something similar, he had always been good with his hands. But lately, I had to admit things between us were deteriorating. He violated the midnight curfew more often than not, and as much as I wanted to believe his explanations, I couldn't completely. "Because you'll have to follow rules?" After all, Hank would be putting him through college.

"Mom, I have nothing against Hank. I just don't want to go."

It was late July. In a few days, August 5th, he'd turn eighteen. I could hardly force him. "But what will you do?"

"I'm moving in with a friend."

"But…" Because of the trauma of the first five years of his life, was he blaming me for Bill and I breaking up? Didn't he know I'd walk through hot coals for him? Irrational thoughts like kidnapping him flew temporarily through my mind. The wonderful future I envisioned for him was evaporating faster than water from the sprinklers.

"It's just too soon, Mom. Please, I don't want to talk about it."

I took a deep breath. "Well, maybe you can come later, when summer ends." My words sounded lame, as crippled as I felt. I'd send him transportation money, meet him at the airport, enroll him to William and Mary, whatever. But would it happen, I wondered as we drove out of Las Vegas and into the rest of our lives.

Two

"Man is neither an angel nor a brute, and the very attempt to raise him to the level of the former sinks him to the latter."

BLAISE PASCAL (1623 TO 1662)

As Hank and I traveled a southwest route east, it reminded me of my first cross-country trip. World War II had abruptly ended. Americans danced in the streets. No more gas, sugar, and shoe rationing. No more worrying about men at the front. My mother took the card with the star, showing she had a son in the service, from her front window. My brother came home from Europe; neighbors arrived from the Pacific. During the war, my sister, Mavis, and her husband had gone to California to help build ships. Dick had been one of the last Americans to suffer polio, including time in an iron lung. The military hadn't wanted him, although he would eventually recuperate fully.

Throughout the war Mavis had written about California towns with Spanish names, about scenery that encompassed desert, mountains and seashores. About no snow. Winter was whistling around the corners of the house when she arrived in Ohio with tales of balmy weather. The day Dad picked her up at the train station he backed into a snow bank and had to dig out. That incident had Dad questioning Mavis minutely. Before she returned to California, he announced he and Mother were moving west. Those old enough to be on their own could go or stay.

In 1946, I couldn't contemplate living without my parents. I had been working for the Navy Department in Cleveland, but with the war over, things were winding down. I resigned and it was decided, I would ride west with Lenore, my oldest sister, her husband Ed, and their children. The others would travel west with Mother and Dad.

Heading for California in his big old Chrysler Air Flow, Dad never looked back. Mom feared she'd never see her Ohio relatives and friends again. California was like the end of the world. But it was an adventure I looked forward to. I was going to the west of my childhood dreams!

Despite long hours in the car, pulling a trailer with Lenore's china, silver candlesticks and whatever else she prized, didn't dampen my enthusiasm. From the width of the Mississippi River, to every conceivable historic site, I was enthralled. The wide-open spaces of the prairie, wind ruffling the grasses, all held their own fascination. I imagined the wagon trains, the Indians, Lewis and Clark.

We added a flat tire to the hundreds along the route bordering the shores of the waters of the Great Salt Lake Desert, the white glare not dampening my spirits.

Highway 40, a two-lane road, led over the Sierra Nevada Mountains. Sheer drop-offs, tree tops dwindling away below, had me sitting on the edge of my seat in awe. At times I could not see to the bottom.

As we rounded one hairpin turn after the other, Lenore's voice shook. "Slow down, Ed, I mean it." A film of sweat rode her forehead as we left the tree line, her curly hair curlier. Granite cliffs and boulders rose majestically above us, and we kept climbing higher.

Ed said, "I'm going as slow as possible."

Lenore whispered, "Oh my, I don't think so."

Turning around a switchback, we came face to face with a truck dwarfing Ed's Chevrolet. He steered closer to the edge, the bottomless slope opening up below us. The gentle hills of Ohio hadn't prepared us. No grass, no dirt, nothing showed between us and the bottom. Lenore whispered, "Oh, God help us, please, God, please."

I had never heard anyone pray or call to God before, if that was praying. During family dinners, sometimes Ed would say, his eyes shining with humor, "Bless the food, damn the meat, those who are hungry, let them eat." "Now, Ed," Lenore used to chastise him, mock seriously, careful to be socially correct. Her house, her children, and herself were always spotless, the children well-mannered, perhaps to make up for Ed's fondness for gambling and booze. People said you could eat off Lenore's floors.

"Better call on someone a little closer." Ed gave her a teasing smile. "Characters spouting invisibility not needed."

I thought he was very clever, but Lenore certainly didn't. "Oh, hush!" she cried.

After a truck passed with only a hair's breadth between us, a line of cars followed. A half mile up the grade, we were flagged to a stop and sent on a detour. Quickly, the road narrowed, got steeper. "If this is what it's going to be like, I don't want it," my sister said. "Ed, if you don't slow down, I'm getting out. You never learned how to drive on roads like this."

"Will you please be quiet?" It was not a question.

Open-mouthed she stared at him and then fell to her knees.

"What are you doing?" I asked. Lenore was often like a second mother to me, but unlike mother she had a penchant for bossing me, as if I were one of her children. I was only five years oldest than her first born.

She snapped, "If you have any sense you'll get down, too."

Ed cried, "For Christ sake, don't you think I know how to drive?"

"Not in the mountains. And stop taking the lord's name in vain." She glared at me over the back seat, reaching back as if to shove me down.

"What in the hell are you talking about?" Ed sounded exasperated.

"Safety!" she muttered and then in a louder voice ordered her children to the floor.

Not wanting to add fuel to their argument, I fell to my knees, and remained there until she got up. I didn't know what to think. If there was a god, was he really able to see everyone at once? Or were the random deaths and miraculous savings people spoke about because he really had to keep switching his gaze from one place to another? No one had yet given me any concrete arguments for belief. Now that I was on my own, I was trying hard to figure things out for myself. Why was Lenore suddenly so religious sounding? Were we on our knees because she figured it was safer than sitting up or was she hedging her bets? Lately she had made friends with a woman who called herself a "church-going sinner."

Lake Tahoe saved me from having knees so sore I'd never be able to get up. The setting sun dappled the cobalt and turquoise blue waters with light so sparkling Lenore couldn't help but get over her fears. And Lake Tahoe cemented my love affair with the west.

Shortly after our arrival in Oakdale, Mavis, who was nothing but enthusiastic about California, had us on the road again. Before we could catch our breath, we crowded into two cars and wound our way to Yosemite National Park. Awestruck, we stood at a view-point looking down at the valley, me doing most of the ohing and ahing, the older family members too tired to say much.

Taking pictures with my box camera, suddenly, I had trouble framing a scene. Half-Dome and the other peaks were taking my breath away when two pickups came to gravel-spinning stops at the scenic stop. A group of young men spilled out. I gathered from their conversation, they had been fishing for golden trout in the high Sierras. Fit looking, with better than average features, the one addressed as Bill seemed to be the center of the group.

Smiling at me, he apologized for butting in. "But, over there you can get a better picture." He framed a scene with his hands.

I nodded and snapped the shutter and then turned to thank him.

Holding out his hand, which seemed to me like a very adult thing to do, he introduced himself. "I'm Edgar A. Hall, better known as Bill."

Belatedly, I put my hand in his. A reasonable facsimile of a young Marlboro Man – he was twenty-five – he had the look of the west: year around tan, hard muscles, a slight swagger in his walk. I was interested. He seemed straight out of the western novels I'd read.

He asked if he could call me some day.

Before the age of cell phones, smart phones and e-mail, I glanced at Mavis. She gave her phone number and later told me she thought he was part of the Hall family of ranchers. She seemed impressed.

He called a few days later, and I agreed to a date. We sat in the smoking section at the movies in Modesto and ate hamburgers later. On subsequent dates he took me to the local bar where he hung out. Already I'd learned he had an exaggerated politeness with women, apologizing if he swore, opening doors, walking on the outside of the sidewalk as if it were necessary to protect women from problems from the street. At the bar I learned to play shuffleboard and liar's dice with him and his friends as we fed the jukebox, and the men drank beer. He played country-western music, talked rodeos and roundup and threw in talk of ancestors who rode wagon trains west. I was fascinated.

As summer edged toward fall, Bill told my sisters he was going to marry me. That annoyed me considerably. I was getting used to the wide open spaces of the west, the green and golden colors of California, a relaxed way of living. My job in admittance at the local hospital took care of my needs. I was dating other men in addition to Bill and enjoying the single life. "I'm not marrying him or anyone," I told Lenore and meant it. But Bill had rugged persistence. After a steady campaign of polite perseverance, catering to me, Bill finally wore me down. I consented to go steady with him, see no other men. At that point, he took me to meet his family.

I almost tripped over myself when we topped the rise after the long drive from the road. "It's a village," I exclaimed. In an offhand way Bill identified a carpenter shop, blacksmith shop, tackle shop, barn, a bunkhouse and other buildings. At a gas pump he filled his Buick before driving over to a low bungalow and parking. Beyond an orange grove adjacent to the bungalow, a big white house appeared on a slight knoll. "Granny lives there," he said when I asked. "My grandmother. I live with her."

Before we could get out of Bill's Buick, a man came from the front door of the bungalow that was half hidden in olive trees. "It's the old man," Bill said in an offhand way.

It would be exaggerating to say the elder Hall sauntered, but there was something of the dandy in him. While Bill was a white shirt and jeans man, as was the style among young ranchers, his father wore a scarf tucked into the open collar of an expensive shirt, and with his soft-spoken way of speaking, his almost flamboyant way of dressing, his casual reference to famous places I'd never seen, entranced me. This was the West I'd read about, imagined, seen in movies.

His second wife, Ruby, who met us at the front door, coke bottle in hand, looked as if she had stepped from the pages of a 1920's magazine. Extra slim, she wore a 1920's hair bob, had big eyes, skinny legs, and was addicted to Coca Cola. Unless she was going to the city – San Francisco – she wore wide-legged pajamas made especially for her. One-piece cotton, they had a flowered pattern. In her strange way, she added to the story-like surroundings, everything blending in a montage, glamorous because of its difference.

Before leaving the ranch that first day, we went to see Bill's grandmother who called me a darling and wrote a check she handed to him. "For your wedding," she said telling us about her second wedding to the foreman of the ranch. Her eyes twinkled as she admitted he had been the love of her life, edging out her first husband.

I tried to protest we were just dating, but she didn't listen. Neither did Bill. After a few weeks of that, it was hard to resist. I consented to marry Bill. Doing the popular thing, we went to Reno for the wedding and then went camping on our honeymoon.

Back at the ranch a week later, we stayed with Bill's father and Ruby because the autumn hunting season, when all the family – aunts, uncles, cousins and friends – went to the family cabins in the mountains. It was an entirely different world I'd discovered, and I was enthralled.

In the mountains I found a four-room house an ancestor had homesteaded, a large cabin and three smaller cabins, all under sugar pines. It was an idyllic time, sitting around a campfire at night, listening to stories of the early years before Yosemite was a park, breathing in the crisp morning air, learning to savor the outdoors.

My father-in-law took me on walks where he explained how to stalk game and not be seen, spotting them before they spotted you, soft-stepping and alert. I enjoyed it all. Life was good and Bill was at his most loveable. Most days, even Sundays, the men went hunting early in the morning. I saw deer, their glossy eyes glazed in death. I watched them being skinned and cleaned and fought back squeamishness. Soon, I was cooking venison on a Coleman stove, frying fresh caught trout and eating up the family praise.

Like my own family, no one seemingly believed in a supernatural being. None of Bill's family and friends attended church, and the only time I heard a deity mentioned was when one of the men swore. On one of my walks with my father-in-law, he told me anyone who appreciated nature had no reason to worship a god. "If there's a god, he's here in this place. In nature." I agreed immediately.

A month later we came down out of the hills and returned to the ranch in time for Bill to work the fields. I was checking out rental housing when one of Bill's cousins bought a ranch with an elegant old house that she eventually planned to remodel. She offered it to us rent-free until we could find a permanent home.

The house sat on a small knoll surrounded by fields that would be yellow with grain later in the year. I felt as if I were playing house. We used the kitchen, dining room, and one of the downstairs' bedrooms. Like all the bedrooms, it had a marble fireplace, a vanity sink in one corner, and high ceilings with crown molding. A chair rail and faded embossed wallpaper lent fading glory to the dining room. The decaying luxury, reminiscent of the Victorian age, intrigued me. We lived there a few months only.

One day, after Bill left at dawn, I hurried through my chores and drove over the dirt roads to the ranch. Ruby was in Georgia visiting her niece. I didn't miss her at all, but I really liked my father-in-law, eating up his polite phrases and his charming ways. I looked forward to a visit with him.

At The Ranch, I slowed down near Bill's grandmother's house. She loved telling me about the days when mules pulled the plows and the bunkhouse was filled with men, and I loved listening. But she was not on the side porch or visible in the front windows. I went on to the bungalow and glanced around, but no cars or trucks were parked anywhere near. If he were home, Bill's father would be alone. Smiling I approached the bungalow with its big screened-in porches and called out, "Anyone home?" No answer. At the front door I called again.

Still no answer. No one locked doors in those days. I went in.

In the living room a half-dozen mounted deer-heads looked down at me, their glass eyes dim. The window blinds had been drawn. "Hello," I called again.

"Well, well." A slurred voice came from the master bedroom. "So the little lady comes for a visit."

I blinked and peered toward the sound, spying Bill's father as he slouched into view. It was clear he'd been drinking. With the exaggerated walk of the inebriated, he approached. No longer did he look like a movie star of the twenties. His clothes were wrinkled and soiled, and I could smell his breath before he got to me.

"I came for some of our venison." I lied and half turned toward the front door. "Bill said you had it in your freezer."

He cocked his head in a semi-flirtatious manner. "I'm crushed, I thought you came to see me."

I felt sick, and started toward the door. "It's all right. I can get the meat some other time."

"Now, now, I'm not going to bite you. Damn it, maybe I've had a couple drinks. Maybe a couple too many, but Mr. William Edgar Hall knows what he's doing. I always know what the hell I'm doing." He straightened as much as possible, looking down at me. "To prove it, I'm going to write you a check. A thousand dollars to Mrs. Edgar A. Hall, wife of my son, Bill. William, that's me, but they call me Edgar. Damned re-dic-u-lous, if you catch my drift." He staggered to the desk in the corner.

"Really, I have to go." I started out, keeping to a measured walk, not running as I wanted to do. I would act as if nothing was the matter, while all the while I wanted to scream.

He caught up with me as I started out the door and thrust a hastily scrawled check into my hands.

"Here, for imposing my dissolute self upon you."

I learned later that Bill's father was a periodic alcoholic, staying sober for months before going on a binge. "Why didn't you tell me?" I asked Bill that night. The dimly lit chandelier didn't penetrate the gloom beyond the table, reach the corners of the room.

"Because you'd find out soon enough." He pushed his plate back and got up. Feeling left out and wondering if my anger was justified, I watched him walk down the hall to our bedroom. I followed, leaving the dirty dishes in place. In the bedroom he was throwing clothing into a suitcase. "What are you doing?" A late fall breeze was fluttering the curtains I'd hung the previous day, using a ladder to get high enough. They added to the look of permanence in the room, but permanence was rapidly going. I put a hand to my mouth.

Bill paused to fix me with a look. "I'm leaving and you can come with me, or act like the old man's king of some damn something and stay here."

It was the beginning of our stay in the high Sierras, Bill helping put in a road and drinking beer on weekends. When it became evident he didn't care if I was along or not, I stopped going with him to the local bars and read most evenings.

Days, I tramped the mountains and waded streams, closing my mind to everything except nature. Water poured from the heights, gushed and foamed over boulders. How could I face that the marriage had been a huge mistake? That Bill had been spoiled by his grandmother, and jerked around by his father, was sad. I felt sorry for him. His father was a drunk, and his stepmother one strange lady, but marriage was forever. No matter that my family had kept religion from our home, they had gone along with societal norms. No one divorced. A divorced woman was suspect. Breaking up a marriage had to be her fault. It took many years before that thinking no longer had a hold on me. I realized many Christian precepts had crept into American life and clung like a fungus.

I had less than two years to dwell on the strange turns life can take. One day the sheriff notified us my father-in-law had died in a fiery plane crash. He had attempted to land at the ranch after dark. The lights on the landing strip had never been turned on, and he crashed, alone and possibly inebriated.

The next day we were back at the ranch. Except for the short talk we'd had in the mountains and the time Bill's father ran off Jehovah's Witnesses, it was the only time I heard religion mentioned by the extended family.

Everyone had gathered at the ranch. A great aunt came from San Luis Obispo or was it the hotel suite she maintained in Los Angeles? A grand dame with an authoritative voice, I kept expecting her to have a lorgnette, but she didn't even wear glasses. She said even though my father-in-law's drinking was not to be condoned, he deserved a proper burial. After all, he was family. It was one thing not to attend church, but being buried without a religious presence was gauche. No one argued. A minister was contacted. After the dry and formal ceremony and weeping at the cemetery, we rode in big cars back to The Ranch.

Days after the funeral, Bill's grandmother arranged to have the bunkhouse remodeled into a modern house for Bill and me. Open concept before that was popular, the kitchen, living room, bedroom and bath flowed toward the back porch where we sometimes sat after dinner. It was a relatively quiet time, Bill running through his inheritance like it was water. I read books and went to see my family as often as possible. But then Granny died, and the ranch as The Ranch was no more. Although she had said frequently, all she owned was to be Bill's after she was gone, she had died in-testate. Her money, house, land and antique furniture went to her remaining children.

Even though stone cold broke, except for what he earned working for others, Bill lived as if nothing had changed. Borrowing money, for hunting or fishing trips, from more affluent family members, he spent what he wanted to spend when he wanted to. My sympathy for him eroded seriously. But I was stuck. "You made your bed, now lie in it," was the mantra people respected at the time. Women were responsible for holding a marriage together.

All these things and more went through my mind as Hank and I drove south from Las Vegas. Had I made the same mistake again, marrying too soon after meeting? No, I told myself, this time there had been a meeting of the minds.

Three

*Americans are so enamored with equality that they
would be equal in slavery than unequal in freedom.*

ALEXIS DE TOCQUEVILLE (1805 TO 1859)

For miles Hank and I paralleled the Mexican border. We'd played in the swimming pool at our motel in Tucson, took pictures in Apache land, and now the quiet hypnotism of open space set in. In this sparsely settled land, we seldom passed another car. Radio programs told about the local grange meeting, who was sick, who had traveled to Santa Fe for a festival, who had made the honor role at school and who had found the lord.

"What do they mean, finding the lord?" I understood so little about religion, and now I wanted to know.

"I can only guess." Hank explained. As a Catholic the main thing was to do what the church wanted, go to confession and mass, listen to the priest, stay away from birth control, go to confession. No one read the bible.

"Did you pray?"

49

"Maybe, as a little kid. In school you learned to follow directions or get smacked with a ruler. "

After a while, long, comfortable silences developed between us before I spoke my misgivings about the move.

"I hope Virginia isn't too Southern," I said. "people fighting the Civil War again."

"It's not the deep south, if that's what you mean. More outsiders are moving in, but people are people." He told me about his college friend from Mississippi. "He actually slugged someone who called him a racist."

I told him that was good to hear. "Especially now that Martin Luther King was shot."

"Unfortunate incident? I'd say King was a moderating influence. Now the blacks won't have that guiding hand, no telling what will happen. They already have their hands out."

Unfortunate incident? Or was it just an unfortunate figure of speech? "What do you mean they have their hands out?"

"I mean they can pull themselves up by their bootstraps like everyone who came here had to do. My father really worked at getting a high school education. Like I said before, he was born here but grew up in Poland. It wasn't easy for him."

I stared at Hank's profile. I saw the same smooth face I had so admired. He couldn't be saying what I thought he was saying. "I don't understand."

"The Poles, like my family, had to make it on their own. Like the Irish and all the other ethnic groups before them."

"You mean so can the blacks."

"Of course."

"That makes absolutely no sense," I said, shaking my head. Outside the air-conditioned car heat shimmered the highway ahead. A sign warned it was a hundred miles to the next gas station. "No one forced your family to come to America. Or the Irish or anyone."

"No, but once they got here they worked at any job they could get to feed their families. My parents scrimped, went without, and they got ahead."

The scenery was blurring by, and I was feeling light-headed. "They certainly weren't brought here in chains. They certainly weren't treated as property. They certainly weren't whipped, beaten and sexually abused."

"Oh, come on, I think you're confusing apples and oranges."

"I think you are."

"It's what a lot of people believe."

"A lot of stupid people."

He glared at me. "My family is far from stupid."

"What! I wasn't talking about your family."

"So, just me? You were calling me stupid?" He glanced at me, surprise on his face.

"You're way off." I tapped my feet on the floor mat. "How anyone can believe such rot as what you said is beyond me, and you know very well you're not stupid. I never meant that."

He shot another look my way, his eyes narrowed. Emphasizing each word and pausing between words, he said. "Then what in hell did you mean?"

I opened my mouth to speak but before I could he shook his head. "Don't say another word."

I wasn't sure I'd heard correctly. I left several beats go by before I said, "Don't worry, Mr. Kocol, I won't" It was my best put-down voice. Damn him! I'd never during the days I'd considered his attributes and liabilities ever concluded he was racist. But that wasn't the kind of talk I was used to. I could see it would be no use to say anything now. For miles, the landscape blurred by as neither of us spoke. An ache stabbed me deep in my chest. All kinds of possibilities raced through my mind before it settled into a waiting game.

At the motel near the long-anticipated gas station, we ate dinner without our glances ever meeting, saying nothing more than "pass the salt" and "thank you." We were extraordinarily polite.

In our room, one step up from Motel 6, the only one available in that long stretch of nothingness, I took my overnight bag to the bathroom, took a shower, and got ready for bed. I'd placed my book on the bed closest to the bathroom. When I came out he was standing looking out the window to the parking lot. His suitcase sat on his bed, unpacked. It wasn't like him. He turned. "We need to talk." His tone was even.

"Okay." I sat down on the edge of the bed and waited. I would not make this easy for him. I had lived alone before; I could again.

"I've been thinking."

Again I said nothing.

"I'm sorry if I gave you the wrong impression." His voice grew in intensity. "I'm serious. I never thought it through, just repeated what I heard people say."

"It? You mean slavery and the strange slant you seemed to adopt earlier?"

He spread his arms. "Please, you've got to realize, I grew up in a Polish Catholic world. People talked like that. Everyone went to Catholic schools, including college. My mother thought the Irish Catholics should stick to their own parishes and not go to St. Stevens. She thought the world was coming to an end when a non-Catholic moved into the neighborhood. She and Dad wanted me to be a priest, but when I balked at that, stating from age six or seven that I wanted to be a scientist, they eventually stopped arguing. Science and Catholicism have an uneasy relationship. My father understands and believes in evolution because he says it makes sense. My mother believes because the priest says so. Otherwise they both have a vague feeling that science would create problems."

"I thought they sounded proud of you."

"They're responding to success, not to science. You have to understand: everyone we knew was Catholic. In some of the areas of the city where we lived when I was little, everyone was also Polish. You couldn't buy a loaf of bread unless you spoke Polish. Now my folks live in the place they bought when I was eleven or twelve. We never knew any black people, except I was aware I shouldn't drive through the slums on Chicago's south side." He shrugged. "My mother said Martin Luther King had to be a saint." He paused. "You see?"

"I'm not sure I get the connection."

"She and everyone said slavery was wrong. But that's as far as their thinking went."

"You never questioned?"

"Not until you shamed me into it."

I debated mentioning again my younger sister's two half white, half black daughters. Then I blurted it out. In those days it was far from ordinary to cross the color line. One niece was studying to be a fashion buyer, a career that eventually took her to the fashion houses in New York City. The other was deep into ballet, dancing with Moscow's Bolshoi when they came to America, heading for a career that eventually took her to New York City, also.

He struck his head with the flat of his hand. "I feel like a prime idiot. Of course I was wrong. I was so damn arrogant, never questioning the status quo. It's a wonder you're still sitting here."

He looked so sad I wanted to run to him, soothe him into feeling better. But I didn't.

"When I left the church, it took time to rid myself of all the doctrine that was drilled into me, things I took for granted for almost twenty years. Let's talk about it again later." He came over to the bed and sat on the end. I was near the head

I nodded, added a smile, "Your mother wanted you to be a priest? I don't think she knew you." I grinned. I'd never seen anyone make such a quick turnaround.

"First choice was a doctor. They make more money." As he repeated the old cliché, which I think was true in his case, we both began to chuckle. That was the end of the discussion that night.

But the next day as we drove through Missouri and little towns, "civilization" getting closer, he said. "I never realized what a closed world I lived in, what I subconsciously accepted until I started thinking on my own. Obviously some of that indoctrination holds on. As a scientist I realized that the god element was unnecessary, but some of the other things took longer to combat for it works its way into the culture."

I told him there was only one religious phrase I wanted him to hold on to – "until death do us part."

We both had to laugh, and we were closer than ever as we continued to our new home.

A few years later, wondering how far Hank's new thinking went, I saw proof at a South American jungle camp on a tributary of the mighty Amazon River.

About twenty other people arrived at the same time we did. Native people lived nearby, and at night we heard the jungle drums as one group talked to another. It was tremendously exciting. The whole tourist complex was built on a series of pilings, with walkways leading to the dining room, the dance hall, and guest rooms.

The people who came on the boat with us from Iquitos, Peru, were Caucasian with the exception of two African/American women from Philadelphia. A shared toilet joined every two rooms.

From this group of strangers we all chose with whom to share a toilet. About five couples had selected when Hank asked the two women of color if they would mind sharing with us. Before he spoke their faces were non-committal, afterward they blossomed with smiles. I have never seen expressions change so fast. They said they were truly honored. They'd been afraid they would be the last selected, forced to share with someone who objected silently. I squeezed Hank's hand, my admiration for him deepening.

In Virginia the honeymoon atmosphere continued. I sent Steve a letter to accompany the cards I had sent along the way. We picked Henry up at Dulles International Airport, and at home let him pick between two bedrooms. We all looked forward to a new life.

Within a few days, I met the neighbors, many of whom were moving into the new housing development at the same time. Amy Brown, whose back yard butted up to ours, had a son Steve's age, another Henry's age. We spoke the same language and soon became fast friends. She was there to commiserate when I learned Steve had received greetings from Uncle Sam. He told the army he was a conscientious objector, but before admitting he had no religious reasons for saying so, he went to see the local navy recruiter who welcomed him with open arms. He would not be in the front lines in Viet Nam.

Life soon had a rhythm suiting Hank and me, a two-year honeymoon. We visited all the historical sites, almost camped out at the Smithsonian museums, and patronized the best restaurants in the area. It was a time of discovery. Hank, if not reined in, debated most points in a conversation. Because of his views, I cut him slack and teased him about his Socratic method of romance. He had been in the forefront of so many social events, a member of the National Abortion Rights Action League before I knew of its existence. During my high school years, a young couple, the boy, a senior, the girl two or three years younger had been forced into marriage when the girl became pregnant. I had accepted the action without thinking it through although neither was mature enough to be a parent. Adoption was barely discussed, and abortion was verboten. My mother told me women died in back-alley abortions. To get pregnant and not be married was the demon that lurked over dating couples.

Hank learned to put a bridle on his penchant for debate, but he never put a bridle on his addiction for learning. That suited me fine. When we visited George Washington's birthplace as well as Mt. Vernon, his mansion on the

Potomac, we were also reading in various media stories that this was a Christian country and quotes from the Founding Fathers seemed to back up this assertion by the religious right. We began reading and educating ourselves, learning that most quotes were taken out of context. Washington, for example, went to Anglican Church services only because his wife, Martha, was a fervent believer. But he left before taking communion and waited for her outside.

In Washington's day, when people lived in small villages and on scattered farms and plantations, the churchyard was comparable to meeting places of today. People met there to exchange news, gossip, confirm deals, and socialize. Washington, who was an ambitious man, although hating what he termed politics, had to engage in some activities that came under that description. In his letters, however, he used the term "providence" instead of god. The crowning example for me of his disbelief in a living god, a supernatural being, came when I read about his death. Because of his desires, Martha did not have any priests or ministers in the room as he lay dying. She recited no prayers, and neither did anyone else present. No one appealed to god. How great to read facts to counteract the ubiquitous cherry tree myth circulated in my childhood.

Of course, Hank and I went to Thomas Jefferson's Monticello and almost genuflected at the thought of this genius who showed his very human side. Not only did he question religion, he read the new testament of the Christian bible in English, French, Latin, and Greek and then cut and pasted together his own bible. The details regarding miracles and the resurrection were omitted. "Faith, "as we read later in a quote by Mark Twain, "is believing what you no ain't so."

Reading these things and visiting places where the Founding Father had lived, gave me a tremendous feeling of freedom, more than I'd felt before. Becoming educated about my non-theism made me infinitely more aware of how "going along" without protest can hold society in a religious bind. But life went on, and I was part of the 1970's and not the 1700's.

After the draperies and paintings were up, I signed with a temporary employment agency that sent me on a job the very next day. We had been in Virginia a week. The job was in Arlington, Virginia, just over the Chain Bridge from Washington, D.C. Before leaving for work, Hank traced a route on a map I would follow. Because he had worked in the District before, he knew his way around. But he wasn't aware that several streets had reverted to one-way traffic in the early morning rush hours. I had to be at work at eight in the morning. Hitting my first one-way, I struck out blindly and ended up circling the Lincoln Memorial, which you could do then. I imagined Old Abe scowling at me the third time I passed. Finally, in a panic, I found my way across the bridge to Arlington. By now I was five minutes late. Parking in the underground garage, the only place I spotted, was expensive and ate up any profit I would have made.

I took my name off the register and looked for something much closer. A doctor advertised for an assistant. I applied and got the position. The first day the girl who was leaving handed me a pile of envelopes to be mailed. She described where she had always dropped them off. It took me a little time to locate the mail box. Three days later, I realized I was spending an extra half hour each day posting the doctor's mail. It seriously cut into my time at home, making me practically race to get a meal ready early enough so we could relax a little in the evening.

The next day, a Saturday, Hank was attending a radiation health convention, and Amy's husband, Paul, had Naval duty. Amy and I dropped the kids at a movie and went to hear a speaker. We'd read that the woman favored women's rights. We weren't quite sure what that meant. The woman, who spoke like an academic, asked, "Why are men identified as John Doe, but his wife is only Mrs. John Doe? Why identify women by their marital status, Miss or Mrs.? But men are never anything but Mister, impossible to tell if they're married or single." She told us about Lucy Stone, who lived in the mid 1800's, the first woman to keep her own name after marriage. Amy and I exchanged significant looks. Neither one of us had ever questioned such troubling things before.

After the talk, we sat in McDonald's and sipped cokes. For a while we were silent, watching the crowd of young people ordering hamburgers. When Hank was gone, Henry and I did the same, but otherwise I cooked my version of gourmet meals, enjoying the challenge and surprising Hank.

"Quite a talk," I said, wondering what the speaker would think about time I spent on showcasing my culinary achievements.

Amy nodded. "It's too late, and I'm too timid to do it, but I would have liked to have kept my own name."

A rose is a rose is a rose, I muttered, while my own mind raced remembering all the speaker had said. I t had been a lot to absorb. "Really?" I'd been happy to shed Bill's name, take Hank's.

She shrugged. "I like to think so. Think about it. Why should women be recognized by the world as only an adjunct to a man?" Her gaze was semi-challenging. She'd had polio at a young age, and, of necessity, walked with a hip-tossing motion, that managed to look snazzy on the dance floor, but when we went shopping, she pushed a cart that made it easier for her to walk.

I told her about my first marriage. Gushed a bit about Hank and listened to her elaborate about Paul.

"But we shouldn't be only their wives," she said.

I agreed, and then told her about the extra half-hour daily I spent posting the doctor's mail. After being practically on a par with the psychiatrist I worked for in Las Vegas, it felt like a definite come down.

Amy's mouth fell open, and her voice, which was always soft, rose. "Does he pay you overtime?"

She knew he didn't. Why hadn't I questioned it before? The next night as Hank unpacked his overnight bag, I told him about the mail drop.

"Isn't that usual?" he asked. He didn't seem perturbed.

I frowned. Was I going to hear him defend the doctor? I still couldn't entirely shrug off his racist background even though I understood it. "Do you have to do after hours stuff for your boss?"

"Of course, I give talks at night. You know that." He took dirty clothes to the laundry.

I followed. "Yes, but do you make your secretary fix your coffee? Pick up your dry-cleaning?" An edge had crept into my voice.

He took off his suit coat before turning back to me, a slight smile parting his lips. "You make me think about things I never thought of before. I think your situation is slightly different from mine, but you make a valid argument." He smiled at me. "He can only fire you."

"So you want me to speak out?"

"I know you will, and you should."

We both laughed. Although the honeymoon period had passed, the sparks that had brought us together were as strong as ever.

The next day at work, I spoke out, explaining that making coffee and taking the office mail after working hours was not in the job description.

The doctor said, "What is it you gals want today? My girls have always taken the mail. I'm sorry but that's the way it is. If I say, okay, what will you want next? Those lab results need getting out immediately. My patients need knowing. But, you girls have some kind of bee in your bonnet."

I closed my eyes for a second sensing that if I apologized, the job would be there. No problem. But his words suddenly showed me what I'd always wanted and not always got: that was respect. Working for him would be an emotional disaster. "I think you'd better look for another assistant."

His head, always carried high, went higher. "It's good you quit before I fired you."

"I'll get my things," I said.

"Oh," he called as I went out the door, "don't expect a recommendation."

I didn't bother answering.

A few weeks later I took a temporary job at the United States Wildlife Federation. It was neither demanding nor boring and was the first time I encountered computer printouts. The job ended in six months, time enough for Amy and I to go shopping while swapping women's rights talks. We agreed it was time for many changes. We let our husbands know our thoughts as we danced at venues like the Holiday Inn where Metro Melodies, Amy's oldest son's band had engagements. We followed them from one hotel to the next. It was a fun time. The men didn't quite know what to make of our women's rights talk, and we weren't totally sure of everything we were saying.

One day Amy confided that she had qualms about religion. We were sitting at my round kitchen table. Two or three mornings a week, we got together before starting our days. She'd never looked at the parts of the bible where women were raped, sometimes at god's command, but now she had. "Paul," she said one day, "wants the kids to go to catechism. He reminded me that he wanted to raise them Catholic. I promised that when we married."

I didn't know what to say except that Hank and I weren't religious. Amy never said anything more about it, but I think for a while she was disturbed and later on she told me she believed in birth control and abortion. "I don't think unmarried popes and priests should control my body." That night I told Hank and he said most Catholics were going in that direction

One day Hank came home from work to announce that he wanted to march in the anti-war protest the day Richard Nixon took the oath of office for president. Neither of us had been involved in local politics. Although we both had never failed to vote, and he had a long record of letters to the editor that were political in nature, neither of us had marched or carried signs of protest during the Vietnam War. I had not known enough to come down strongly on the side of those who spoke out vociferously. I had come to my firm stance against the war only after it had been going full bore.

Hank had a purposeful look on his face as he made his announcement about marching. He told me he heard that photographers in police helicopters were going to photograph the protesters. "Who knows what they'll do with the pictures."

"Maybe you'll lose your job." The sun was shining brightly although the air was crisp with January cold, but no snow covered the ground, and the breeze that had rustled the trees at night had dissipated.

"No problem. I'll go to work in the private sector. Make a hell of a lot more money."

Despite his seeming laissez faire attitude, I realized he was dead serious. If he could risk a job, I could risk whatever happened. "I'm going with you," I said.

"I was hoping you'd say that."

The day of the inauguration dawned chilly but sunny. I wore a heavy jacket with a hood, made sandwiches we planned to eat on the steps of the Lincoln memorial, and found myself astounded by the crowds of people.

"Excuse me, pardon me," I said moving through a gang of young people of all stripes from hippy to college student and laboring class who were invariably polite, asking if we needed assistance or wanted to carry a sign.

Everyone seemed embroiled in the anti-war movement. I passed women in fur coats and high heeled pumps, both men and women in wheel chairs, husbands and wives with their children in tow, as well as the stalwarts who led the anti-war chants. A girl gave me a print out of chants. I read it while I gulped my tuna sandwich. I turned away from Hank to answer a woman who asked how many marches I'd been in.

"This is my first," I said.

She said it was her sixth, and she'd been among an anti-war group arrested at the Pentagon.

"Gosh," I murmured, in awe of her bravery. When I glanced back, Hank was no longer seated beside me. Feeling a frisson of panic, I finally located him at the bottom of the steps snapping my picture. Automatically, I smiled.

As people began to line up, we joined them and slowly began marching, leaders with bull horns leading the chants. No one evoked the supernatural. No one suggested we pray. "Get out now," we repeated over and over. A rhyming poem about Tricky Dick got lost in my memory of a rewarding day.

Hank estimated we were larger in number than those in the stands listening to Nixon take the oath of office, but there was nothing in the Washington papers about our protest. And Hank didn't lose his job. I congratulated him for realizing that it was time we got involved, got quite flowery in my praise. I felt energized, as if woken from a long sleep. I kept talking about "we the people." He seemed embarrassed by my outburst of praise, but he, too seemed changed, both of us discussing each scrap of political news we heard from then on.

He was so modest; it always astonished me. He told Paul that he knew nothing about cars. I couldn't understand that at all. He changed his own oil, rotated his tires, kept all kinds of modest mechanical things going. If he didn't know everything about a subject, he claimed he was not knowledgeable about the matter. It was the same with sports. Although he made it clear to everyone that he didn't like football – he considered it a potential medical problem – it took time before I realized he knew everything about baseball, had played softball in college, and knew more about obscure sports than I ever would.

While Hank and I were changing in important ways, recognizing connections between politics, religion and women that had whizzed by us earlier, we were still learning about one another. But life didn't stand still and let us examine our knowledge in leisure. Hank's burgeoning career had us moving again. Hank's office would be in Philadelphia, so we contracted to have a house built in the suburbs of New Jersey. Amy and I bid a tearful farewell and off we went.

Four

*"All children are atheists and were not religion
inculcated into their minds, they would remain so."*

ERNESTINE ROSE (1810-1892)

While our house was being built in Mount Holly, New Jersey, we spent a fascinating month in a cottage on Long Beach Island. Just across the bridge from the mainland, the island is twenty miles long and a half-mile wide. Each morning Henry crabbed in the bay and every afternoon he and I cavorted in the ocean. Hank, who drove to his office in Philadelphia each morning, said when the waves got too rough and the water too cold, only the teenagers and Cleo and Henry were there. It was a slight exaggeration, but mostly true. Weekends we drove north on the island, past the stilt houses where the waves sometimes lapped at the foundations, to see the Barnegat Bay lighthouse or to eat at a crab shack on that part of the island.

It was a fun time. We put our names on a waiting list for the Surflight Theater. Actors of renown, also stage presences of the day, came down from New York City to entertain. We'd wait outside until everyone was seated and then invariably someone didn't show, and we got seated. Among the other well-known actors, we saw Lauren Bacall reprising her Broadway show, Applause. When Amy and Paul visited, we had marvelous fun on the beach and at night after the kids were asleep with a sitter, we found a piano bar where we sang as if we knew how. None of us were gifted vocally, but that didn't deter us.

After that fun time, we moved into our house in Mt. Holly. Situated across the river from Philadelphia, the town had houses built in the mid 1800's. They would have been of historical interest out west. Here they were considered close to contemporary. The oldest buildings were pre-Revolutionary. Our house in a new subdivision a couple miles out of the small town would not have fit in. Gray shingle and very, very modern with two and a half baths, its entrance hall held a wide staircase leading to the four bedrooms upstairs. That and a sunken living room and long narrow windows gave the house distinction, that and the many trees we planted.

But all the historic spots in the area screamed to be visited. In Philadelphia I stood in Constitution Hall where the country's wise men deliberated about the laws that would govern our nation. I felt goose bumps locating the seats of James Madison, Benjamin Franklin, and John Adams. By my reading I knew that the Constitutional Summer was hot, and after their workday, the men often supped at Franklin's house – he could seat 20 at table – or gathered at the local taverns. I imagined the people of the city gossiping about them. They still do, but now their facts are often skewed by political ambitions. None of our founders championed forming a Christian nation. In fact, much earlier, in 1758, Franklin had written in Poor Richard's Almanac, "The way to see by faith is to shut the eye of reason."

No matter their religious bent, all of our founders were men of reason. They understood that the only way for a government to work properly was to separate government and religion. Thomas Jefferson in a letter to Peter Carr, said, and I quote, "if there was a god, he would follow reason rather than blindfolded faith." Seeing the room where he penned the Declaration of Independence made the top of my head go prickly.

After our first foray into Philadelphia, I hurried to the local library, got a card, and came home with books about the founding fathers. Once again the infusion of facts bolstered my non-belief. Each day when Hank came home from work I met him with a quotation from one of the founding fathers. When he didn't respond with a fact about our country's early days, he had to pay me a quarter. When I forgot to greet him with a quote, I had to pay him a quarter. Neither of us got rich, but life went on in its fascinating ways.

When wind driven cold began to whistle around the house, the furnace purring heat into every room, Hank came home with tickets for a lecture by Isaac Asimov at the Franklin Institute in Philadelphia. Fans of Asimov's novels as well as his essays, we were thrilled to find he, too, was a non-theist.

The night we met him it was snow-blowing frigid, the skies dark, the streets icy. We hurried up those steps Slyvester Stallone had climbed in the movie, "Rocky," pushed through the big double doors and went in shivering. Leaving our coats with an attendant, we preceded to a line we assumed was one of the drink lines. We needed something to take away the chill.

The line moved faster than expected, and suddenly, I was face to face with Issac Asimov! We had inadvertently joined the reception line! Shocked, I stared at the mutton chopped man. I had worn a fetching wool dress with a matching scarf artfully fastened with my best jeweled pin, and I could see I had captured his attention as I gushed, spouting words that at least were truthful. "I love your work; it's so prophetic and interesting and…" As I hesitated, he smiled broadly.

"And readable?" he suggested.

"Oh, yes!" I cried.

Married to Hank I had met and was meeting many men and a few women who were big names in the scientific world, but Asimov was more than a scientist, and I was like a young kid mooning over a rock star.

Next thing I knew, Asimov had leaned forward and was kissing me.

My eyes zoomed to their largest. "Oh, my," I said, suddenly remembering he was a bachelor and consequently I fiddled with my hair like a girl on a first date.

"One kiss deserves another," Asimov said, and before I could collect myself, he had kissed me again.

I couldn't help thinking how far this little girl from Chagrin Falls, Ohio, had gone. I glanced at Hank and he was looking on with pride.

Asimov was hardly a slow learner. Quick to account for his spontaneity, he assessed the situation and said, "Your wife is a good kisser."

Hank took my arm with a proprietary look, and we proceeded down the line, the heads of the various scientific societies almost irrelevant to me.

Escaping the line, I declared to everyone we slightly knew, and to others who overheard, including the woman Asimov was dating, that I'd never wash my lips again. It was a facetious statement, said without thinking, both Hank and I getting a "charge" out of the incident. Of course when you're on that sort of path, it's almost impossible to change. In the dining room, we committed the second faux pas of the evening, sitting : at the same table with Asimov's lady friend who gave me a tolerant smile that managed to make me feel silly and childish, not worthy of more than a nod. After his witty speech, Asimov joined our table, but did not acknowledge me. I expect he was feeling a bit silly, too. I was grateful the large round table made conversation impossible except with the people on either side of me.

At the same time I was chaffing at staying home, being a housewife. I had tried various temporary positions that didn't work out. Now, Hank suggested I give up looking for a job and become a full time homemaker as well as a scholar. Although frightened about competing with young people, I went to college and added to the feeling I'd already had that learning was fun. My major, social science, was just taking hold in academic circles.

At the same time I immersed myself in the women's rights movement, Amy's and my discussions and her subtle questioning of religion had helped move me in that direction. I was realizing that religion was often the catalyst keeping women in a second class status. That American women had it better than women in many other countries was due, not to religion, but to our economy. I saw that women in tribal conditions were held down by religious beliefs, that women in Muslim countries were held down by religious beliefs, that religion of all kinds said women were inferior because of a god's dictates. I felt personally affronted.

Our first Thanksgiving in Mt. Holly, not fully unpacked yet, we went out to eat. The area specialized in Italian, and the only restaurant open was in Cherry Hill. We had been seated and had given our orders (I was still traditional enough to order turkey) when I realized, we were the only blondes in the room. Our new neighbors said we'd probably dined among the Mafia.

It was a story that brought smiles, even in the Alice Paul Chapter of the National Orginazation For Women, Now, which I joined. Alice Paul who had grown up in nearby Moorestown, NJ., had gone to Britain to observe the suffragists, came home and led women in picketing the White House during Woodrow Wilson's administration. They called for votes for women.

My marriage had settled into a very nice middle-class existence, Hank and I meeting people, exchanging dinner parties, and of course he and I going to the reenactment of Revolutionary battles and marches. I saw that the lay person most often likes to believe the most dramatic historical elements presented, which often are not true. Ladies of the night did not follow George Washington's army, as many people believe today. Why? Because he did not allow it. But women and children who would be penniless without their husbands, followed their men into battle, the women cooking, doing laundry, and often taking up their fallen husband's musket when he was killed. Only the British allowed camp followers. Unfortunately, we saw camp followers attached to all American reenactments. So much for historical truth!

But the truth smacked us in the face during our first international trip. We were in Mexico City walking near our hotel on the De la Reforma, that very wide main street, when our eyes were drawn to a kiosk and a newspaper. The large type headline read "Nixon Renuncio." Astounded, we looked at one another, bought a copy of the paper and hurried back to our hotel. Everyone in the elevator was talking about what had happened. We realized we were living through history. No president had ever resigned before.

I was learning so much. My friends from the Alice Paul Chapter of NOW, were fonts of knowledge about women's rights, feeding me books about women's history. Mid age, upper and middle class women, they knew how to fix yummy canapés, bake luscious bundt cakes, win contests for their cooking, and spout the feminist line.

We talked about our pasts, conceding that boys were favored over girls in our growing up years. Girls were supposed to work as a nurse, secretary, or teacher for a year or two, or if she came from a more "liberal" household she could even attend college, the goal being marriage. We discussed everything including religion. The Jews among us said that in traditional Jewish families, a man thanked god each morning that he wasn't a woman. It was the first thing on Jewish women's "hit list." Many of us were non-theists, although we called it "not being religious." The mantra for my feminist friends was: "Not the church, not the state, women must decide their fate."

The first march I participated in as a feminist was on the 4th of July. Bright summer. Flags everywhere. The people living near where our country was born, seemed to make more of the fourth than I'd seen out west. It wasn't hard to enjoy the beauty of the scene, everyone thrilled to be celebrating another birthday for America. We feminists wore white pants, white tops with a purple sash that honored the suffragists' colors.

Properly dressed and properly excited, I joined the other women.. We followed cars holding town leaders, bands from adjacent towns, church choirs, and boy scouts. The mayor and his staff rode in open cars followed by the Junior League. Women from St. something or other altar society marched early in the parade. Behind them came the American Baptist Church women. Women and girls in all the traditional roles showed up. We were the aberration.

Our leader, an attractive blonde woman who made the best éclairs around, gave our small group of a dozen women pins that said Americans Need the Equal Rights Amendment, the ERA. We walked beneath elm and oak trees shedding dappled sunlight, families sitting in folding chairs, or perched on the curb or standing in groups, kids waving small American flags. We were to hand the pins to watchers along the route.

As people said over and over again we were lucky to be Americans, I felt a thrill run thought me, but the thought of handing out political pins startled me, jolting me out of my reverie. I had to force myself to run to the side of the street and hand a pin to a man. He glanced at it and mouthed an obscenity. Even women watchers frowned when I held out the pins. They didn't know what to believe about the budding women's movement. Secretly some voiced anger at their place in life, but they seldom put the facts together. My heart did its usual leap. But I felt proud when I spotted Hank taking my picture and signaling his approval. He never held back support or praise, and was an outspoken supporter of women's rights.

71

That march began a flurry of activity for me. With the Alice Paul Now I went to Washington, D.C. to lobby and march for the Equal Rights Amendment. At legislator's offices we said "Men, their rights and nothing more; women their rights and nothing less." Equality for all took hold in my mind like a leach and never left, no matter that only one of my sisters supported it. After moving to Oklahoma with her new husband, Lenore, who was the most tradition bound of my sisters, had found religion, and it was the kind that said woman's place in life was ordained, second place.

My youngest sister, Dale, a single Mom, feared that women would be forced to do jobs they hadn't before. She wore blinders when it came to anything beyond her own sphere. Only Mavis agreed that women were given a poor hand to play. If only she could agree with me about religion. She jumped all over the place exploring one church after the other.

But I was looking at the larger picture. Infused with energy, I was feeling empowered, my days filled to overflowing. I almost jumped out of my shoes when I heard from Steve. He seldom wrote or called, but now he was getting married to Rhonda, a girl he'd gone to high school with. A letter a few months later had me smiling when Hank came home. "Guess what?" were my first words. "I'm going to be a grandmother!"

I half-expected him to say, I'm too young to be a grandfather, but he said, "That's great." At times I concluded he'd never been a child, just hatched fully formed, talking and walking. He'd been reading at four, and as he told me, words had gushed from him spontaneously until he came home from Holy Innocents' kindergarten crying.

His mother had turned from the stove where she was preparing lunch, pierogi she'd made from scratch, dropping the filled dumplings in boiling water and then frying them in butter after they rose to the top. "What happened?"

Seeing the look of concern on her face, Hank said, "Sister Cecelia hit me with a ruler."

Before he could confide that he had done nothing wrong that it was another boy who had knocked over the box of toys and he was just picking them up, his mother smacked him across the face. "If the sisters hit you, you had it coming. Don't ever talk against those good women."

The incident taught him to be selective in his pronouncements, to put words into proper sequence. What he hadn't realized until later, a seed of doubt had begun to form about the infallibility of the Catholic Church.

All that evening Hank's response to my news about Steve and Rhonda sang like a song that would not let up. That our family was increasing thrilled me. Steve would be a father. Whatever had come between us was in the past. His youth would be tempered by fatherhood. It would force him to be responsible. He would write me sweet notes about the baby, send pictures. My excitement spread a light-centered glow over everything.

When Steve got stationed in Oakland, California, I flew west at the first opportunity. Rhonda had made their apartment near Lake Merritt homey with potted plants and photographs. Gracious and sweet, she was shy in front of a mother-in-law she did not know. I liked her immediately and also managed to refrain from saying Steve looked cute in his sailor suit. Again, I was carried back to the day I first heard about him.

That day moved like a slide show in front of my eyes. Bill and I were living in Battle Mountain, Nevada, Bill involved in mining, I working at the doctor's office. The M.D. was the only doctor in the whole county, his day starting with rounds at the local hospital before he got to the office. His girl Friday, I did everything from managing the office to assisting with patients, sterilizing instruments, developing x-rays, and acting as receptionist.

At times we could hardly work fast enough, rodeo contestants breaking legs or getting in fights, local hypochondriacs insisting on medication, children needing preschool examinations, high school football players getting their annual physicals, and the "girls" from the "line" coming in for their weekly or monthly tests.

"Girls" came from Stockton, Angels Camp or other northern California cities to the two houses across the tracks from the central district. Restricted, not allowed up town except when escorted by the police for their examinations, people had a tolerant attitude toward prostitution. It was said that one of the older women in town had come from one of the houses, married and settled down. Fathers said nothing when their teenage boys were seen heading across the tracks. It was a facet of the old west that both intrigued and repelled me.

Life with Bill was increasingly unsatisfying, and I asked myself, is this all there is to life? More than once a friend said, "Why don't you go to church?" I never had and saw no reason to begin, but she pointed out that I was abysmally ignorant about religion. At least I should find out what it was all about. I finally agreed. There was a Catholic Church and an Episcopal Church, as well as a hell and brimstone local church. The loud music emanating from the local "god" house repelled me. I was not going anywhere near the Catholic Church, which in the protestant surroundings of my childhood town, was looked upon as Rome's child. By default, that left the Episcopal Church.

I knew nothing about the history of the Episcopalians. Vaguely, I recalled reading that they were an offshoot of the Anglican Church, but that was all. The small congregation greeted me with open arms. Good people, I enjoyed their company, and the better parts of religion, which to me were their concerns for the poor, the sick, and all those in need. I helped with the Indian children the church took under its wing, and I went through the whole baptism, communion ritual. But the hard questions, the real probing

I eventually brought to religion never brought the kind of answers I wanted. I was still a nominal Episcopalian the day I first heard of Steve.

That day the office was inordinately quiet, and I was doing make work, cleaning out old patient files, packing them in boxes the doctor would put in storage. When the bell on the outside door rang, I looked up. One of the small town elites, the district attorney entered. Along with the judge, the doctor, the hotel and casino owners, and the big ranchers, they made most of the unwritten rules. Some celebrated a birthday or other important occasions on the town, but mostly they socialized at home.

Only the banker, a widower, spent his Saturday nights going from bar to bar with the young crowd from the mines or the cowboys in from the ranches. Age was not a barrier. Gossip said he also made it across the tracks where the two non-descript houses became emblazoned with neon after dark. I was the only "good" woman in town who saw the "girls." They came to the office from the Desert Inn and the Green Lantern for a weekly swab and a monthly blood test. I sent both to the state laboratory for analysis.

The D.A., a man about forty, paused at my desk and exchanged a few words before he asked, "His nibs busy?"

I gestured to the empty waiting room, the same one I decorated at Christmas because that's what people did. "No one's with him, if that's what you mean." Not a stickler for staying on schedule, the doctor visited with favored patients until I had to remind him about the schedule. Sometimes as many as eight or ten people filled the waiting room.

"Thanks." The D.A. disappeared down the hall to the examining room, and didn't close the door behind him. I heard the creak of the doctor's chair, and scraping sounds as the D.A. made himself comfortable in the other chair. In addition to an examining table and small tables with tongue depressors and the minutia of the medical trade, there was also a cabinet filled with dental supplies. In an emergency the doctor pulled teeth. A short man in his early fifties, his girth was partially obliterated by a while coat. The DA by contrast was a tall man of average weight.

The next patient wasn't due for forty-five minutes, so I expected they'd exchange a ton of gossip. I worked with one ear cocked toward the hall, catching most of the conversation, filling in the gaps with logic. A woman at the other end of the county had walked out on three children and a baby. Left them alone.

The D.A. announced, "We have the kids in foster homes."

"Hell of a note," I heard the doctor say.

There was silence and then a spate of words, not all clear. I gathered the kids were quite young.

The D.A.'s voice had a firm, this is it, quality when he said, "We're going to put them up for adoption."

Silence, and then the doctor cleared his throat and said, "Isn't that soon?"

"Not with her record. As I make it, four kids, three different fathers. Left those kids alone for days. A neighbor saw the boy climbing up on a chair and then up on the counter to get oatmeal down from the cupboard. Or maybe it was rice. She wasn't sure. But he was fixing a meal for the others when she spotted him through the window."

Another silence while the doctor apparently assimilated the news. My own heart was doing its typical dance as I pictured that little boy. I wished they would speak louder, but I couldn't make an excuse to go to the x-ray room which was closer to them.

After a long pause, I heard the D.A. say, "You interested, Doc? That boy's a charmer. Guy who owns the bar said the kid would come in sometimes. The men coming off shift would pretend to box with him for pennies. Same age as your boy."

"That so?" I could imagine the doctor nodding. "I'm too old to take on another. You got any prospects?"

"The Mrs. has taken a shine to that youngest girl. And there's a couple I know who probably would jump at the chance of getting a baby."

"So that leaves what?' I heard the doctor's chair creak, and knew he was getting up to close the door, knowing the next patient, one of the town's hypochondriacs, usually arrived early.

Before the door closed I heard the D.A. say, "The boy just turned five."

My son, I thought. He's going to be my son. The doctors I'd consulted because I hadn't gotten pregnant had said they couldn't determine what was wrong unless Bill was tested, too. Bill wouldn't go, saying crudely, "I will not jack off in a cup." Always I'd dreamed of a family life with Sundays like I'd had as a kid. I wanted a child.

When noon came, I wasted no time leaving. The office would be closed until I returned an hour and a half later. I rushed home, cutting through vacant lots and left a note for Bill who got home before me. We have a good chance to get the boy or the oldest girl or both, I wrote.

That night Bill let me talk him into seeing what I could do. "But only one," he said in a voice that meant he didn't want to discuss it further.

In the morning, I was leaving the house at the same time the judge's wife was walking by. I fell into step with her, and within a short time had steered the conversation toward those children. Before I veered off towards the doctor's office, she said she certainly would put in a word for me with her husband. A religious person would say god had made the coincidence happen. Whether her speaking out had any bearing on the ultimate outcome, I don't know, but it was a great example of coincidence and 'guts' on my part. If I had hung back and let her walk alone, I would never have learned the boy's name was Steve.

The first time I saw him I was hooked. He was cute, smart, and charming. He had learned to use his wits, and he certainly knew how to turn on the charm, and I was ready to receive it.

Not long afterward, Bill and I, with Steve between us in the pickup, rode the 90 miles back from Austin, the county seat where we had been all day. The night was dark, the pickup's lights occasionally highlighting sage brush or the turnoff to a dirt road. Steve, who had been looking straight ahead, turned to me and then to Bill who was driving. "Mama, Daddy?" he said. I could have cried with delight.

In that apartment in Oakland, I realized again how hard it must have been for him in those early years. That he had my unconditional love I'd thought at the time would see him through separation from his siblings, from the only life he'd ever known. I was as naïve as most women of the nineteen fifties. We were spoon fed the story that a loving family would fix everything. (God was looking over and after us.) Be good, kind and fair to others and the world would treat you well. While I ignored the god part, I ingested the loving family part with alacrity.

As Steve and I, without Rhonda, drove the Oakland hills, seeing the luxury homes that perched on the heights, he told me he felt trapped. He and Rhonda weren't that compatible. Intellectually, she wasn't his peer. Her interests were on a strong family life. He hadn't wanted children yet. He wasn't ready. What he really wanted to do was have a career in the navy. He'd told

Rhonda, and without telling him, she had gone off the pill. He didn't know what to do. That I couldn't help him saddened me. Like it or not he had a child on the way.

I went home and trusted that the future would work itself out. When Terran was born, Steve was ecstatic and I never heard anything more about his feelings regarding Rhonda. And like always, I seldom heard from him. Shortly after his stint in Oakland, he was at sea again, and Rhonda was back in Las Vegas near her mother. The two women were exceedingly close, Rhonda relying on her mother. With her mother's backing, Rhonda convinced Steve he belonged at home, not in the Navy. He left reluctantly. He loved his daughter without restraint and thought he was doing the best for her. I hoped it would be enough for the three of them to go on, forge a good family life, and for a while it seemed to work.

As soon as possible, Hank and I drove to Las Vegas to see Steve and Rhonda, and above all our grandchild. It was a fun time, Terran learning to walk, little Henry guiding her first steps, Steve looking young but capable. We picnicked at Mt. Charleston, ate on the strip and enjoyed shows at Caesar's and the Sands through complimentary tickets Steve managed to get for all of us. He had gotten into the air conditioning field before he went into the navy and resumed it six years later. With Rhonda working at the Review Journal, helping put out the paper, they appeared to be doing okay economically.

A few years later we went to Las Vegas again. It, too, was a fun time, playing Marco Polo in the backyard pool with Terran, reading the Judy Bloom books with her. Rhonda's day ended before Steve's, and so she was home when he arrived. Having put a meal in the slow cooker before she left for work, she was checking on it when Steve arrived. Neither spoke to one another when he came in, shocking me completely. Hank and I were constantly stroking one another verbally if not physically. Although Steve said everything was fine, I could see it wasn't. It began a time when I couldn't count on hearing from Steve, and Rhonda, fighting her own demons, didn't write either. She couldn't help feeling Steve's less than full bore love for her. The two were in a losing situation

The divorce came when Terran was eight. He and Rhonda got joint custody, and for a while this seemed to work. I visited Steve and Terran during that time, walked Terran to school in the morning and read with her and mostly enjoyed my time. But to my eye Steve seemed troubled, and it began a time when as much as a year would go by without my hearing from him. It was the sour note in my upbeat symphony.

Our life in the tree-shaded area of New Jersey proved interesting and at times exciting. But Hank and I missed the West, its grand vistas. No more driving miles on a whim. Congestion and inbred tradition forbade it. People said, "But that's twenty miles away!" As our years in New Jersey approached seven a slight claustrophobic feeling set in. We had taken advantage of the great theater, museums, and historical sites in Philadelphia and New York City, had walked the boardwalk at Atlantic City, ate its famous taffy, and attended shows at the Steel Pier.

But we were used to pedestrians having the right of way, not drivers looking as if they wouldn't mind plowing into us. We were used to hills and mountains and skies that went on and on. We were used to people who had come from other places to make up the montage of the West. And we were not used to the vast numbers of people per square mile. My farthest view in Mt. Holly was three houses down the block. Although Hank loved his work and said he'd learned more from his boss and mentor, Bob Frankel, than anyone in his career, he began putting out feelers for a position in the west where he preferred to live.

We were still learning things about one another Hank was like a kindergarten child confronted with college courses when trying to identify the garden I planted at the property line of our Mt. Holly home All his life he'd been surrounded by buildings, pavements, sidewalks, stadiums, and traffic.

My small town life had included vegetable gardens and open fields. I assumed everyone recognized carrots, green onions or peas by their foliage, that they recognized queen anne's lace and buttercups. He didn't. I got a kick out of teaching him something, for he was certainly helping me

In college, while the idea of attending with 'kids' had troubled me, I had no trouble getting A's. But when it came to grasping Categorical Propositions in Logic, I floundered. My instructor didn't seem to know how to explain it so I could understand the concept. Hank took time out of his busy schedule to explain in terms that I understood, and I ended the semester with an A.

But we were both feeling boxed in. He said he had felt truly free for the first time when he had encountered the west with its great sweeping dimensions. He'd bonded with the live and let live philosophy and fallen in love with the desert, could identify ocotillo, saguaro, cactus and succulents of all kinds, but not the lowly vegetables he ordered with ease at fancy restaurants. I loved being able to help him achieve the one dimension he lacked. But I, too, missed the West.

Feeling nostalgic, I hosted a Western party complete with chuck wagon food cooked in my kitchen. I made "wanted" posters of all the guests and tacked them up throughout the house and Hank and I dressed in proper western wear. Few of the guests went that far, the men's version of casual being a shirt without a tie, the women's version was sandals instead of high heels. One guest, Jack, whose acerbic wit skirted social norms, liked to be on the vanguard of things. He invested in a pair of jeans and for days he boiled and bleached that new pair so they would look properly "worn." Unfortunately, another guest had a horse farm and arrived wearing boots as well as a vest and bolo tie. Jack took his defeat gracefully. "Curses, outclassed again."

Jack also nailed us about "the meaning of life," maintaining that religion was the answer. Knowing he didn't really believe that, we let him play devil's advocate several times, he and Margaret and our friends Peggy and Al adding to the discussion.

"So what will you do if God suddenly appears, or Jesus comes back to earth?" he asked Hank one night while we were all sitting around after I'd fixed a Greek dinner, Hank and I having been to Europe by now, my culinary efforts pairing well with the red wine someone brought.

Hank laughed. "What else but say I was wrong. But I doubt very much that will happen."

We all agreed and concluded that life had the meaning we put into it. Al worked for a big tobacco company, and everyone except Hank and I smoked at that time, no one questioning the smoke curling to the ceiling as we discussed religion, politics, children, and what to believe and not to believe. We felt as if the Watergate affair was the worst thing that ever happened to America. As the wine and after-dinner drinks flowed, we mentioned, facetiously, moving to another country. But where? What other country had our democracy, our constitution, our separation of church and state. We were Americans through and through. Yet, as knowledgeable and liberal as we were none of us knew that secular, non-theist national organizations existed. Hank and I discovered them a short time later.

Five

"No citizen enjoys genuine freedom of religious conviction until the state is indifferent to every form of religious outlook from atheism to Zoroastrianism."

HAROLD J. LASKI (1893-1950)

In 1976, when summer made the northern hemisphere a delight, Hank said, "How would you like to take a trip, to the Soviet Union?" With thoughts of returning west still simmering in my mind, the glamour of a place few Americans had been since the Cold War intrigued me. Having already been to Europe, Mexico, and Canada, I felt like a seasoned traveler. Hadn't I sat in Constitution Square in Athens sipping ouzo and reading the London Times? Americans still feared the ever growing arsenal of nuclear weapons, school children doing "duck and cover" exercises, but by now we were separating the Soviet people from the government. Everyone we knew was talking about going to the Soviet Union. Hank and I had read about Americans who managed to get past Soviet security and meet ordinary citizens.

"What would you say if I suggested we do the same?" he asked while we were lingering over dinner, splitting a bottle of wine, getting slightly sloshed.

"You mean try to blend in?" I asked, my thoughts zipping. "If we're apprehended, all we have to do is say we're American citizens. Right?"

"Exactly," he said grinning at me.

"But how?" I asked gulping the last bit of wine in my glass, cabernet sauvignon we had bought on a splurge one day, spending more than our usual stipend.

"Looking like the Soviets for one."

Looking out at the row of poplars that separated our yard from our back yard neighbors, I saw a magical sight, lingering twilight lighting the trees with silver. "And two?" I asked, enthusiasm kicking in.

"Not speaking English."

"Speak for yourself. I don't speak Russian."

"Leave it to me," he said getting up and returning with a world atlas. He had studied Russian in college.

As we perused the maps, a sense of adventure filled me. If we pulled it off, we would be doing something few Americans achieved. By the evening's end my determination to do it matched his.

Hank memorized streets and locations in Moscow. I bought clothes at a thrift store that resembled what I'd worn in the 1950's. I also bought pants and shirts for Hank. At a Sears budget shop, I bought eight-dollar dresses, and at Woolworth's I found beads for 88 cents, both for "dress up" times, never realizing that in the Soviet Union, those Sears sale items would look like Paris originals.

When we notified Hank's parents, they announced they would be in Poland at the same time. We immediately made plans to meet them in Warsaw.

Hank had no problems booking a flight to Moscow and, like we'd always done on foreign travel, prepared to see Russia on our own. It had been a very successful way of travel for us. Ahead of time we boned up on the culture, history and geography of where we were going, and I made cheat sheets of the foreign language phonetically so I could at least know how to get along without asking Hank every minute. We secured a baby-sitter for Henry, put the still green tomatoes from my garden in the refrigerator and set off.

Arriving at Sheremetyevo Airport in Moscow, we followed other passenger down the plane's steps to the tarmac. I almost called out, "We're here!" It seemed like we'd been preparing forever. But I clamped my mouth shut and suppressed a startle reaction before taking another step. Soldiers with guns watched us from a few yards away. For a few seconds I stood perfectly still.

"Pretend they don't exist," Hank whispered, coming up behind me.

Still shook, I said nothing. I'd never expected such blatant militarism. Belatedly, I realized Hank was hurrying toward the terminal. I followed. Inside, a preternatural quiet hit me harder than the noisy airport terminals at home. No one was talking, and no one was smiling. Added to the guns I'd just seen, my excitement at having arrived in Russia evaporated and a feeling of utter strangeness made me wary. I glanced at Hank, but he ignored me as we both identified our suitcases and took our place in line. I realized he expected me to follow his example and not draw attention to ourselves, not to do or say anything that would make us stand out as he preceded me in line. Standing quietly, I said nothing.

Ahead of us, a sturdy Russian woman, evidently returning home, unlocked her suitcases and stood quietly while attendants riffled through her luggage, two cardboard boxes and a worn suitcase held together with a man's belt. The officials appeared to be interrogating her at length, their Russian reminding me I wasn't at home. She answered in a monotone, never smiling or frowning. Their voices rose as they pulled her clothes and toilet articles out while continuing to question her. They rummaged through her belongings thoroughly, missing nothing, asking questions now and then, she answering in a stoical manner, only her hands pleating her scarf betraying her true state of mind.

I tried to look as disinterested as everyone around me. A quarter hour later, they waved her on.

Again, I glanced at Hank, but again, he didn't return my look. Stop carrying this so damn far, I wanted to shout. Couldn't he see the quiet was getting to me? Behind us, two Americans, the man wearing a Beatles haircut, the woman wearing wildly-teased hair, were shifting from one foot to the other. They shrugged when my gaze crossed theirs. Then it was our turn. The attendants waved us forward. Hank moved into place, me close behind.

In broken English, an unsmiling man asked for our passports. Hank handed them over, apparently forgetting he had stuck our visas for visiting Poland inside. After an agonizing long time, looking from our passport pictures to us, the man indicated we should unlock our luggage. Quickly, Hank complied and turned back to the desk in time to scoop up our passports. Then he frowned.

"What's the matter?" I whispered.

He made a shushing motion and turned back to the counter. "May I have our visas for travel in Poland, please," he said in English. At the same time another airport official began to riffle through our belongings. A cold shiver passed over me. I had read that Russians unhappy with the regime tried to get out of the country any way they could. Our visas would bring a goodly sum on the black market. I tried to show nothing of my feelings as Hank asked for our visas again. It was unnerving enough seeing the ham-handed man's fingers catch on my lingerie. "Please give me our visas for travel in Poland," Hank repeated.

The counter man didn't reply and kept his gaze averted. It was as if nothing had been said. At the same time, the man riffling through our possessions discovered the novel I was currently reading – E. M. Doctorow's book, Ragtime. I held my breath. Would they confiscate it, send us home on the next plane? What? I kept my face noncommittal as the stocky man going through my belongings waved another man over. This one, slimmer and taller, adjusted his pant legs, sat down, opened the book at random and started reading. I figured we were in for a lengthy wait.

Pushing down panic, I glanced at Hank, but again he did not meet my eye as he repeated, louder now, a request for our visas. The man behind the counter shrugged as if to say he did not understand.

The official reading Ragtime, suddenly nodded and put the book back in my suitcase. I suspected he had opened the book at a place where socialism was presented in a way acceptable to the Soviets. I felt only a little relieved. Hank had a Playboy magazine in his suitcase, and they hadn't gone through that yet. We had planned to leave the magazine in a hotel room knowing that a maid would pick it up and sell it for cash in the underground. Again I turned to Hank.

He was leaning over the counter now and talking earnestly, this time in Russian. He told me later he'd demanded our visas. Before leaving home he'd planned not to let Soviet authorities know that he understood and spoke Russian. He had not wanted to break his cover, but it had become necessary. Eyes opening wide, the counter man, saying nothing, turned aside and turned back with the visas in his hand. Without comment, he put them on the counter. The man who had read the novel for at least ten minutes, hearing Hank speaking Russian, looked from him to the counter man, a frown growing on his face. Giving Hank's suitcase a cursory pat or two, he waved us on. We were through customs!

I wanted to laugh, make a joke, say something, but as we moved toward the doors leading out, we were stopped by another official. "You will be staying at the Metropole Hotel," he said. "The Soviet Union, in an effort to make your visit more enjoyable will make sure you are part of a sightseeing group of people from the western world. We will also provide a guide who will speak English. You will enjoy."

Hank nodded, and belatedly, I added my nod, too. Later he whispered that arguing the point would have been useless. "You will enjoy."

I almost laughed out loud.

Guided to a taxi, we were told we were going to the hotel situated not far from Gum Department store, a store equal to the shopping centers in America and a hotel as good as any five star one in the world. I hardly listened to the spiel and hardly noticed the elegance of our lodgings as we entered. Built in 1907, the Metrople had hosted most of the world's celebrities of the past, its art nouveau style magnificent at the time. I was too undone by what had happened at the airport. Now it's main attraction in my estimation, was its location – kitty-corner from the Bolshoi Ballet and a block from Red Square.

"You'd think they'd let us know before coming here we would be put on a tour," I said testily. We'd assumed flying over without being on a tour meant we could travel within the country by ourselves.

We checked in, left our suitcases in our room and went out to reconnoiter. Although we had been restricted from the minute of our arrival, we were still determined to get out on our own as much as possible. Walking down Tverslaya Ulitsa, the central thoroughfare, I was surprised that no one stopped us. I had to pinch myself. We were in the Soviet Union, our country's long-time enemy. We'd been second in the race into space, and the Soviets had been boastful. Nikita Kruschev had told us they would bury us. Both countries had arsenals of weapons of mass destruction that could annihilate life on earth. Yet nothing like that entered my thoughts as we walked down the block, passing a few pedestrians, Slavic appearing men in well-worn suits, work-worn women who avoided eye contact. Being tired, we didn't stay out long.

The next day we met the fifteen other Americans on our Soviet imposed tour – older women, couples, and a young man from Chicago. He consistently lightened the grim atmosphere by making jokes about everything as we toured the city by bus. Standing next to the driver, Luda our young, slim tour guide, contrasted greatly with the plump women we saw on the street.

From the Bolshoi to the Kremlin we viewed famous buildings from outside, Luda explaining what we were seeing. On Red Square, we all clicked photographs of St. Basils with its gaily colored turrets. It added color to the grayish city, the drab clothing, the uniformity of men in military uniforms, and the blurred glimpse we got of officials zooming in and out of the Kremlin in large black cars, all blending with an overcast sky. Only St. Basil's turrets and Victorian style trim brought relief to the landscape. Painted red, burgundy, salmon, yellow, blue, green and gold, it looked like a fairy-tale building, and Hank clicked several photographs of it and me.

From Lenin's tomb we were rushed on, Luda keeping a tight schedule. At the Armory she said we could view the degeneracy of the czars, the relics of the Imperial Age. It was easy to imagine the last Czar and Czarina, their daughters and their son riding in one of the huge wooden carriages, the gold and gilt detail augmented with bud vases of crystal.

Two days later, after a day of seeing what Luda called Soviet triumphs, she announced the next day we would see the great stride forward by the Russian people since Lenin liberated the country. She would explain the five-year plans and other great accomplishments that had brought the communist state to its present great place in the world. As she spouted propaganda, pausing now and then to find the right English word, Hank squeezed my hand once and then twice. The signal meant we would dodge the tour in the morning. At dinner while we all picked at what we called "mystery meat," I began planning my "Soviet" wardrobe and polished off the ubiquitous cabbage, potatoes and beets as if they were gourmet food while I complained of a queasy feeling in the stomach.

Early the next day Hank sent a message to the desk for Luda. Jet lag and the threat of colds would keep us in. Hopefully, we'd ward off a virus with rest and see her and the group when we felt better.

As soon as the bus left, I put on a long skirt and a plain blouse, circa the 50's. With my hair skinned back unbecomingly, and wearing no makeup, no one in the hotel gave me a second glace as Hank, in a yellowing white shirt and dated pants, and I left the hotel behind. I'd already learned the Sears budget clothing put us in a category we didn't own. In the great subway system, Luda keeping us all together, I had stood, clutching a strap near a seat where a woman with large knuckled hands sat. She looked up at me with a gap-toothed smile, her broad face thinning a network of lines and wrinkles. With gestures, she offered me her seat. I shook my head, muttered spa-see-buh, thank you in Russian, and smiled in what I hoped was a friendly, appreciative way. She looked sixty or so, but I expected she was no older than me. My short red dress, set off by the 88 cent white beads, were far from grand. But in that train, I personified a woman of the rich upper class. I thought it ironic that in the land of supposed equality, a tired woman offered me a seat. Was the so-called classless society a fraud?

At least the subway lived up to its reputation. No graffiti, no hooligans hanging around, everything clean and attractive, so deep in places the escalators leading to the streets were exceedingly long and exceedingly steep. I kept feeling as if I'd fall backward.

Now on our own, using his memorized knowledge of the city, Hank led us through Gum Department Store – no great shakes according to American standards – by the notorious Lubyanka Prison where I, foolishly, snapped a photo, and hesitated near the American Embassy complex. We could see little beyond the entrance and tried to get closer. In Russian, a Soviet guard told us to move on, this place belonged to Americans. We held our laughter in until we were out of his sight. We had passed! Hank reminded me not to smile so much and not to hold his hand. He said we should not speak English. If necessary he'd speak to me in Polish. I had learned enough of the language to get the gist of whatever he said. Otherwise I'd be silent. We'd probably not draw attention to ourselves if he spoke quietly and I added a Polish word occasionally. Inasmuch as Poland was under the Soviet fist, we could be Poles visiting Moscow.

Silently, we wandered over to the Moscow River where a line of people waited to buy tickets for a boat ride. A gentle breeze was ruffling flags at the Kremlin, the Soviet summer in full sway. We joined the line and others crowded in behind us. The line stretched out, broadened. We all waited, and then waited some more for the ticket booth to open. We could see someone inside.

A murmur began to grow, children grown restless, strained at parents restraining hands. A few people began to complain. Even though I didn't understand the words, I could tell by the tone. Ahead of us a young man in a blue work shirt spoke to a woman wearing a summer dress with puffed sleeves, something I hadn't seen in years. I assumed she was his wife for a child in a colorful playsuit clung to her hand. The woman looked to be in her twenties, her face round and without a line, her sandy colored hair obviously had been set in pin curls, like the bobby pins we'd all used in the forties and early fifties. Her tow-headed daughter, glanced at us with suspicion. An older man, his hair liberally sprinkled with gray, spoke to them both, his voice deep with a warning edge.

Comments from up and down the line got louder. The young man tossed a sentence over his shoulder, clearly meant for us. Fearing he would address me if I made eye contact, I glanced at Hank, determined not to blow our cover. Hank had boned up on his Russian before we left New Jersey. Now he was answering without hesitation. The young man nodded as if in agreement, his broad Slavic cheekbones almost casting his face in a perpetual smile of happiness. I hoped he actually was.

Abruptly, the man selling tickets waved the first people forward. Soon the whole line was moving, only murmurs discernible now.

As Hank bought our tickets, the couple with the older man stood nearby, the rest of the line boarding the boat. The woman smiled at me; I smiled back. The younger man spoke, asking something for his voice rose at the end of the sentence.

Hank said yes. It was one of the few words I knew. As we climbed the gangplank of the sight-seeing vessel, I poked him and Hank whispered that they wanted us to sit with them. He began threading past people settling on seats big enough for only three. He pointed to two bench seats one in front of the other, and indicated we would sit behind them.

We all slid into place, and as the boat left the pier, the young man leaned over the seatback and said he was Dimitri and his wife was Eda, their little girl Galina. The older man said he was Boris. Hank gave them the Russian versions of our names.

Dimitri asked another question. I thought I recognized something about location. Again, I glanced at Hank.

He looked as if he was preparing to speak, weighing what to say, but the older man spoke before Hank could. "Czechoslovakia, Poland?" he named Soviet Block nations. Although the names were pronounced differently from the way I would say them, they were similar enough that I understood.

Glancing first at me before adding a shrug, Hank said with pride, "American." Later, he told me he had felt a surge of patriotism and knew he could not pretend when asked straight out. They had actually thought we were from one of the Slavic satellites. We had passed close scrutiny

Taking my cue from Hank I nodded affirmation, adding "American."

"No," came from all three adults, and Boris sniffed as if the idea were preposterous and looked down his considerable nose at us.

Both Hank and I were smiling broadly now. "Yes." We had hoped our faded and out-dated clothes would let us blend in, and apparently it had. It probably helped that with no makeup, I fit in well.

They shook their heads adamantly, repeated nyet, no.

"But we are," I said in English.

They glanced at one another before turning back toward us. By now the other passengers were talking to one another, no one paying us the least attention as the pier disappeared behind us, the decibel level drowned out our talk

Dimitri said in stilted English. "I think you Poland. Nyet America." The older man nodded.

"Why?" I asked. The boat was gliding through the city, but I saw little of it. We were achieving our goal, talking to ordinary Russians.

Dimitri pointed and continued in English, "Your shoes. Too good."

We'd never thought of that. I glanced around. All of our new acquaintances wore cheap sandals.

Hank looked pleased that it was our shoes that had given us away. "So my Russian was understandable?"

"Was clear, with, how you say... ?" Speaking English, Dimitri moved his hand in an arc.

"Accent?" I brought my gaze from the other passengers and their poorly shod feet. I was rewarded with instantaneous smiles from our new Russian acquaintances.

Boris said, "Accent like Poland." His face wore a look of superiority. Under the domination of the Soviets, Poland gave the Russians something to feel better about. We found out later that trucks full of meat and vegetables went from Poland to Russia weekly.

Looking shyly at me, Ada pointed to apartment buildings, "Moscow. Nice." Her voice did not rise at the end of the words, and I gathered she expected me to feel the same admiration she obviously did.

I mentioned the Bolshoi, said "Great dancers."

"Yes," she agreed. The men nodded. Boris's head went higher.

I said, "St. Basil's," and smiled and nodded.

They smiled and again said yes.

It was slow going. I mentioned the Gum department store, although it had not overwhelmed me in the way I'd expected. I pointed to the older man and then to Dimitri. "Are you father and son?"

Hank translated the words into Russian.

Nodding, they followed with Russian that Hank translated for me.

I glanced out the right side of the open-air boat. The sky had few clouds, the air was soft, the temperature hovering around seventy degrees Fahrenheit. Passing a narrow, pebbly beach where men and women of all ages, sizes, and fitness sunbathed or waded near the shore, Eda said, "Is nice." Most of the people wore their underwear; bathing suits were few. I nudged Hank and repeated "Nice," to Eda.

For a time the shore claimed our attention, as it did everyone in the boat. The excited talk of the early few minutes descended to quiet comments. Dimitri said it was their first time in Moscow, but Boris used to live there. He named a city forty or so miles away that he, Eda and Galina called home. They were on holiday and going to Gorky Park.

"Come with?" Eda suggested.

"Yes, please," Dimitri added, looking from me to Hank and back.

Our being with them would be a tale repeated often when we were home again. Would they be as free to talk about it?

"Yes." Hank and I answered almost simultaneously.

"Is good," Boris said, and we all settled back in our seats.

At the park, Boris led us to the children's section. Exclaiming about everything they saw, it was clear the younger couple had never been there before. They were as excited as their daughter at the sights and sounds. Boris said little. I could not figure out whether he disapproved of us or just liked feeling superior. He seldom smiled while Dimitri and Eda smiled constantly.

Today Gorky Park is as sophisticated as any amusement park in the west. Then, it wasn't. All three Russian adults appeared naively proud of the elementary rides and proud that we were with them. I heard Dimitri say "America" to several bystanders and point at us. Boris shrugged as if everyone could see Americans were no better than Russians. One ride had both adults and children vying for the seats. Riders sat in individual swings that went round and round moderately high. As Boris engaged Hank in deep conversation, Eda and Dimitri insisted I ride, too.

I allowed myself to be strapped in. "Is nice?" Dimitri called as we floated above the crowd. Eda waved at Boris and Hank talking below. Boris was gesturing broadly, his head inclined toward Hank. My husband would never have let anyone stand that close at home. I would never have been per-suaded to ride something I considered for children. But here old women with lined faces and white hair, men stooped and palsied acted as if they'd never enjoyed anything more. They laughed and waved at us as we went round and round.

The rest of the afternoon became a montage of strolling, riding and eat-ing. As the sun began to dip, Boris led the way to a restaurant set among the trees. Although crowded and noisy, it did not spoil Dimitri's and Eda's spirits. They commented on everything they saw, sometimes saying "nice," or "good" in English. It was easy to see they were thrilled by everything.

As the afternoon progressed, Eda lost much of her shyness, commenting almost as much as Dimitri. Chattering in Russian, she took my arm, held Galina in the other. She only let go of my arm when Galina's head began to nod and she fell asleep. Dimitri stayed in step with Hank, and he and Boris took turns paying for everything. They would not let us spend a kopek, no matter how we tried. "My treat," Boris would say each time he paid for an orange soda or a souvenir, his head going high.

At the restaurant, we followed Boris past tables full of celebrating people to a table for six. By now the warmth of the day was receding, and I was glad I'd brought a sweater. Boris ordered, and soon plates of pyrogy, sausage, beets and potatoes, served with heavy black bread appeared in front of us. A bottle of vodka was put in the middle of the table, along with orange sodas. A sprin-kling of dim lights went on, leaving the corners dark, the people at other tables in silhouette, faces lost in shadow.

I ate and praised the dumplings. Hank talked about the difference between Russian and Polish pierogi. He told them his grandparents had been born in Poland, that we were going there when we left Russia. Boris's superior look fell into place. "So, you Polish."

"No, American," I said, adding we lived in New Jersey. They stared at me blankly and asked if we lived near Hollywood. Had we been to Las Vegas? We explained we had once lived in Las Vegas. Admiringly they nodded their heads as if this verified their knowledge of what Americans would be like.

A temporary quiet descended as Dimitri lifted his glass of vodka and saluted us. Hank lifted his glass and in Russian said it was a pleasure to be with them. I clicked my orange soda glass against Eda's.

We all turned to the blintz that Hank had ordered and insisted on paying for. Neither men argued with him, and I surmised it was a real treat. The pastry had little of the flakiness I expected but was moderately good. The three Russians ate it with gusto. Afterward, Boris refilled the men's glasses, the level going down in the vodka bottle. Almost all tables had a bottle of vodka and some men clearly felt the effects of the liquor.

Boris suddenly asked about liberty.

Hank and I tried to explain. Again, it was more difficult than I had perceived at home when we'd planned the adventure. I talked fast and convincingly, but Hank had to explain English words in Russian, and sometimes there were no adequate translations. At times we stared at the Russians, and they at us, neither side comprehending what the other had meant. At such times Boris would hold up the vodka bottle and laugh before filling glasses again, now even including Eda and me. They laughed as I demurred, but my new friends gestured that I should drink.

I sipped the vodka.

"You have church America?" Eda's voice was as soft as the child she cuddled.

I nodded.

"Many churches." Hank said in Russian.

"Christ church?"

Did she mean the Church of Christ or was it her way of saying Christian? Figuring it had to be the latter, I said, "Yes."

Her smile broadened. "You Christ church?

It was not what I'd expected. Remembering my own foray into religion when I was married to Bill, I glanced toward Hank who was saying something about Lenin calling religion the opiate of the masses.

A short silence followed then Boris frowned and said in Russian, "Women." He shrugged, spread open his hands. "She hears foolishness from her Babushka."

While Hank translated, I looked at Eda. She would not meet my gaze. A man in the corner was playing an accordion, and a middle-aged couple were dancing in the space between two tables, stomping their feet and laughing, people at the tables laughing, too.

Dimitri leaned toward Eda and said something in a low voice. I gather he was telling her to lighten up, at least that's what Hank overheard. He told them we didn't go to church.

Both men smiled again.

With his hand, Boris began keeping time with the music, tapping the table on alternate beats. "Is party," he said.

Dimitri repeated the words, and soon the two began singing. Eda smiled and lifted her head and looked at me shyly. Soon we were all keeping time, they singing, I humming. Hank picked up the bottle and, bypassing his own glass, filled the Russians glasses with the last dregs.

Everyone laughed.

Eda said, "Poland Catholic."

Hank and I reminded her we were Americans.

"Americans, Christ church," she said.

It was impossible to answer. "Some," Hank said, but by now Boris and Dimitri were singing again.

Later, in the taxi taking us back to the hotel, they told the driver we were Americans, and he, too, showed his surprise. The streets were practically free of traffic. When we pulled up in front of the Metropole, our new friends, including the taxi driver, took turns kissing us on both cheeks, all of us spilling out onto the empty pavement, the grand façade of the Bolshoi gleaming, the Metropole imposing in the moonlight. We had taken the architecture for granted when we'd arrived. Hadn't we known the palaces of Las Vegas? We waved as we went in, turning to look back and wave one more time at people we'd probably never see again.

Seeing no one in the lobby, we hurried to our floor, having taken the key with us in the morning. The key lady, a broad-faced bully who had glared at us previously, jumped up from behind her table and put her considerable bulk between us and the door to our bedroom. "Is American room," she said smacking her hands together.

"We are Americans," we both said in English. Snatching the key from her hand, Hank added a few words in Russian about contacting our embassy. I wanted to giggle, but knew it was important to keep my dignity. I'd never said American so many times in one day before. "We're Mr. and Mrs. Henry Kocol of the United States of America," I added, my head high, the thought of being top dog in a world of many dogs giving me strength. I could have taken on the Russian army.

Frowning, she took her seat again. Although she said nothing, I could see we had gotten through.

The next day at the Bolshoi, in the red velvet and marble splendor I was lost in admiration of the dancers, the music, the artistry. At that time Russian ballet dancers were leaping higher, staying on point longer, electrifying dancers in the West. The Russians were at the pinnacle of world ballet

While I watched transfixed, I was shocked out of my dream of being part of Russia's royal past when the house lights went up for intermission. So much had happened so soon, only days since we'd arrived in Moscow. As people edged by us, Hank and I were virtually alone in our seats. Shaking off fatigue, the day before playing itself through my mind again, I asked Hank what he made of Eda's questions about church. "Do you think maybe it's wrong to ban all religion? Eda certainly had a longing for it. Don't you think so?" He was wearing a sport coat, white shirt and tie, I had donned the fanciest dress I'd brought with me, the splashiest necklace, my makeup impeccable. Eda would never recognize me.

"Out of ignorance. And of course it's as wrong to ban religion as to force it on anyone." He spoke as if that was all there was to it, and it certainly was an American reply, but I had thought we could discuss it more.

I frowned and looked around before speaking again. No one seemed to be paying the least attention to us, people talking to one another, Russian landing on my ear like a drum. We were a few steps from the refreshment stand, caviar and toast points available with vodka and the over-sweet orange soda pop. One of the American women in our tour group had approached the stand. Wearing New England tweeds and pearls, she leaned heavily on a cane, her fingers bristling with jeweled rings. "Look." I poked Hank. The woman I recall as Martha had bucked the long line that staggered a considerable length. She had the attendant's attention immediately.

Hank shrugged. "I doubt she realizes what she's done. Like Eda"

"You may be right about Martha." The attendant stood at the end of the food stand rather than the middle. "But Eda's really young. She has to know what's going on. Do you think she has a gene for religious devotion, like some Americans say?" I opened my evening bag, checked my makeup in the mirror. My hair was now loose and waving becomingly.

"I think the answer is she was raised by her grandmother." He stood. "Let's get in line before the caviar is gone."

"Okay, but first tell me what was eating Boris? It looked like you were having a heated discussion while I whirled around and around." I rolled my eyes.

"Oh, that. I suppose the obligatory debate over communism versus capitalism. He made his points; I made mine. We did our duty for our countries." Grinning at me, he started off.

I hurried after him, past men in shiny serge suits, women in cheap floral jersey dresses. A few men looked as if they had just come from London, the women from France, the men in three piece suits and shiny shoes, the women wearing Chanel and pointed-toe high-heeled silver pumps. Undoubtedly, they were visiting diplomats or Communists high in the party. I said no more about Eda's religious bent, but it seeped from the very walls of the hotel in Leningrad when we ended up there.

The city that Peter the Great built for a window on the west has now reverted to its former name, St. Petersburg. But while the country remained under Soviet rule, it was Leningrad. And it was shivering cold in June. It was also the place where Hank and I continued our talk about Eda. In the northern city, I felt as if the music of Rachmaninov and the literary genius of Tolstoy could sometime prevail, a life of the arts, not communism. And of course the Russian Orthodox religion with its vast ritual, onion-shaped domes that we sighted brought thoughts of Eda to the fore.

Our room had high ceilings and thick walls, the windows covered by a series of small shutters. In order to look out and avoid the deep cold of winter, one could open the tiniest shutter only. Feeling like a prisoner, waiting for Luda – the Soviet tour leader who accompanied us from town to town – I was feeling down. We had toured the Hermitage, its gold and malachite, its sweeping stairways vying for attention with the international paintings and sculptures exhibited. But despite the magnificence and the grand playfulness of the grounds at the summer palace, fountains that went on when someone stepped within their perimeter, I was now seeing the country as gray. The grimness of the political regime had permeated the society. Soviet citizens seldom wore a cheerful expression, and I had ceased smiling at them. To add insult to a trying situation, the food seemed to get worse, not better. I couldn't stand eating the heavy bread or the sausages that were skinny as hotdogs but tasteless.

"Did you really feel that Eda was influenced by her grandmother?" I fished a sweater out of my suitcase. It would be a long day, and I might need it when the sun went down. I reminded Hank I had Eda's address and intended to write. If she answered in Russian; he could translate.

"Her grandmother probably went to church as a girl." He put our suit-cases near the door, checked again to see they were locked and the keys in his pocket. We would be leaving on the train that night for Warsaw where Hank's parents, in Poland on vacation, would meet us.

I thought for a minute. The sun had not yet risen, a dull pewter lit the sky. "And Eda remembered the religion of her grandmother with nostalgia? Is that what you mean? That feeling or whatever rubbed off on Eda?"

"The forbidden always has a powerful pull."

'That's true." How much had the difference in Hank's and my age added to the romance when we met? The town where Dimitri and Eda lived was an industrial center. They both worked at some manufacturing plant, she leaving their daughter at a child care center. At least they were ahead of America in that respect, no other I could see. "Maybe she equates religion with freedom." Weren't the Soviet people's freedoms seriously restricted? She'd probably been indoctrinated in obedience to the state at a young age.

That night after Luda and the tour had gone on, we were alone. Just being led around had left me gloomy as the traditional Russian in novels. Now, I began to feel more like myself again. We spent the evening in the hotel restaurant among the Soviets. People did not come and go, but secured a table for the whole evening. As the night progressed, the room became louder, talk and laughter at times drowning out the music. Bald-headed men became staggeringly drunk while I ate the best meal I'd had in Russia. The Chicken Kiev was delicious, the mashed potatoes fluffy, the broccoli fresh and not overcooked. I savored each bite and finished it off with a Russian torte. It, too, was good. A band had taken up the far end of the room, and couples were dancing. We managed two slow waltzes, but fatigue weighed heavily upon us.

At midnight we taxied to the railroad station to find a myriad of train cars waiting on the tracks. Luckily Hank had purchased our tickets ahead of time. The overcast day had ended in a deep black night, the moon hidden behind a thick layer of clouds. The railroad yard was dimly lit, a surreal painting in black and gray. In the shadowy night, we paused to get our bearings while an attendant took our luggage and placed it on what looked like a very large wheelbarrow. Pushing it, he began running through that large, asphalt-paved lot toward the train. In seconds, I could barely see him and our luggage.

Running after him, I shouted, "Hey, you with our bags." I had no idea how we would locate our car. We needed our luggage in our compartment. Would this man see to that? Ahead of me, the attendant paused long enough to shrug. It was obvious he didn't understand English. As he went off with our belongings, Hank said, "Don't get so excited," and took my arm, keeping me from rushing off again. "All we have to do is get on. Someone will direct us. And our bags will be there."

Seeing how silly I must have looked, I agreed. By this time I had had it with Russia, its regimentation, its gray unfriendliness. Glancing around, I saw no one else. Could we be left behind? "Yes, let's board." We started towards the extremely long line of railroad cars. The few people we had seen earlier had probably boarded. The feeling that had grown through the night struck full force: I wished I were home.

A voice broke into my "pity me" stance. "Americans?" Partially muffled by distance, the words still rang clear.

Hank turned in the direction of the sound, and I gazed past him to where a man was waving. Together, we stepped toward him. He wasn't alone. A woman stood close to him, both of them with heads high. Not even the shadows could hide their attractiveness and the warmth coming from both of them, their smiles disarming. The man said in English, "We are Anna and Jerzy Feiner. We're returning home after a vacation in the Soviet Union."

Surprised, we said nothing.

"We visit – what you say – museums?" The woman's attempt to speak English was endearing, but she had let us know we had something in common.

I said, "Are you from Poland?" That would be a nice coincidence.

"Yes, we are Poles," the man said, and it was clear he was proud of the fact.

"<u>Yestem</u> <u>Ameryki</u>," Hank said in Polish, and explained his grandparents had been born in Poland. For a few seconds we all stood grinning at one another. The two men shook hands. Then the train whistle sounded the alarm. It was past time to get on, and the man with our luggage was nowhere in sight.

Hank said, "Excuse us, we have to hurry."

"We have to find our car," I said.

Jerzy began lifting his luggage. "You are traveling first class, yes?"

Hank and I nodded.

Jerzy pointed out our car. "We will see you later on the train."

We all ran, they burdened with their bags, I trusting our bags would arrive safely, Hank assuring me they would.

At the proper car, an attendant reached out and helped us aboard, and Hank handed him our tickets. He glanced at them and led us to our stateroom. The Polish couple had disappeared.

My fatigue momentarily lifted, I stood by calmly as Russian soldiers entered our compartment, turned our bunks upside down, went through our belongings, and held our passport photos next to our faces, one man looking at the other before both nodded and they departed.

I had no trouble sleeping that night, waking in Estonia when day broke, striking our window with sunrays illuminating a pastoral setting.

Six

*"To require conformity in the appreciation of sentiments
or the interpretation of language, or uniformity of
thought, feeling or action, is a fundamental error..."*

JOSIAH WARREN (1798-1874)

The scene outside moved by at a fast clip. All sleep forgotten, I marveled at how each inch of land, even the strip alongside the railroad had been utilized for growing crops.

Before we left Leningrad, we had learned there would be no dining car aboard. Hank had shopped in three different stores in order to get food for the trip, standing in multiple lines. We had bread, cheese, wine, and cookies. After eating some bread and cheese, food was not our first thought. Leaving our compartment, we strolled through car after car looking for the people from the railroad yard. It would be good to talk to someone from Poland. Neither of us had ever been there, and it would be nice to get inside information. Quickly we passed through the first class cars where foreigners and rich Russians traveled. Most compartment doors were closed. But some Soviets sat with their doors open and nodded as we passed.

"The Polish couple are probably not riding first class," Hank said leading the way from one car to the next as the long line of cars swayed through the countryside. Having no compartments, the second-class cars had people everywhere, jostling one another as the train picked up speed. At times we had to weave our way past people sharing picnic style breakfasts, others attempting to sleep, groups talking in loud voices.

In the third second-class car, again people everywhere, we found Anna. I told her we had a "<u>butelka</u>" of vino and would be glad to share it with them later. I was proud of being able to pull that Polish word from my slim repertoire. Before we left home Hank had provided me words and phrases and attempted to instill in me respect for Polish grammar. His success is doubtful, but I learned enough Polish to follow simple and slow conversations and get the gist of others. Now, the sibilant sounds of Polish and the slightly more militant sounds of Russian had ceased. Everyone had their ears cocked toward us. "Don't speak English," Anna whispered. "Is not safe." She never looked at us.

My eyes widened, and my heart did its little tap dance.

She edged by us as if we were unknown to her. Out of the side of her mouth, she said, "We find you later."

I literally gulped. Alarmed, I exchanged glances with Hank, and we hurried back to our compartment. Throughout the trip we had acted and reacted as Americans. Now we reconsidered. Had our dressing down and going out in Moscow been dangerous for the Russians who spent the day with us? How about us? The cold war still froze trust. Had we been followed, reported upon? We tossed the questions back and forth before deciding no amount of conjecturing could change our actions. We had to put it from our minds. If the Soviets had known about our clandestine moves, they hadn't acted upon it.

Late that afternoon a knock came on our compartment door. Hank opened it to Jerzy and Anna. He was charm personified; his English almost impeccable. Although hers was more hesitant, more accented, her bearing gave clues to her family status, and her classic high-cheek bones were perfect material for an artist. Sharing wine and stories, we learned he was a painter of fine art, an architect, a professor, she a mother of two. At times she spoke about cultural events on Polish television. We gave them thumbnail descriptions of ourselves, and we four smiled at one another and made toasts – in English, Polish, and Russian. Before they left, they gave us their address and asked us to visit when we were in Cracow.

Later as we approached the Polish border, the train stopped abruptly. In a Russian guardhouse I glimpsed a soldier with a rifle at the ready. On the other side of the border, men were waving and milling about. "They're Poles," Hank explained.

The difference between the dour Russians and the smiling Poles made me put my face to the window and watch as the workers changed wheels on the train. "I think I'm in love," I said to Hank as I waved to the Pole nearest my window. "I adore those men out there, they're smiling." I turned to him. "But what's happening?"

"They're changing wheels to fit the smaller gauge tracks in Poland. It discourages escape by the Russians and keeps the Poles relatively safe from a complete invasion by the Soviets."

The Polish workers' smiles undid me. I was sure I'd love everything about Poland. Except when we passed as Polish visitors, everywhere in the Soviet Union, the Russian citizens withheld all signs of friendship, smiles rare, greetings nil. The whole country had a grayness to it that undid me. I'd had my fill of a communist state.

At the train depot in Warsaw, Hank's parents waited. I caught sight of them as the train slowed down in the station. I love color, bright orange, burnt orange, teal, aqua, glittering gold, startling white, black that gleams. In the Soviet State, I felt as if I'd been surrounded by an absence of color, daytime rendering the brightest objects colorless. Hank's parents seemed to sparkle and looked so very, very American, I almost trampled Hank getting to them first. My mother-in-law wore a blazing white pants suit; her hair was fashionably blonde and coiffed, her shoes and purse golden, a blue and gold scarf draped artfully around her neck. My father-in-law, a sturdier, older version of Hank, wore casual tan slacks and a bright yellow shirt under a sport coat. They looked beautiful. They looked American.

"I'm so glad to see you," I shouted rushing at them. I'd never been as demonstrative before. It probably astounded them.

They led us on a circle of visits with relatives, young people, old people, fairly well off, poor, or struggling in the Soviet dominated economy. An ever-lasting array of food appeared on tables in small houses, modern apartments and farms as we made obligatory visits to anyone and everyone who was re-lated to Hank. We watched trucks filled with Polish produce leave for Russia. Sugar was rationed; life was harsh, but the family treated us like royalty. "God will look after us," they said. We said nothing.

I wanted to say God hadn't done a very good job so far. Nor had he looked out for them during the Nazi takeover. One of Hank's relatives had been part of the slave labor force in Germany during World War II. Others had had their lives torn apart, dying in the initial Nazi invasion or afterward during the dark days. None of them talked about it as they served lavish lunches and dinners, urging us to "Eat, eat." I felt as if I would burst in two until I learned to taste everything only. It was not required that I eat it all.

Leon Uris's unforgettable book about the Warsaw Ghetto during World War II, had seared my mind with images, but now I saw no sign of the Ghetto ruins or even a plaque, and no one spoke of it although a very elderly couple, distant cousins of Hank's mother, smirked when we visited them in their small apartment. "Jews used to live here," they said. We said nothing, although again my heart did a dance. A crucifix hung on the wall, a picture of Jesus as a white Caucasian with a beard hung alongside it.

On an earlier European trip we'd been to Dachau. We had been in a rented car, a few blocks from the concentration camp, but no one admitted knowing where the camp was located, although we asked several adults. A teenager pointed out its location. While all aspects of the camp hit us hard, the largest shock was to see the map showing the locations of all the concentration camps in Germany. I had heard the names of the most notorious, but I had not been prepared to see a map showing hundreds of locations. They blanketed the map. I broke down crying. Later I learned the Nazis had established camps, not only in Germany but also in the conquered world, 15,000 in all.

In Poland we went to Auschwitz, walked under that notorious sign, "Work Makt Frei" and saw the exhibits and remains of the camp that was the result of Hitler's Final Solution. If Dachau was hard to see, Auschwitz was heartbreaking. Images of children's shoes, empty suitcases, the crematorium, the barracks and the brick administration buildings are seared on my mind. I stood in the second floor of the building just outside the gate and images of people arriving in box cars, going through the Nazi selection process, and I began sobbing.

Now, I realize being a Christian in those countries did not automatically make everyone good or evil. Jerzy Feiner's aunt, a Mother Superior, hid children in her convent. The Nazis played a game of cat and mouse with her, at odd times descending on her and demanding she give up Jewish children. "I don't have any Jews," she said at first. But the Nazis persisted. Eventually, she had to let them take one and then another and later another. When visiting the Feiners in their comfortable home, Jerzy's studio on the third floor, we told them we were going to Auschwitz the next day.

"Why?" Jerzy asked.

"Because it's important for Americans not to forget," Hank said. I added that we'd lived in the Midwest, knew no Jews and had not known about the atrocities and genocide until after WWII ended.

Jerzy nodded. "Your position is understandable, but I need nothing to help me remember. I spent the war years in my aunt's convent. Others died so I could live." He looked aside. "It is not easy to forget."

Once again I realized how isolated Americans were during that time. Scores of citizens in the Midwest, away from the two coasts were not only un-informed but also naïve. While both Polish men and women put themselves in danger to help Jews, most Catholics went along with the Vatican. When a majority of a population is steeped in Catholicism, disagreeing would have been extremely difficult. In 1976, only twenty-one years after the cessation of fighting in World War II, at least 98% of the Poles in Poland were Catholics.

On a Sunday, Hank and I hosted his extended family at a catered dinner. We arrived near the restaurant as the others were leaving mass. They took it for granted we were sleeping in after our trip. They even said so. Because Hank had exchanged money on the black market, our meal for thirty-five, in-cluding cognac, wine, and many courses cost approximately forty-five dollars Americans. And like the Polish Catholics we knew in America, none of them said grace before eating. Religion for most Poles was a part of life, not a topic to be discussed. No one spoke of religion at any time.

Yet later during the trip, we were not able to avoid a priest who did not speak or understand English. We were site-seeing with Hank's parents who were practicing Catholics, but they never, at home or abroad, suggested we should join them at mass or confession or whatever. At the shrine of the Virgin of Czestochowa we listened to a Polish dissertation about the Black Madonna. The painting had darkened through the years, thus the title. I understood little that was said, and Hank had no desire to translate what he considered mythical talk.

Following the priest's dissertation, my mother and father in law went into the church. Hank and I lingered in the hall outside to wait for them. The priest, who spoke no English, seeing us opened a door that led directly to the sanctuary and indicated we should go in. We shook our heads and said, "No thank you."

The priest, smiling all the while, said we should not be shy and literally shoved me through the door. Not wanting to leave me standing alone in front of the whole church, Hank hurried in behind me. Knowing he was there helped. We learned later that people sometimes hung around in the hall just for such a chance. While liturgy swirled around me, I kept my gaze firmly on the wall in front of me as I stood in front of the railing where the faithful took The Host. *Two atheists were at the altar, and the building did not fall down!* Some believers would have been shocked if they had known. My face red with embarrassment, I listened to the priest drone on in Polish.

I apologized to Hank's parents later. His father merely shrugged. Not your fault; don't worry. I realized then that their belief was part ritual, part tradition, and believing in a god who often goofed. It was more a part of being Polish rather than anything else. The shrine at Czestochowa was part of Polish history, the icon partially destroyed in 1430 by raiders who periodically overran Poland. At that time the icon was painted over. Originally, the icon had been painted on wood that supposedly came from a table used by the holy family. I often wonder why people don't question such nonsense and conclude they don't want to. Once you sincerely drink the waters of faith, you drown in it.

In Cracow we saw this blending of religion and history in the church where every half hour the same haunting phrases of a song are played and cut off abruptly to signify when the original trumpeter died from a Turkish marauder's arrow.

Jerzy and Anna lived not far from the famous square. After we saw the cramped quarters of Hank's cousin, a practicing physician, we realized fully the high status awarded to the Feiners. The doctor's patients sat on chairs in the hall outside his family apartment and consulted with him in the first room of his family home that he used as an office.

The doctor and his wife invited us to a dinner party. Approximately twenty others attended. A large square table took up the majority of the living room, four or five people on each side of the table. When anyone wanted in or out, almost everyone had to get up. Laughter filled the room as the Polish equivalent of "down the hatch" rang out often. Hank's relatives seemingly delighted in toasting us, especially me.

But with the Feiners, space appeared to be no problem. They hosted casually in a home filled with beautiful antiques Anna had inherited from her family. During the evening as our acquaintance grew, and the strongest drink offered was tea, we learned Jerzy taught at Jagiellonian University, founded in 1364, the second oldest university in Europe. The Soviets allowed him to go to countries they controlled, but whenever he had a speaking engagement in London or had an invitation to display his paintings in western cities, Anna and their two children had to stay in Poland as assurance he would return. The Soviets kept them under strict control, considering him too important to let out of the country.

These thoughts colored my thinking as we followed Jerzy up the spiral stairs to his studio, the smell of turpentine and oils I'd noticed on entering the building, growing stronger. Canvasses were stacked against the walls, a half-done painting sat on an easel, a working palette nearby, sable and bristle brushes in a jar. Varnish and other supplies were jammed on a shelf, a few watercolor studies he would use as models for large oil-based paintings hung on a facing wall. The colors were intense but muted. "It is where I hang out," he said, emphasizing the words "hang out," as if proud to use such an American phrase. I immediately said, "<u>Dziekuje</u>," thank you in Polish and then struggled to say "for showing us your studio," and ended saying it in English. We all laughed.

At the front door, as we were leaving, both he and Anna said, "We will see you again when there are no more Soviets."

Our last day in Poland, we drove our rented car to the farm where Hank's mother had grown up. Relatives gathered from all over, one family arriving in a horse drawn wagon. Others crowded into two or three small cars in order to come see us. Once in Cracow, we rode with a cousin, a professor at the university who seemed very fussy, brushing the floor of his car after we'd ridden in it. When he wasn't looking, we exchanged glances. But later we learned that it took years for anyone to purchase an automobile, prospective buyers leaping many hurdles and saving the complete purchase price before they could own a car. In such an economy, we'd keep a brush handy, too.

The gathering at the farm included farmers, small business men, two college professors, and a young man who was giving up his dream to be an auto mechanic to stay on the farm. The collected family had pooled their finances to get him a motor-bike. Because of their munificent gesture, he'd gratefully consented to be a farmer and keep the homestead in the family.

No one talked religion, but it was evident, some making the sign of the cross, all saying the equivalent of "may god bless you," when we said goodnight.

The moon drifted in and out of the clouds, the air soft as we went to our car, everyone following us, some women with gap-toothed grins, others with "store-bought" teeth shining, other women wearing clothes that mimicked my own, men wearing suits that had seen better days, or ones they'd saved for years to buy, and most young people in highly-coveted jeans and t-shirts.

I started to get into our rental car, but Hank shook his head and led me to the large circle the family was forming. They drew us in. As we held hands with people we probably would never see again, Hank's father and mother began singing Sto-Lat and the rest joined in. It meant may you live a hundred years and was the traditional way of saying farewell. The moon shining through an opening in the trees, its shaft, in that instant, covered us with a silver glow. With tears in our eyes, Hank and I got into our rental car and rode away, tapping the horn as we exited the drive.

A half-mile away, the young man on his motor bike awaited, pointing out the route we should take back to the nearest town where we had reservations at the only hotel. I rolled down the window and shouted goodbye several times. Existing under the spell of the evening, I was glad I had said nothing to Hank about the cheap carpet, the harsh toilet paper in the hotel and at the farm.

When we arrived back in New York, I said I wanted to kiss the ground beneath my feet. Hank said I better not. "After all, this is New York." We both laughed. We were home.

Seven

*"The louder he talked of his honor, the
faster we counted our spoons."*

RALPH WALDO EMERSON (1803-1882)

*B*ack home, Hank once again rode the local bus to his office in Philadelphia, and my women friends and I ratcheted up our activities in the women's movement. Fiercely patriotic after my Soviet trip, and fiercely anti-Soviet, I looked at everything in U.S. society through a microscopic lens.

Picketing a Catholic Church gave me a feeling of bravery I hadn't experienced even in the Soviet Union. There it had seemed as if I were playing a game and if caught we'd contact the embassy and plead ignorance or something as ridiculous. The United States would take care of us. But was it taking care of women? And was it breaching the necessary line between church and state? As a child I'd seen my aunt, the one who was fifty pounds overweight in a time when everyone was slender, make fun of priests. While no one in my family ever discussed religion, her words stayed with me from the few times I'd been to her house in Cleveland.

While the main concern of most feminists during the 1970's was equality and choice regarding abortion, mine was two-fold. Churches paid no taxes, so essentially all of us paid for their right to preach their belief. We paid because that land went untaxed, parsonages weren't taxed either. But we paid the firemen who kept their places from burning, we paid for the policemen who protected them and their untaxed property. Hank and I had spent many evenings with like-minded friends deploring such un-American ways.

I'll never forget the shocked look on the faces of the two priests and two nuns in the car that was leaving the church grounds when they spotted us that day. We were less than a dozen women, and our signs said it all. "Keep your hands off my body," read one. "My body, my right," said another. My sign read, "Tax the Church."

About the same time I shocked the Catholics, I had to do an ethnographic study for a cultural anthropology class I was taking. I didn't know who to interview and observe. After all it would be easier if we were in the south Pacific and I was observing a native. What American wanted someone intruding into their life? Hank suggested I get in touch with a cleric. He said he was sure any of them would be eager to go along. I finally chose an American Baptist minister. The American Baptists had separated from the Southern Baptists and I felt would be easier to talk to.

The man who agreed to be interviewed was probably close to my age, rather good-looking, and eager to submit to my prying. Prepared to be objective, I asked the easy questions the first time we talked, and the harder ones the second. He seemed exceedingly honest, and not that radical in his thinking. He even suggested I attend one of his services. I hadn't told him that was my objective all along. It was then Mr. Good Guy became a carnival barker getting someone to come in and see the dog-faced boy. In his sermon, he did all the things I imagined him doing, using words in ways that made people anxious, guilty, tearful, afraid, and finally absolved for their sins by turning to god. The words blood and sacrifice were woven into the life of Jesus Christ and the lives of the congregants. His voice rose and fell. He leaned against the podium and whispered. He shouted. He leaned his head on his folded hands.

It was an illuminating event. I felt as if that very nice man had to be in some way leading a double life, being so intelligent sounding in daily life and then getting so emotional in front of a congregation. I left before he could get to the door to shake hands with the people as they left. I didn't know if I could face him and not show my disdain.

At the same time, Hank and I were finding a bit of the west in New Jersey. We lived not far from horse country and both of us took riding lessons. He progressed to jumping and was a judge at our first local horse show. I was in charge of pinnies, meaning I stood at the entrance to the corral and when the riders came up on their mounts, I pinned their numbers on. After the show, we all attended a bar-b-cue, eating chuck wagon beans, balancing our plates of corn-bread and ribs as we sat on hay bales and drank beer. It was fun and different until one winter day when I rode with others in my beginners' class inside the large barn. It was too cold for riding in the open air. While we were circling, a truck outside backfired, spooked the horse, and I lost control and ended up on the ground. I'd fractured my back.

In the hospital, I requested no visits from the clergy, but I did enjoy visits from friends. Peggy and Al smuggled in a bottle of champagne and poured an ounce into my water glass. While Hank joined them in enjoying the full bottle, I clicked my water glass against theirs and felt better than I had. Life could go on.

After getting out of the hospital, I determined I wouldn't be a cripple; I would walk again. None of the doctors suggested rehabilitation. I don't think it existed in those days. But I was determined I would not hobble through life. So I set myself a walking regimen in the house. Each morning I set the kitchen timer and walked for three minutes. When I could manage that, I upped the time I walked to five minutes, adding stairs and steps until eventually, by the end of the summer, I was walking for twenty minutes inside and upped it to thirty outside.

While I was still wearing a medically boned corset that held me upright, Hank came home one day to find me taking down the chimes I'd collected throughout our travels. They had not been able to withstand the Jersey wind. I announced, "I walked ten minutes today. Without stopping!" The American health craze had not yet taken hold, but I was proud of my accomplishments. I glanced at him, having expected him to say something, but he was grim-faced.

"What's wrong?" I asked, as I followed him into the house.

Depositing his briefcase on the hall table, he shook his head. "My glaucoma medication isn't keeping the pressure down in my left eye."

"So what does that mean?" I asked as we went down the hall to the kitchen. Days when the wind blew and intermittent snow came and went, I usually met him with a hot toddy and we sat in the family room telling one another about our day. I turned the heat on under the teakettle.

"I don't feel like a drink, today," he said.

A third generation Pole turning down a drink? He was really worried. I frowned.

"My ophthalmologist is sending me to Will's Eye Hospital in Philadelphia for treatment. I check in two days from now."

"So soon," was all I could think of saying. My insides were churning.

"It's reputedly the best eye hospital in the nation. It just came at an awkward time."

"You're supposed to go to Texas, aren't you?"

"Right." He loosened his tie, took off his jacket. "I'll have to cancel. Someone else in the department will jump at the chance. I've got to get this taken care of. In one way it will be a relief not to have to take all those drops each day."

I latched on to that aspect, and he was more his old self when I drove him into Philadelphia the next day. After seeing him admitted and officially a patient, I went home. It had been snowing intermittently, but nothing was sticking.

After several days of treatment, Hank came home, ostensibly well. But within twenty-four hours his pressure rose to an excruciating level. It began a time we kept the roads hot driving back and forth to Wills Eye Hospital. Twice he returned to the hospital. Twice he came home ostensibly well again, but within days intense pain always returned. I called the doctors; Hank talked to them. They couldn't believe what either of us said. Reluctantly, they had him return. Reluctantly, they admitted his pressure had risen alarmingly. They kept him in the hospital.

Although Still in a back brace, my back still giving me problems, I drove in from Mt. Holly daily, brought Hank small gifts, books, cards and tried to keep his spirits up. As soon as NOW friends heard what was happening, they drove me, but most of the time I drove myself. I was getting worried. Hank was withdrawing more and more into himself. The staff seldom looked directly at us; the doctors not knowing what was happening, the nurses taking their cue from the M.D's.

One day when I arrived, Hank wasn't in his room. The nurses sent me to another area where they said I'd find him. On that floor I walked by someone slumped over in a wheel chair, someone I assumed was an old man. I went to the nurse. "I was told my husband was here, but I don't see him."

"You walked right by him," she said pointing.

Shocked I ran to him. "What happened?" I cried.

He looked up, his eyes lighting. So lost was he in his own thoughts, he hadn't seen me pass. "They think I'm faking it," he said. "Then they take my pressure, and don't want to concede it, but it's high again. They don't like being wrong."

121

"Oh, honey."

"A nurse asked me if I wanted to go to the chapel, that some patients found comfort there." He grimaced.

"Oh, honey," I repeated, fighting back tears.

"It's better now that you're here." He squeezed my hand, smiled.

Shocked at what I'd seen and heard, and what I had figured was a general cold atmosphere, I planned. The next day I went to see the doctor in charge early, before the hospital officially opened, the only time he could accommodate me, I had been told.

Sitting in front of a bank of files cabinets, and a desk strewn with papers, the doctor looked official in his white coat, a professional smile on his face.

"I'm worried about my husband." I took the chair he had indicated

"Your husband's case is of great concern." He took Hank's chart from a pile and flipped through it.

I'd grown up in the years when everyone thought doctors were gods. Fighting down that false assumption that he knew better than me, I said, "I think there are some misconceptions here. Do you think my husband would make up his pain? Why? He has a good life. He and I get along fine. He likes his job and was looking forward to going to Texas on a teaching assignment for the Radiological Branch of the Food and Drug Administration this week. Saying he's faking his pain makes no sense."

If the doctor was embarrassed, he didn't show it, but he apologized, said he didn't believe they ever used those exact words, but they had never run into a case like his.

"Please believe him. Every time he has said the pain was back, the readings have corroborated his words." I gestured toward the chart. "It should be there."

He nodded slowly. "We've never had such a case. I promise you we're doing everything we can, and we will continue to do so to the best of our ability. I'm sure it isn't easy for any of us." He rose. "I appreciate your coming in."

I could do nothing but leave, but I knew I had made him realize Hank wasn't feigning pain. His face wore a look of concern.

A few days later, they again brought down the pressure. I smiled when I picked Hank up in Philadelphia. It had started to snow, big fat lazy flakes fluttered down, but I felt as if the sun were finally shining. Although neither of us were very chatty, there was warmth in the car from the heater and our shared feelings.

Traffic was slow over the bridge into New Jersey. I crept home to Mount Holly, the snow coming down hard and steady and accumulating in drifts before I drove into the garage. I hurried Hank inside the house and tucked him into bed, told him to get a good rest.

"You're so sweet," he said. "I know I'll sleep now." He looked exhausted.

I went down to the kitchen, made myself a cup of tea. Police Woman was playing on the TV, but I couldn't concentrate on it. I turned on the outdoor flood light and looked out the living-room windows. Snow, falling fast now, obscured the view across the street. But the furnace hummed warm air, the tea was soothing, and the two extra-strength Tylenol I'd taken had partially soothed my aching back. With the television going, I fell asleep in the family room.

About midnight Hank called out. I clicked off the TV and ran upstairs. His pressure had risen again. He told me he was out of his skull with pain.

Outside, the wind had drifted the snow into three and four foot high piles and had drifted into five foot or higher against the house. And it kept coming down. The driveway was snowed in, the road not visible. From television I learned traffic had come to a standstill. Nothing was moving. I called the local eye doctor, explained the situation. He said he would send a prescription drug by the National Guard. I should mix it with orange juice and give it to Hank in small doses. It would be the equivalent of an IV. In the morning I would have to get Hank back to Will's Eye Hospital. The doctor would alert the hospital we were coming.

A huge National Guard vehicle, sending snow in all directions, arrived. As I struggled to open the door, wind and snow entered. I shouted, "Thank you," and took the package from the young guardsman. Shaking, I managed to follow the doctor's instructions and rushed it upstairs to our bedroom. Hank swallowed the mixture a little at a time and eventually dosed off. I went downstairs and fell asleep in the family room. As light seeped into the sky in the morning, waking me, I was stiff, but fully dressed. It had stopped snowing, but a white world prevailed. No traffic was moving anywhere. If I could make it to the highway, a single lane had been plowed into Philadelphia.

With teenage Henry's help, I shoveled the wind-drifted driveway clear. Each shovel full felt like a ton. My back protested, but nervous energy drove me on, my back brace in place. Hurriedly, I put on a clean sweater and alerted Hank who was fully awake. Clutching the wheel, and going slowly, I drove him into the hospital. I met no cars in New Jersey. Philadelphia was deserted, only William Penn looking down from his perch on city hall. No cars; no people, just snow and ice and one lane open. I don't know what I'd have done if I'd met a car coming toward me.

At Wills Eye Hospital I slowed to a crawl, figuring I'd leave the car going while I saw Hank in. But he cautioned me not to stop. "You might have trouble getting traction on the ice." As sick as he was, he jumped out when

I was barely moving. "Don't stop!" he hollered wading through a drift. If I had stopped I could have sat there, wheels spinning forever, he told me later.

Leaving was one of the hardest things I ever did. I glimpsed that very weary man climbing those snow-covered hospital steps and a deep sadness hit me, like a stone hitting my chest. But I had to leave, drive on, not help him. Feeling as if the bottom had dropped out of our life, I returned home. The snow had stopped, and gradually life returned to a routine of going to the hospital to visit. But Hank's eye never settled down and his welfare stayed with me at all times, as I pumped gas in the car – a new innovation that had started with the oil problems of a few years earlier – as I socialized with Peggy and Al, met with my feminist friends.

Fearing the worst, I read everything I could about living with one eye. A person could get along without undue trouble. They could read, pass driving tests, and only an astute person could spot a fake eye. Eventually, Hank lost his eye but had no difficulty adjusting to a prosthesis. Hardly anyone ever noticed any difference between his eyes, the artificial eye was that good.

The fascinating fact for Hank and me – avowed atheists by now, although we never used the term – was the fact that during that whole ordeal not one friend or acquaintance had suggested prayer or a visit to a cleric. Not our friends, Hank's colleagues, my NOW women friends, no one, even the ones who did not know our religious stance. During those years, people went to church or not and no one discussed it. Of course we did not realize that men who had strong fundamentalist religious beliefs were making themselves felt in the political world, bringing together religion, politics, and patriotism. While we were living life, they were, behind the scenes, working hard to change all our lives.

After the "eye" problems were behind us, we received a call from Penn State University from Jerzy Feiner. We were aghast. How had he managed to get out of Poland? The Soviets kept everyone on a tight rein. In the past they had let him go by himself to England, to Norway, and countries in the Soviet Bloc only because his wife and children remained in Poland. He told us he was a guest lecturer at Penn State University. Could he come see us? "Of course," we said, I on one phone, Hank on an extension.

We promised to pick him up at the Greyhound bus stop in Mt. Holly, and talked about the "miracle" all that evening. We had had some contact with the Feiners during our years in New Jersey, but not much. The Russian/Polish incident had been an extracurricular moment in our lives. Once a priest from Europe had brought us small watercolors Jerzy had done with instructions we should sell them if possible. I sold one copy to a neighbor, but paintings depicting Pegasus weren't big sellers in America we were told by the owners of an art gallery. But at least I had gotten fifty dollars for a small canvas. Jerzy would welcome the money. The Soviet controlled Polish State made him travel close to penniless.

Before we braked at the bus stop, I saw a woman standing with Jerzy. Could that possibly be Anna? As we got closer, I saw it really was her. "However did you get out?" I asked, as we jumped from our canary yellow Pontiac.

"We'll tell you later," she said as we exchanged hugs and loaded them and their luggage into our car. At home, after they unpacked, we gathered in the sunken living room while the Feiners explained. Anna's father had been part of the Polish air force in Britain during World War II and settled in Scotland afterward. He'd had enough influence in Poland before the war that a few strings still survived. He pulled the strings, and Anna was able to fly to America. The Soviets were not too concerned as the Feiner's children remained in Poland, a situation that would force both mother and father to return.

When Hank and I toured Scotland, the country of my mother's ancestors, we met Anna's father. He had become a proper Scots gentleman, the picture of a country squire, occasionally dressing in kilts and eating haggis.

126

After Anna was rested from travel, we took the Feiners to see a friend who sculpted busts of Lenin and Trotsky and painted pictures of Scottish castles. He and his wife lived in a three-story house that had more charm than substance, shingles needing replacing. But his paintings and sculpture decorated walls and crannies and Jerzy and Anna said it reminded them of their younger days and student "digs" in Paris.

We also took them to Washington, D.C., for an extended stay, proud to show them our capital city. Like tour guides we took them to the Smithsonian as well as several art galleries. Back in New Jersey, we could hardly neglect historic Philadelphia, showing them important sites before hosting a party and inviting a slew of friends. It was a fun time.

One night, while the Feiners were still with us, our friends Peggy and Al had us all to a dinner party complete with escargot at their house. Petite, pretty Peggy had planned a festive affair, inviting another couple, choosing the proper wines to go with her excellent dinner. It was a fun affair. But it wasn't hard to recognize the sense of unease at times between Al and Jerzy, all because of cultural differences.

Tall with a decidedly American look, Al was very much into American fads and actions in all areas of life. Jerzy, while very cosmopolitan, and always well dressed, was only partially aware of American customs. Before dinner, when Al asked Jerzy what he wanted to drink, Jerzy said, "Whatever you have," most likely thinking in an Eastern European way. Few people behind the Iron Curtain, no matter their status, had more than one alcoholic beverages in addition to the ubiquitous vodka. Throughout the Soviet Union we had never seen a well-stocked public bar. Empty bottles sat on the shelves, adding color to the bleak surroundings. Jerzy was doing what was polite in Soviet dominated states, but Al, who was typically American, hoped to please his guest. "No, it's what you want." For the only time in our acquaintance I saw Jerzy look uncomfortable. He didn't know what to say. Hank cut in with, "Al, if you can still mix a good martini, I'll have one." Jerzy said, "I'd like one, too."

After the Feiners were gone, my worries about Henry rose to the top again. Teenaged Henry and his father butted heads often. Henry was far from sympathetic to what his father had gone through with his eye, and Hank had trouble understanding that teenaged boys always tested the limits as part of eventually becoming their own man. In addition, Henry had difficulties keeping up in school. He had attention deficit before people were talking about it, and in addition, I discovered he was epileptic, which required medication. None of that helped during his teenage years. We arranged for specialized schooling for him that he held against us, although I believe he blossomed in the new school surroundings.

Our trip to eastern Canada had been a wonderful family time. A high point for all of us was the day we spent observing nature at the northern-most point of our trip.

Picture a beach with large rocks, rounded stones and gravel, a narrow strip of sand, high bluffs, and large, silvered driftwood.

While I cooked fish Hank and Henry had caught, wrapping it in foil and placing it among the coals of a fire between large rocks, a pod of whales breeched and cavorted only a few yards off shore. Deer grazed the hillsides, gulls swooped and the sun threw just enough warmth for me to be bikini clad. Despite the frigid temperature of the water, Henry waded the shallows and Hank recorded it all on his latest camera. We all declared it one of our best days as a family.

We were still talking about it after we were home again. One day Hank zoomed into the driveway, rushed into the house, grabbed me up as we met in the front hall and swung me around. "We're moving to Seattle,." he announced, a big smile on his face. He would run a program for the state of Washington as a liaison from the federal government.

To me, it sounded wonderful. I had broken a bone in my foot that required an equine cast and it had taken a hard few months to heal. As I hobbled around in that horrid cast my sister Mavis arrived for a visit like a breath of fresh air. A fancy scarf blowing in the airport breezes, she looked very West Coast. I was ready for all her scarf had implied.

I remembered this as I prepared for the western move and was shocked when Henry declared he wasn't going with us, that he wanted to spend time with his mother. He left for Chicago shortly afterward, hardly saying goodbye.

Saddened, but excited, we put the New Jersey house up for sale and left on a house-hunting trip to Seattle.

Eight

*"Reason and free inquiry are the only
effectual agents against error."*

THOMAS JEFFERSON (1743-1826)

From the beginning I was intrigued with Seattle, its glory of hills almost as famous as the Seven Hills of Rome. The city's year around greenery, evergreen trees, both indigenous and imported, seemed great after that long and horrendous winter we'd spent. The realtor we consulted, and Hank's colleagues, steered us toward the north of the city, and we lucked out, finding a new house tucked among the cedars and pines in a settled community.

Of redwood and cedar, our new house had a marvelous fragrance and a completely different look from the New Jersey house. With a split-level foyer, an upstairs deck, and shingled siding, it fit beautifully with the pines and cedars on the lot. Later, we added a down-stairs deck. But no screens covered the windows! The realtor wore a smug look as he told us flies and mosquitoes were unknown in the Pacific Northwest. Screens weren't necessary.

No one mentioned spiders. Early the first year, we left on a trip and returned to find our downstairs powder room had become a fantasia reminiscent

The Last Aloha

of the haunted house at Disneyland. Spiders had spun their webs everywhere. We had screens installed immediately.

Perched on the edge of Puget Sound, Seattle's streets ran north and south with small divergent east and west locations. Like my friend Peggy had always done during various moves with Al, I studied the Seattle map and soon knew my way around.

Soon, in environmentally friendly Seattle, Hank and I were both riding public transportation. In the downtown area anyone could ride the busses for free. We checked out the theaters, traipsed all over the Seattle Center, and investigated the Cascade Mountains, falling in love with the views, the trees, the water, and in no time, the people.

One day, about a month after we moved in, Hank came home with a newspaper in hand. "Look at this." He held out the paper as if he had found a modern day Rosetta stone.

I didn't know what to expect. He had the paper turned to an article about Richard Alvord of Seattle. Alvord, it read, looked to reason, science, and logic for answers to life's problems, not some super power. I had no idea that what I was reading would thrust us into the world of organized secularism. The unknown man had started a local chapter of the American Humanist Association, a national organization. The AHA, in addition to being non-theist, worked to right social wrongs. It had been around since 1941 in its present form, more loosely before that

"So what do you think?" Hank asked, an expectant look on his face. The article showed a photograph of Alvord, a scholarly, pleasant-looking man, in the basement of his home. He'd transformed it into a library crammed full of multiple shelves of books all properly catalogued. I glimpsed books by Isaac Asimov who had turned me into a gibbering juvenile. On an adjacent shelf,

Carl Sagan's Cosmos showed plainly. Sagan ran neck in neck with Asimov in my hero worshipping lexicon.

I grinned, understanding Hank's beatific glow. "Sounds like a man we might want to know."

"They give a meeting date," Hank said pulling out his calendar and scribbling in the time. "A man who reads Asimov and Sagan can't be all bad."

We both laughed, high in a dither of discovery. We had thought our nontheistic, liberal-thinking ways had no official name, and here was an organization that mimicked our own slowly-developing philosophy.

"Nothing attempted, nothing gained," I said in a tone that made Hank laugh again.

That week we read the AHA got its beginning when ministers of the Unitarian Church started the official organization. Annual awards honored Humanists of the Year and had been given to Margaret Sanger as well as a full list of male scientists and other well-known people, including Betty Friedan, who founded the National Organization for Women. I was impressed.

The night when we went to the Humanists of Seattle (HOS) meeting, our ebullient mood had become one of caution. Maybe these people were just a bunch of shouters and haters wanting to get even for a religion they felt lacking. But Alvord certainly didn't seem that way...if the article had portrayed him correctly. If so, we were the stupid ones, just now learning about a movement that had been around for years. We'd thought we, and the few outliers we met, were it. We assumed there were others in little pockets around the country, but we might never meet them. People kept their non-theism as secret as a clandestine love affair. It was fall, the leaves of the deciduous trees starting to lose hold, the air chillier than when we arrived. We hoped to meet other progressive people at the meeting. If we were disappointed, we would never return, find other outlets for our freethinking during the winter months.

Arriving just in time for the meeting to begin, we ducked into seats in the back, making sure we could make a quick exit if necessary. Recognizing no one but Alvord, who stood at the front of the room, we kept a low profile. Slowly, we relaxed. It was easy to see that Alvord knew what he was talking about and that everyone respected him. Dick, as most people called him, and his wife, Sue, a pretty blonde woman, were unassuming people, quietly living the life they espoused, we discovered later. Now we were glad to see he was not a shouting, bible destroying zealot.

The evening was heady stuff. Sure we had thrown around words of unbelief in the Soviet Union, but that was different; it wasn't at home where people acted as if one had to genuflect at the word god. We had never heard anyone say publicly there wasn't any, but Alvord began the meeting with something like, and I'm paraphrasing. "This group is non-theist, meaning we don't believe in tooth fairies any more than we believe in a god. What we do believe is honoring humanity, being charitable, kind, and loving. If a god exists, there is absolutely no proof of his or her existence."

Someone called out, "Hear, hear."

The speaker, Bette Chambers, represented the AHA and had some position of prominence in the national organization, carried out Alvord's theme. We later learned she was president emeritus.

I looked around, thirty or so people apparently had no difficulty with Alvord's statements or hers. The group had been meeting in private homes for a few months. This was their first public meeting in a hall.

As soon as the formal meeting was over, Hank introduced himself to Dick, and I tagged along. But other people were crowding forward, and Dick, after welcoming us and exchanging a few words, was engulfed by others. A similar group crowded around Bette. Hank and I started toward the back when the man and woman who were sitting directly in front of us, called out, introducing themselves as Randy and Betty File.

A couple roughly our age, he held out his hand, saying "I'm here because I'm an agnostic, and probably a humanist. I guess I'll find out." A fair-skinned man with pleasant features, he smiled at us in a friendly way.

"We saw the article in the paper," Hank said. "Sounds like our type of thing."

We both glanced at Betty. She said in a teasing tone, "Randy thinks I'm a radical because I call myself an atheist, but humanism really attracts me because they have a Women's Caucus. It's time someone paid attention to the ladies."

My own smile went full watt. "Remember the ladies," I said quoting Abigail Adams who had used the phrase to John when he and the other Founding Fathers were putting together the Constitution.

Betty and I exchanged smiles, and she looked at me in a way that showed she was serious. Fresh from the tutelage of the Alice Paul women, I loved her enthusiasm. We immediately made plans to get together and through the years became fast friends, an improbable visual duo, she tall, brunette, me short and blonde.

Energized from the meeting, Hank and I set out on a path of discovery, reading books we had missed, and checking out various organizations. Happily, we discovered the Freedom From Religion Foundation, another national atheist organization, but one not as in your face as the American Atheists. FFRF had the sensitivity to mail their material in plain covers. I was really intrigued when I read that the founder was a woman. Anne Gaylor not only commanded the respect of the non-theist world, but also she actively helped women needing abortions! Another feminist! For years women had died in botched, back-alley abortions. I was amazed. To add to the appeal of this group, Anne Gaylor's daughter, Annie Laurie, was a feminist, writing a feminist newsletter. The frosting on our freethought cake had gotten thicker. FFRF's concentration stayed on church-state issues while the AHA took strong social stances from a secular viewpoint. Feeling the two organizations complemented each other, Hank and I joined both.

After that initial meeting of the Humanists of Seattle, we gathered informally with the members at private homes to socialize, laugh and joke and end up discussing topics that we'd never heard discussed.

Most of us were neophytes to organized non religion. Many times, from the centrally located Files' condominium in Seattle's Capitol Hill area, we held forth in their beige, white and tan rooms, the lights of downtown Seattle glittering below. Their condo was convenient for people throughout Seattle as well as the small neighboring towns.

From their apartment, Hank and I sometimes went down the hill to the Pike Place Market. With its salmon, halibut, fresh vegetables and home-baked bread as a magnet, we branched out to prowl the aisles of the antique stores, the fake jewelry emporiums, and smile at one another, displaying our thrill as the fish mongers tossed salmon around like they were rubber balls. After all, we had grown up in the Midwest where salmon came in a can and our mothers molded it into salmon patties.

Enthralled with Seattle and the people, for a while the members of HOS comprised our complete social life. Admiring both the city and the people, we felt as if we had found a home for life. We drank wine, munched guacamole dip and chips as we talked about all the things that had bothered most of us for years. If there was a god who was supreme, why did that god have such a hands off attitude while Jews were being killed in atrocious ways and in atrocious numbers? Why did this god divide himself into three? Which one of the three was in charge, or was it a divided leadership? Was that why God wasn't helpful? Too many gods spoiling the broth? And, what in heck was the Holy Ghost, anyway? Nobody could find a logical answer to any of those questions. Hank and Dick explained there was no need for superstition because we had the Big Bang, science and reason. Everything about those words shouted logic.

Former Protestants were the loudest when we discussed the Bible. Wasn't it supposed to be the be all and end all book, giving people the answers to life? Absolutely not, someone would holler and we'd all chime in, laughter and outrage in equal portions.

Except for my brief time as an Episcopalian, I knew very little about the bible. The Episcopalians I knew had shrugged off the Old Testament with the words, it's ancient history, but the gospels were the important part of the bible. My family's births and deaths were recorded in a bible belonging to my aunt. Once a "funny uncle" had licked his lips and said there was "hot stuff" in the Old Testament. It hadn't given me a good feeling.

With the Humanists of Seattle, I learned the Bible was written by several writers, over many, many years, thousands of years ago. Superstitious people, they had none of the knowledge we have today. The air might be chilly outside, but it was positively tropical inside, we were so fervent in our rush to learn everything we could about theist and non-theist thought.

We laughed often, a little uneasy at displaying our ignorance, but delighted to repeat what we learned. We were speaking with one tongue, even though Hank came from a Catholic background, Betty from a Lutheran, the others from various protestant traditions, some like me from a childhood without religion. We were a diverse group, but tightly knit through our new-found awareness.

One day Fay, who had lived in a rigid "thou shall" and "thou shall not" home as a girl, looked puzzled. A middle-aged woman, she had seldom spoken except to agree with statements others made. "But doesn't the Bible teach morals?" She looked around the group, a wan smile on her lips, her eyes wary. Fay had driven several miles to the Files condo from a small town south of Seattle. She had never questioned religion in her earlier years; now parental anxiety was settling in. She leaned forward in her eagerness, wanting to know how to advise her children. "It's supposed to be the moral compass of the world."

"If the Bible is so moral, why didn't it condemn rape or slavery?" Randy asked.

"Because the so-called god didn't give a damn. He, or she, or it never said a word against either." Barbara Dority, a young single woman in a committed relationship, shook her head, her long straight hair lifting and falling like a waterfall, framing her face. She had come from a strong fundamentalist background, but rebelled at the upbringing. Whether she was wearing beaded moccasins or thigh-high boots, Barbara always drew attention with her waist-long, shiny hair, her youth, her passion. But it was her probing words that lingered in everyone's mind.

"So the Bible isn't that moral?" Fay ventured.

Round faced and round bodied, she contrasted vividly with Barbara who said there was no evidence anywhere of most of the things mentioned in the bible. No world-wide flood. No Jacob, Isaac, etc. "And the gospels contradict one another dreadfully. So why should we think such a book is a moral authority?"

A few people, who had read the Bible from cover to cover, shouted "No way." They shivered in exaggerated disgust as they rolled their eyes.

Rain tapped against the windowpanes in the drizzle that personified Seattle as Fay ventured, "But wasn't Jesus a good man?"

Well, yes and no, we agreed as a group, analyzing each of Jesus' actions through the lens of our own experiences as well as where our new-found questioning had led us.

Frank, a member who had made a study of the gospel of Thomas, one of the gospels left out of the cannon at the Council of Nicea when Catholicism decided what to include and exclude from the "greatest story ever told, " wondered how many people knew about Thomas. A former longshoreman, he reminded me of philosopher Eric Hoffer. Retired now, Frank still looked as if he could unload a whole ship by himself, hoisting it unto his shoulders as easily as I unfurled an umbrella.

Hank had scoured the history books, and none of them mentioned Jesus, although the historians of the day had not been quiet about any of the other famous people. "We know a hell of a lot about the Romans for example. We know about others who were supposed to take part in Jesus' story. But there's no mention of Jesus in any of the official records. Nothing leads to a historical Jesus."

Dick pointed out that the paragraphs generally attributed to Jesus in the history of the age by the historian Josephus had been proven false, the passage added by someone else and clumsily at that. Experts regarding the era, knowledgeable about writing tools and ink in ancient writing, knowledgeable about the style of ancient writing, and scholars who looked for proper transitions in any writing, had made it clear: the Jesus entry was a forgery. If he had lived and his life followed that shown in the Bible, wouldn't the Romans as well as the local people have mentioned him while he was living? Certainly, they would have recorded his crucifixion.

While a variety of opinions arose, we were all agreed on the bottom line. There may or may not have been a Jesus, but if so he certainly didn't perform miracles. We concluded the Bible was a combination of history and myth. Studying the different religions of the world, we found ourselves both admiring and condemning various aspects of all. We felt as if we were seeing clearly for the first time in our lives, that a blurred lens had been cleaned.

Betty said she felt as if a big weight had been lifted from her shoulders when she realized she didn't have to go around feeling guilty – for her thoughts as well as her actions.

Suddenly Andy spoke. A medium sized man in his mid forties, he had a forceful way of speaking. "I hate to say it," he began, "but my thinking varies from most of yours."

Everyone settled back in their seats. "I do believe in god. Don't get me wrong, I thoroughly reject that god in the sky stuff. I maintain that god lives within me. I have no idea if he resides in you, too, but I know he dwells within me." He looked supremely confident, looking around the room from one person to the next. He wore jeans that had seen better days and a bright colored T, his bare feet in sandals. He looked as if he were a holdover from the 60's Summer of Love.

This esoteric belief in a god amazed us all. "I'm afraid I don't understand," I said. Others nodded agreement.

"Let me explain. My background includes theater. One time I was going for a tryout for a play in Appalachia, and I had worked on that sucker for days, memorizing lines, saying them out loud until I knew them forward and backward. And it all came back to me like gibberish. Let me say it straight out. I sucked. But Gloria," he gave a cursory tilt of the head toward the bra-less woman who apparently lived with him, "said I had to go, that it would be okay. I had the ability in me. I thought she was having pipe dreams, maybe too much pot. Anyway I went." He paused looked around the room, gazing from one person to the next. "You know the ending. I landed the part. I did have the ability in me."

We all said something appropriate, although we all wore a look that said we didn't quite follow.

Andy said, "The god inside me came through." His head went up. "I don't expect any of you to understand. That's okay, it's my belief. You don't have to share it."

We all agreed the bottom ethical line was not to harm anyone else by our actions and for a government to maintain separation of church and state. The thing that I came away with was that Andy had a background that included theater. I'd always had a sneaking suspicion that in another time and place, I could have been an actor.

By this time winter with its gloomy days, relentless drizzle and occasional downpours, had ended.. Seattle's rhododendrons and azaleas added color to the hills, the blackberries were ripening, and whenever the sun peeped through the cloud cover and we saw Mount Rainier and repeated, "Life is good."

But despite our personal good feelings, far right religionists, like Jerry Falwell were infiltrating schools and preaching in the public market places. Randy said if they took over the government, he'd join the Unitarian Church, the least "churchy" of the churches.

"And when they come for the Unitarians? What then?" It wasn't something that worried us a lot. We still lived among the echoes of an America we all loved.

As the summer solstice approached, I wrote a short script for Andy and I to perform at a summer solstice party for our group.

When, at my suggestion, Andy and I rehearsed, I was shocked. He read the lines in a monotone, showed me nothing that would verify his statement about his acting career. I was not looking forward to our performance. But the day of the party his voice had nuance, his pauses appropriate. And above all he had me rising to heights I would not have attempted otherwise. I realized I had a talent for acting. It was a thought I kept to myself.

At the same time I was bolstering all the facts I'd read about women – that they were paid much less – 59 cents for every dollar paid men. They were secondary citizens under the law in most all aspects. I'd never known the extent that women had been treated shabbily, belittled, blamed for actions not of their doing, a second class status coded into law in many states as well as the federal government.

The more Betty and I learned, the deeper feminist credentials were emblazoned on our foreheads. We were no longer pushing our feelings down but were reaching past the fog and finding our voices. Boys were favored in most all cultures, girls dealt a losing hand. The only reason women and girls in the United States had it better than in other countries was because our economy was better. Men were boys for a short time only, but women were labeled girls their whole lives. We were women, not girls, and we didn't want to be belittled any more. From the time men had realized they had a part in procreation, it had become a man's world, condoned by religion. Women were patronized and stuck in a second-class status. We wanted the same respect men got. We wanted to be paid the same. We wanted the Equal Rights Amendment.

It was hard for some men of the late nineteen seventies and early eighties to wrap their heads around the rapid changes. Soon after moving to Seattle, I began volunteering with Dejah Sherman-Peterson at the National Abortion Rights Action League's office in the back of a small office complex on Lake

City Way.. There was just enough room to park off the busy highway. If I hadn't had such a strong belief in women's autonomy, I wouldn't have worked after daylight disappeared, which happened early in the winter. Leaving the brightly lit office and stepping out into the dark wasn't easy. Then getting my car into the traffic on the busy street was harder.

But I could not conceive of anyone else telling a woman what she could do with her own body. While few women opted for abortions except in circumstances that were intolerable – rape, incest, poverty, her health – neither would those women force anyone to have an abortion. That decision should be made with the man in her life and her doctor.

It wasn't difficult to see that religion was behind the anti-abortion crowd's vitriol. I saw it as a wedge into separation of church and state. But I enjoyed working with Dejah and meeting Margaret Okamoto who also volunteered with NARAL. Margaret and I clicked from the beginning, doing what we could to help. Dejah at times debated in public forum the spokespersons for the far right wing, Dejah's logic impeccable. So was Margaret's and eventually, she, her doctor husband, Deems, and Hank and I became friends.

One of the first things I did at Dejah's suggestion was to get signatures on a letter she had penned about the right of women to access Roe V Wade, the Supreme Court decision making abortion legal. I called well-known people in the city – state legislators, the mayor, and various clerics.

Because of my one time connection with the Episcopal Church, a church I had joined when my life with Bill had constricted me like a boa, I knew the Episcopalian thinking about cultural events even though my association with the church had been short-lived. I realize now I needed out of that marriage. I hadn't needed religion. Then I'd been grasping at straws. All religions would hold women in intolerable situations, so I called the most famous of the Episcopalian clerics in Seattle. Episcopalians were known for their liberal stance regarding social issues. But this priest displayed decidedly conservative views. He wanted nothing to do with abortion. A baby was a baby at all stages of gestation according to him. He would not sign the letter.

I was learning that people cannot be put into pigeon holes. This became clear in another way, too. Hank and Randy had trouble understanding Betty's and my antipathy toward Playboy and Hustler and similar magazines. We tried to explain that having thoughtful articles in Playboy didn't make it all right that women in the magazine were viewed as objects.

While most all women and men are sexual beings, we didn't like being only sex objects. We wanted to be whole persons, just like men. We wanted society as well as the "men's" magazines to address us as complete persons, not important for our looks or sex appeal alone. Most women liked looking "sexy" and wearing pretty clothes. I certainly did. But what about women who did not begin to fit the Playmate of the month model? And most of all, what about those meat grinder covers on Hustler, which made Playboy seem as innocent as a kindergarten rhyme?

The men would not discuss it with us, but sometime later Hank told me he had thought it through and realized that what Betty and I said made sense. My regard for him soared again.

One day Betty called to tell me a far right religious group had advertised an open meeting. She suggested we attend. "It would be informative to see how they operate."

I told Hank that night, and although he was far from enthusiastic, he agreed to go along to please Betty and Randy.

We took our seat midway in the hall and listened to various members expound. And then suddenly one rose and began "talking in tongues." It sounded like gibberish, and Hank, who spoke several languages, said it had no basis in any language he knew. The most startling part was when others began translating what the gibberish meant! Cries of "Praise the lord" rocked the hall. Applause thundered. When we did not applaud with the others, or call out, "God bless you" the parishioners began to glare at us. I nudged Hank.

"I think we need to get out of here," he said.

As the next speaker in tongues rose, we hurriedly left the hall by the nearest exit.

I had read about cults and snake handlers, but never thought I'd witness any of the aberrations in religious devotion. Now I had. I was smiling even as I realized what a serious threat such nonsense posed for America. We had to keep religion out of the schools, and it had started to encroach.

While my mind swirled with these new problems, my personal problems stayed the same. Henry did not join us in Seattle and Steve seldom wrote. If I hadn't been so busy I would have been devastated. I had always wanted a warm family life, but it seemed that wasn't in the cards. But Hank bolstered my confidence daily, liking what I said and did, liking me. That others did, also, was like mulch around a plant, making it grow.

Nine

"Religion is a bandage that man has invented to protect a soul made bloody by circumstance."

THEODORE DREISER (1871-1945)

When Seattle's hillsides were covered with full-blooming flowers, lilac bushes perfuming our yard, showy rhododendrons adding color, we hiked the area, learning early on that Seattleites didn't let the rain bother them. In ecologically conscious Seattle, our new friends and acquaintances were pleased that Hank rode the bus to work, and I used it to go downtown. An early treat was taking the ferry from downtown Seattle to Bainbridge Island and coming back after dark, Seattle's skyline like a jeweled necklace against the sky. Quickly, our love affair with the city deepened.

In addition to my feminist, non-theist activities, I had found the oldest writing group in Seattle. Having started my writing career in New Jersey, writing for the Burlington County Times Sunday supplement, I was eager to find other writers. The Fictioneers met in a meeting room on the second floor of the downtown library. Hank was almost as excited as I was when I won first place in a short story contest before I fully knew my way around the area. I still remember the story's title, "A Real American." It referred to a character with Mexican heritage who found her American self without abrogating her

Mexican customs. I don't know what happened to the story, but I realized my liberal leanings had grown. Growing up, I'd never seen anyone who wasn't white, Anglo-Saxon, protestant. Jews passed through Chagrin Falls going on vacation to Geauga Lake during the summer months. Looked upon as an oddity was a girl in high school who admitted she was Catholic. No wonder my mother had cautioned me not to advertise my non-religious views.

In Seattle, I loved watching the sun splash rose, pink, and violet across the sky as it took its dip behind the mountains of the Olympic Peninsula. The clouds were suffused with radiant color. Usually, I would be taking dinner out of the oven as Hank came home from work. A few times his secretary called saying he would be late. She had a low mellow voice and I imagined a face and body to go with it.

What a surprise when I saw her. She would have had a hard time being a contestant in a beauty pageant. But, in a way I'd never expected, she was aggressive.

I held a small dinner party; she was among the invited guests. Afterwards I discovered hand-written notes in our clothes closet. Tucked into pockets of Hank's pants and coats, into my clothing were sayings such as "Jesus Saves." "Your salvation comes through the Lord" and other far from subtle messages. Everyone working for the state of Washington knew Hank and I followed Thomas Jefferson's words, "Question with boldness even the existence of a god."

As soon as we arrived in Seattle, I had gotten in touch with NOW. Unfortunately, at the time, the dedicated Seattle members were not very well organized. After my positive experiences with the Alice Paul NOW in New Jersey, I was definitely disappointed. But at a NOW meeting I heard about Mary Whitmore and her ERA Action Line. When I got home, I called the number listed. A recorded message said Mary would be picketing the Mormon Temple that was being built in Bellevue, Washington, across Lake Washington from Seattle. She picketed because the LDS Church actively worked against the Equal Rights Amendment, the ERA.

Grinning like the proverbial Cheshire cat, I told Hank that night. He grinned, too, and we both started laughing. What an opportunity to make a statement about women's rights and our non-theist beliefs at the same time!

That Sunday, Hank drove us across Lake Washington to the looming edifice. The exterior of the temple was in place, all the way to the top where the angel Moroni perched. The Mormons only needed to put the finishing touches on the interior and wait for the Prophet's dedication before the temple would be "open for business."

We parked and walked over to where three women and one man were picketing on the sidewalk adjacent to the temple. Honk if you believe in the ERA, Mormons stay out of women's lives. Tax Mormon Million, read the signs the people were carrying. Mary Whitmore turned out to be an attractive young mother who was fed up with women's lot and had started the action line on her own. She met us, wrote our names on a clipboard and handed us signs before introducing Ruth and Betty, the late middle-aged sisters who made the signs.

Mary made sure we knew that none of them were connected with any of the women's organizations and their actions weren't backed by any church or civic group either. The weekly demonstrations appeared to be a real populist movement. The local chapter of NOW had not yet seen the need to go outside established channels.

Each Sunday, for a year Hank and I joined Mary and the handful of others picketing the Mormon temple. Winter held us in its grip, the air filled with moisture, heavy coats necessary. When rain became more than a drizzle, Mary handed out umbrellas that had ERA emblazoned on them. Most cars zooming by, slowed and honked their horns, showing they were on our side.

All the polls showed Americans supported the amendment by a large plurality, sixty some percent.

Few drivers gave us the finger. But once, to my amusement, a man walked by mouthing "dyke." At first I was amused, but then later on when he walked by again mouthing the words, it ceased to be funny. While few people were talking about gay or lesbian rights at the time, we heterosexuals were surprised that his sense of equality was so skewed. Equality seemed a no-brainer. But those dedicated to the status quo had powerful spokespersons in congress and in the state houses. Some were virulently against the amendment.

At the same time Hank and I became an integral part of Seattle's activist community, in Sterling, Virginia, Sonia Johnson, a member of the Church of Latter Day Saints, was ex-communicated for her support of the ERA. Testifying in Congress, she debated the merits of the amendment with Utah's chief Senator, Oren Hatch. He patronized; she made sense. From coast to coast, Sonia had women agreeing with her, among them the activists of Seattle. Much later many of us purchased her book, "From Housewife to Heretic", and much, much later applauded when she also ran for president.

Women, for and against the ERA, came to Seattle to make their points. The first time anti-ERA activist Phyllis Schafly spoke, it was summer and Hank and I both were in the outdoor audience. On the radio and television she had continually preached her message: Women should stay home. Now in person, Phyllis reminded people over and over that women did not belong in the work place. They were needed at home. Women were the bulwark of family life, she explained. The traditional American family would suffer if the Equal Rights Amendment was passed. With an ERA in the Constitution, women would be forced to lift heavy loads at work. With an ERA women would be forced to serve in the military. Traveling from state to state, it was the same message she gave throughout the nation.

In a brief lull in her talk Hank called out, "Why aren't you at home?" People around us nodded, some repeated his words. Schafly ignored him, but the audience who got the point, cheered.

I remember feeling so proud of Hank as we walked hand in hand toward the bus line that would take us home, several women saying the equivalent of, "I envy you!"

After I left home, I never lived near any of the family. Now, with both Mom and Dad dead, I was delighted that my sister Lenore came to see me. Looking back I can see she was probably shocked at what she experienced with us. Although she was thirteen years older than me, she was also the shortest, two inches shorter than my five foot two. Because of this and her hesitant way with strangers, I had always felt protective of her. Her first and most charming husband had been abusive. Her second was a jewel. But he had taken her from California to Oklahoma, and she'd had trouble adjusting to the differences in lifestyle. When I visited her in Oklahoma, she seemed depressed, but she showed more than a spark of life when she clicked on the television one day.

"You ever see this news show?" she asked.

It was the first time I'd seen Pat Robertson's broadcast. Watching the tel-evangelist, I was appalled.

Lenore's husband's kind, but far-right-believing sister had introduced her to Robertson. The next thing I knew Lenore was a member of the Southern Baptist Church. Trying to maintain a relationship, I carefully ignored any mention of religion in our few phone calls and letters. She had been through so much in her life that wasn't nice, she didn't need me adding to it. Many times during her first marriage she fled beatings by going home to our parents. No one ever mentioned why. If so they would have had to face what was happening.

In Seattle, I wanted so much to show her a good time. I felt an emotional closeness with her even though we had never been close, partly because of the age difference and partly because she was very much a traditionalist, and I always pushed at the boundaries, literally or in my mind. Wanting to please her and knowing she'd never been to Seattle, Hank and I took her on the ferry to Bainbridge Island, had a typical salmon dinner before returning to Seattle after dark so she could see the glittering skyline of the city. We went up the Space Needle to the revolving restaurant and ate succulent seafood, and she said she felt like a queen viewing the city from on high. We showed her The Mountain, as everyone called Mt. Rainier, driving as high as possible. We took her to Snoqualmie Pass when snow still made a tunnel out of the highway. We took her to the theater, and we let her accompany us to a street fair where we handed out flyers about women's rights.

The next day, after Hank left for work, we took our second cups of morning tea to the upper deck and watched the squirrels dart in an out among the cedars and pines, the bright pink azaleas and deep red rhododendrons adding to the color palette. "It's so pretty here," she said, a soft look on her face. After a while she excused herself, and went into the house, saying, "Be right back." Less than a minute later she was pulling the slider closed behind her. "Have you thought about the future?" she asked flashing a booklet.

"What?"

She handed me the booklet. I glimpsed a Christian cross and words asking if I had been saved. I quit reading. "I'm not sure what you're meaning." Trying to keep a frown from developing, I glanced toward her, seeing first the neighbor's rooftop, the house sitting farther down the hill from us, facing another street. When my gaze found hers, she was smiling. "I mean Jesus. Once I let him enter my heart, I was filled with happiness. Jesus Christ. is the gateway to God."

I didn't know what to say. I didn't want to insult her because of her life choices, but I couldn't go around with my mouth closed either. The church crowd was perpetuating their lies because we in the non-theist movement seldom spoke out. I wanted to say, your heart has nothing to do with your beliefs, it's your brain, your reason, your critical thinking. Instead I asked, without planning, the words bursting forth, "Do you really believe the earth was created in seven days?"

"Cleo, it says so in the Bible."

I glanced away, up to the sky showing its blue, not a common sight in Seattle where gray days predominated. "But the Bible was written by ordinary men."

"God inspired men." She was still smiling.

"What about the Big Bang?" Did she know about it? Of course she did, but I wanted to get back at her for that "Cleo" said in a way she had scolded me when I was a kid.

She checked the crease in her pedal pushers. "I may not be as smart as you, but, of course, I've heard about it. So who was behind it?" Her tone grew sugary again. "Some people say there was no such thing as a big bang, but if there was, and I'm not saying there was or wasn't, but who made it happen?"

"No one, it just happened. Chemical reactions, that sort of thing." I was looking up the hill now to the street. The houses on the other side looked down on Lake Washington.

"That's ridiculous. You always have to have someone to start things. You should know that. If we hadn't had Benjamin Franklin and his experiment,

Thomas Edison wouldn't have made the light bulb." Her look became triumphant.

I looked at her. During my childhood and youth, she had liked to scold. Now she looked like what she was, a woman who had struggled to find happiness, finally found it, and who was I to take it from her? She had adopted and adapted the fundamentalist way of thinking, and no amount of scientific facts I could spout would change her.

Once she had confided that many of her church friends were racists, a position she felt wasn't Christian. But otherwise she seemed to follow the Southern Baptist thinking wholeheartedly. The Fundamentalist beliefs were not far from the beliefs of the ancient peoples of Babylon. Fundamentalist members declared they'd found human footprints and dinosaur footprints side by side in Texas. Although mainstream scientists debunked such thinking, and proved it, the fundamentalists continued to spew such nonsense, teach it to their children. My heart was racing furiously now.

I wanted to get all the books on our downstairs shelves, books by leading scientists and philosophical thinkers like Bertrand Russell, books written for the average person. I wanted to bring all the scholarly texts up as well. I wanted to shout, "You're the one making ridiculous statements," but I realized I could talk myself blue in the face and she'd never concede a point. I could show her all the facts and she'd find an illogical argument to refute them.

Religion, no matter how far-fetched, had brought her happiness. No, I should save my "ammunition" for where it would do the most good for society. The fundamentalists were attempting to get their beliefs into the schools. Separation of church and state meant nothing to them. They were calling for equal treatment, their beliefs to be taught as well as Darwin and evolution. My efforts should go in that direction, not in alienating family.

I looked at her again. Her natural curly hair was drifting out behind her. She looked small and vulnerable, but the daily breeze was also riffling the rhododendrons with their large, showy blossoms. The afternoon would be beautiful for our outing to the Japanese gardens. "Let's not talk about such things ever again. Okay?" I went to her and gave her a heartfelt hug. "We could talk forever, and neither one would convince the other. The bottom line is, I love you, and I think you love me."

She agreed and the rest of her visit proceeded without incident, and during her lifetime, she never again tried to proselytize me.

After she left, the summer had an up-tick in marches through the streets of Seattle and adjacent small towns. During those balmy days Betty and I made all the many events that usually began or ended at city hall. We staffed feminist phone banks, and Hank and I continued picketing the Mormon temple while famous, socially political women from throughout the nation appeared in the area, including Bella Abzug wearing her trademark hats. She and many others supported passage of the ERA and toured the country giving speeches, holding rallies, speaking out. Those blazingly busy days also brought Sonia Johnson.

After testifying in Congress, Sonia had become an outspoken advocate for women's rights. While NOW called for equal rights, other national groups were springing up faster than anyone could count and asking for the same thing. Among them were Homemakers for the ERA, the National Women's Political Caucus, Mormons for the ERA, Catholics for a Free Choice and a flurry of other groups. While different in minor ways, they all had the same goal. Inequality in pay became one of the first talking points.

Soon, the lot of women historically began to surface. In 1980 I was shocked to hear the state of Mississippi had never ratified the 19th Amendment giving women the vote. I learned about women kept prisoners in their own homes by abusive husbands. I learned so much I was ripe fruit when Sonia showed up, and all of this came together near the time the LDS church's Spencer Kimball, the head prophet, was to appear and dedicate the temple in Bellevue, Washington.

On Saturday, November 16, 1980, Joan Schramack of Seattle, and Colleen Miller of Kent, two young women who had at times joined our picket, said they were chaining themselves to the temple gates to bring attention to the Mormon Church's active role in trying to keep the ERA from becoming a law. During this whole era, the Mormons, in a very concerted effort to defeat the ERA had been sending their women, accompanied by husbands, brothers and sons, to state, national, or international feminist meetings. The women were advised to vote against the measure and spout the LDS line.

To defeat the ERA, Mormons were also doing things that were legally questionable. Although their former actions were socially disgusting, they weren't illegal. The latter was. An investigative reporter had found out they were laundering money in their zealotry to defeat the ERA, sending it from California to Florida and other states. Joan and Colleen vowed to stay chained day and night for as long as it took.

Hank and I arrived at the Temple early the day Joan and Colleen chained. Joan, a very attractive single woman dedicated to social justice, Colleen, older but equally dedicated, were indeed chained to the Temple gate, and they were surrounded by people, Mary and the temple picketers among the crowd. Again, I was in awe of the fact I was witnessing history. I had no idea at the time that I'd also be making it.

Looking around, I was astounded. Women and men Hank and I had never seen before were arriving. Our lonely, quiet year-long picket had morphed into something quite different. As people from adjacent suburbs arrived to see what people were talking about, local media arrived. Reporters with TV cameras perched on their shoulders staked out strategic positions. Others holding tape recorders or scribbling in notebooks asked questions. The parking lot was jammed; people everywhere, cars parked on the street.

With our fellow picketers, we handed out pamphlets and bulletins, talked to reporters and curiosity seekers. A circus atmosphere began to prevail. Hawkers appeared with donuts and coffee. Someone handed out sandwiches. People, who had never seen either Joan or Colleen before, who had never picketed at the Temple, were suddenly pretending to be insiders. Astonished, Hank and I whispered our surprise to friends as we marveled at the ever-increasing crowd.

The day passed quickly, becoming dark and cool as the sun set. The parking lot began to empty. Joan's and Colleen's closest supporters stood close by ready to supply food and drink, bring potties and arrange sheets that would give them privacy. Men, not frightened by the thought of women gaining equal rights, stood nearby, ready to protect the women from harassment and worse. Reporters and photographers from the Seattle Times and the Seattle Post Intelligencer newspapers took pictures showing Joan chained to the fence, the temple spire in the background and left. As real night descended, we lingered. When only a handful remained, we left, too.

Sunday morning I practically leaped from bed, eager to see the coverage in the paper. Not as much as we thought should be. We scoured the nation's press looking for a story. Joan's photo had been picked up by other papers in the nation, but we found little about the whys of their protest. While both women were attractive, Joan's glowing face, her figure constricted by chains made a dramatic photograph. But for the most part, the women were ignored nationally.

And then Sonia Johnson arrived. I'd never met her before. Attractive, slightly taller than me, and a mother, there was nothing stereotypical about her. She was fervent, outspoken to a degree few other speakers were. Most of us were slightly in awe of her.

That Sunday night all of us who had been working for ratification of the ERA for a long time congregated for a rally. I knew many of those in the audience, others I'd seen. They came from all over the greater Seattle area and a few from other states.

Hank and I found seats near the front of the hall and nodded agreement as Sonia talked. She spared no words. She said the church had no right to tell women what to do, that government should quit trying to order women's lives, that women should decide what they wanted to do with their bodies, their lives. We all cheered.. It was a philosophy we had promoted all summer

But Sonia had more than facts, she had fervor, and she had ideas that could be implemented. But most importantly, she didn't pussyfoot around. Women were given the shaft, not only by society but by organized religion. She got to the bottom line faster than any woman or man had before or has since. Women had to stick together against the patriarchal churches and the patriarchal attitude that persisted.

Applause was deafening. I felt on fire, inspired. Sonia voiced thoughts that even I had never contemplated speaking out loud. Then, halfway through the evening Joan and Colleen came in dragging their chains. Everyone jumped to their feet so fast a few chairs tipped over and the room exploded with applause, people shouting praise, some crying silently, tears like jewels on their cheeks.

When the pandemonium ended, and the women had been praised, Sonia proclaimed, "We should all chain."

It was a thought that had never occurred to us. We looked at one another. We were old; we were young, we were affluent or living on the edge. We were pretty or homely. We were Christian and Atheist, we were Jew and Gentile, we were American. "Yes," someone shouted, and two or three echoed that word. No one else said a single thing. The silence bore in. No one stirred. Then as

Joan and Colleen left to get some sleep, we jumped to our feet and applauded them from the room.

Now, Sonia repeated her message, leaning forward, clutching the podium to accentuate her point, "We all need to chain, show we mean business."

Some women nodded emphatically; others looked disturbed. Most were stunned.

"I can't break the law," one woman said, raising her head and voice as if daring anyone to oppose her.

"No one has to do anything," Sonia said. "But the opportunity exists." Her voice was firm. "Joan and Colleen have paved the way."

Realization came to me like a shot. The media followed Sonia. She made copy. She made headlines. If we all chained, the nation would listen because she was among us. We would be striking a blow for feminism, but also, we were "outing" the Mormon Church.

A few women began taking her proposition seriously. I nodded agreement. Not pausing, Sonia began ticking off the things we'd need. We'd need people to chain, people to support them, people to help them in any way necessary. We'd need chains and locks, and we'd need nerve. We had no idea how long we'd be chained. Before we did anything, we'd need an attorney. We might be jailed.

Someone went to contact an attorney known to sympathize with women's rights.

Sonia continued talking. "We need to be prepared to go to prison," she said, her voice losing its upbeat sound, almost going flat.

Again, there was silence. We avoided looking at one another.

She pointed out we'd have our attorney bail us out, but after that we would probably have to testify in court, show how the church had brought this on with their anti-woman agenda, their dishonest and illegal actions.. The LDS church had gone easy on the two women, actually ignoring Joan and Colleen, but they would not be inclined to be as lenient now. We had one of their former members among us, one who had thumbed her nose at their beliefs. They would want to retaliate.

I looked at Betty. "We've already gone through a lot together," I said.

"We have," she acknowledged, adding she couldn't take a chance on losing her job. Hank admitted he had the same problem. I understood both answers. People began to leave.

"What do you think of my staying?" I asked Hank, the two of us moving a little apart from the main group. Would my actions impact his job? He loved his work.

"I admire your dedication and bravery," he said taking my hands. We stood there looking at one another for a few seconds. Then he said. "Whatever you do, I'll back you. I understand why you're doing it, and I love you."

I felt the sting of tears, but I held them back. By now we were walking lockstep, finishing one another's sentences. We had become very close.

"Just be careful," he said leaning close and giving me a quick kiss, his hand lingering on my face.

I pulled myself together and looked past him to Betty. Bidding both of them goodnight, I added in an attempt at levity, "I'm not going to break windows or throw stones at the Mormons." The words fell flat. Neither Hank nor Betty laughed. I watched them go.

The crowd had dwindled, and the hall began to look big with all the empty chairs. Cheryl Dalton had come from California, another woman from Oregon to attend the rally. One woman was from Wyoming. They added their voices to the one or two women from Utah, and Sonia's friend, Hazel Rigby, from Washington, D.C. who had come west with her. Although she had never been involved in the women's movement, Hazel quickly added her name to the supporter's list.

Most of us had never committed civil disobedience. I had read about it in Thoreau, but it had seemed remote in the reading, an intellectual point to discuss, never something to do. The women who had been active during the Vietnam War had no qualms. Others had questions.

Finally there were approximately fifty of us sitting in a loose circle. The circus atmosphere had gone completely. People spoke in whispers to friends. "What do you think? Should we?" Sonia passed around a sign up sheet. "Indicate whether you will chain or support," she said. "And don't forget someone has to give me some clothes!" People smiled. She had arrived looking like the college professor she was, not dressed to commit non-violent civil disobedience.

I put my signature under the Chain column. Marion Nelson, another woman shorter than me, signed as my supporter. She'd become famous among the picketers as the woman who left radical statements about feminism in history books in public libraries and book stores.

When everyone who wanted to had signed to chain or be a supporter, it was time to go home. We would meet in the field adjacent to the Latter Day Saints temple before dawn in the morning.

Feeling strange, as if I were contemplating jumping from a bridge, I went outside. It had started to drizzle. The weather forecast said rain tomorrow. The streets were wet, streetlights reflected in the water, the city an impressionist painting.

At home, I put out clothes to wear in the morning and went to bed. Hank was already asleep. My eyes felt scratchy, but sleep would not come. I had never broken the law. Once I was cited for driving too fast. I had left the Nevada line and entered the slower moving traffic of California before I realized it. I had not slowed down early enough and got a ticket. But that was it. To deliberately break the law was another thing. I'd always looked askance at those who did. What was the matter with them? Didn't they know we were a country of laws? Was I going too far? Should I back out? Who could hold it against me? After all, most of the women at the rally had gone home, some going without a word when Sonia suggested we all chain.

I argued with myself for hours, being careful not to wake Hank. It was my problem, not his. No, I couldn't back out now. Women had waited too long for equality. I would be letting down all those courageous women who had gone before me, working 72 year to get the vote, Elizabeth Cady Stanton, Susan B. Anthony and all the rest, Elizabeth calling attention to patriarchal attitudes. I had to do this. Once the decision was made, I slept, but I was so edgy, I woke up an hour later and couldn't get back to sleep again. I remained quiet as Hank left for work, probably thinking I was sleeping. After he left, I got up and stood for ten minutes in the shower, but it did little to help.

My eyelids heavy with the need for sleep, I almost missed the note Hank had taped to the bathroom mirror. "You make me proud," I read, and thought about it as I drove out to Bellevue to join the others.

Ten

*"I submit that an individual who breaks a law that conscience
tells him is unjust and who willingly accepts imprisonment
in order to rouse the conscience of the community over its
injustice, is in reality expressing the highest respect for the law."*

MARTIN LUTHER KING, JR. (1929-1968)

Rain was coming down steadily. In the hard, fast dark; I had trouble seeing who was who. We huddled under umbrellas, a scruffy looking bunch, Sonia in clothes much too large for her, the rest of us bundled up for the weather. It wasn't summer anymore. And we weren't picketing and marching. This was the real thing. My heart thumped wildly.

As Sonia talked strategy, the Seattle mist became a downpour that almost drowned out her voice, but slowly the rain let up. I heard Sonia say we needed to secure all gates and entrances to the temple. Our chains were case-hardened. The police would have to cut us from the fence. We should give our padlock keys to our supporters. Supporters should leave when the police arrived. Anyone still standing around would be arrested as well. There were guards at the temple. By splitting up we might avoid them, but we had to be prepared for them to do everything to prevent us from trespassing. We were twenty women and one man that November 17, 1980. The idea we were about to commit civil disobedience sliced through me like a knife through water. I unfurled my umbrella and handed it to Marion. I didn't need to be encumbered by anything. I would keep my eyes open for temple guards and head in a direction away from them.

"So, we're all agreed we're going to do this?" Sonia asked.

We cried "Yes,"

"Then let's go."

We ran out of the woods where the trees dripped moisture, unto the paved parking lot and on to the temple. Sonia headed for the front gate, others close behind her. Seeing no space left there and catching sight of a guard tussling with a woman, I veered left to the next entrance. With Marion's help I chained myself to the fence and handed her the key. Day was beginning to lighten the sky to a slate gray. The rain eased to a drizzle. I glimpsed other women running. Everything seemed unreal, like something happening in a dream. Time stood still and then leaped forward with agonizing speed.

Marion asked if I was all right. I remember nodding. "Good luck,' she said and left as the limousine with Spencer Kimball, the LDS prophet, entered the parking lot. I was too tired for my heart to do anything. I looked up, and one of the picketers, Willie Woolslayer, had come to stand beside me. She said I looked so small and so alone, she had to do it. Like I was drugged, I nodded, overwhelmed by what she was doing. Of all people, she was the unlikeliest to commit civil disobedience. Heavy set and already gray-haired, her husband's Mormonism had pushed her into being an activist for women's rights. Past her I saw police arriving. Soon, law enforcement cars were everywhere. What was happening? I couldn't see the main gate. Where was everyone? Had my picketer friends been arrested?

I glanced up at the rapidly lightening sky. Was I really doing this? Oh, yes, this was me, Cleo Kocol, middle-aged, middle class. I looked down at my waist at the chain holding me in place. I had acted, not just for myself, but for all women beginning with the mythical Eve. I felt as if I'd been chained to that gate forever. Cars with television logos appeared; the media had arrived but were being kept back by the police. I saw telephoto lenses. Now what?

Still no blue appeared in the sky, just this shadow-less early dawn. An unbearable sadness gripped me. While I was telling myself to snap out of it, the paddy wagon arrived and the police with bolt-cutters cut me down from the fence. Someone read me my Miranda rights, and the blue coats escorted me to the wagon. I felt very alone and wanted to cry. I was so damn tired and nothing seemed clear. I was getting arrested because I wanted equality for women. I climbed up into the paddy wagon, and half a dozen or so women who had already been cut from the fence, were already there. As I entered, they sang, "Just like Cleo Kocol we will not be moved." What a wonderful feeling that gave me. I was part of a historic moment, working like Elizabeth Cady Stanton, my hero, like all the women who had gone before me. No, I was not alone in this, no one was. We were part of a link in the wonderful chain of historical happenings, the actions of brave women who had gone before us. When the paddy wagon picked up others further along the fence, I was smiling and singing, too. Women – students, homemakers, professionals, including a protestant minister, and one man – had been arrested.

My short-lived elation ended at the jail. We were fingerprinted, our mug shots taken. A policeman asked me for my home telephone number. By this time I was so physically and emotionally exhausted, my mind had gone blank. I couldn't remember it. When I was locked in a cell with three or so other women, I will never forget the sound of those bars clanking shut. I began to cry. Karen Beard who had picketed with me, gave me a hug, and whoever else was in that cell joined in. We were one. Karen was as dedicated to the cause as I was. Six hours later we were released.

Afterward the group enjoyed a late celebratory lunch, but while the others laughed and joked and planned, I was so sleepy I was almost comatose.

But I promised to be on the picket line early in the morning to keep up the pressure. I went home and literally slept for ten hours. This time when I woke in the morning, Hank gone again, his note had turned into three, one in the bathroom, another in the kitchen, and a third in my car. All said how proud he was of me, and every year on November 17 for twenty plus years he sent me a card lauding my actions and saying how proud he was of me. (When the cards ceased to come, I began to notice the first signs of his dementia.)

When I arrived at the temple with the signs, women who had not taken part in the picketing or chaining, who in the past had felt we went too far, were already there. Now that we had paved the way, they wanted to join in. After all, Walter Cronkite had reported our chaining on television, and articles were appearing in the Seattle papers about our actions. Picketing was suddenly the thing to do.

The next day, as planned, I met my friend Margaret Okamoto in downtown Seattle. We were soliciting for help for NARAL, the free choice organization. She was waiting when I got off the bus, and the first thing she said was congratulations. Deems, her husband, had asked her why she hadn't been with us. It was a great thing to hear, another man supporting us. Another thing that stands out about that day was we went to Starbucks, which was just getting its start in Seattle. It was also a sunny day, an uplifting day, and Margaret and I believed women's lot would improve.

Back home, I barely had taken off my coat when my friends from the Alice Paul NOW in New Jersey called. "Cleo, are you okay?" And almost before I had time to reply they were picketing LDS churches in New Jersey. Not only did NOW chapters act in solidarity with me but Humanists in Arizona also picketed LDS churches, and various Humanists joined in as news of the chaining spread nationwide. I can imagine how surprised Mormons throughout the country were when they saw people with signs outside their houses of worship.

We who had chained were dubbed the Bellevue 21 and given a court date. Each of us prepared our testimony. But before we went to court, the LDS Church dropped their charges. They knew we had facts that showed they had used all their vast resources to defeat the ERA, and not all of their actions would face scrutiny. At this point their actions weren't universally known; if we went to court they would be. Now, we who had been arrested could come off in Mormon history as a wild bunch of misguided women, and they could maintain their church superiority.

By now many of us were wildly enthusiastic about activism. Our activities escalated. In July Karen Beard and I went to Washington, D.C. Sonia met us at Dulles Airport and took us to her place in Virginia in Loudon County, not far from the plantations of antebellum days, and not far from where Hank and I had lived in Virginia.

It was a busy, exciting time. In D.C., we participated in meetings with women historians from around the country who stressed the continuity of action I had already felt. In one of the meetings we resurrected The Congressional Union, Alice Paul's organization during the World War I era. Paul, a Quaker, had observed the militancy of the British women asking for equal rights. She came home, and said we had not been forceful enough in our quest for the vote. Although she didn't advocate throwing bricks through windows she said we had to make visible statements where it would count. Picketing was not being done, but she and the members of the Congressional Union (CU) began picketing the White House, asking President Wilson to include women in democracy. In Washington, D.C, in 1981, the CU was resurrected, and Karen and I became co-chairs for the Pacific Northwest.

It was a busy weekend that Fourth of July in 1981. Gloria Steinem gave a talk that blended humor and common sense. Other stalwarts in the movement, like Robin Morgan, also spoke. We rallied in front of the White House, picketed in front of the White House, and sang in front of the White House to the music of Cheryl Dalton of California playing her guitar.

After the planned agenda had taken place, Sonia said, "Let's go," and those of us who shared her philosophy, followed her into the street – not just any street but Pennsylvania Avenue in front of the White House. Stopping the ever-flowing traffic, that still drove by, could bring the media. They had studiously ignored us until that moment.

While press coverage was still scant, our actions brought police in full force: in cars, on foot, on horseback, and on motorcycles. It was a formidable sight. Yet, I felt energized as if I were doing what needed to be done. At this time Sonia no longer attended religious services, but she had not fully shucked off the god segment, although she routinely excoriated religion in general. Later, she boldly defended the case against god.

That day as she and the others kneeled in the street, some praying, I stood tall, the only one standing in that long line covering the width of Pennsylvania Avenue. I felt I was doing it for all secularists who backed the feminist movement. While roughly half of the protesters were not religious, they went along with the religious bunch. It's not easy to overcome social pressure. I was proud that I had the strength to be different. I had had plenty of sleep and I was feeling strong and triumphant in the bright-sun day, the White House gleaming, the signs we carried announcing to all, we were women determined to make a difference.

I called Hank that night. He said I had justified his pride in me. It added to my already strong flights of fancy. I felt as if I could do anything. Hank said he and Betty and Randy were sitting on the balcony at the File's condominium watching Seattle's fireworks light up the sky. I told him in detail about the day and he repeated it to the others, their support palpable.

But, of course, our bravery, our actions didn't make a difference on the national scene. The talk against women's rights escalated. In the nation's capital, the police let us off with a warning, leaving many of us knowing we'd commit civil disobedience again. Life was good; good had to prevail. Most people didn't notice that the Republican Party had dropped their support for the Equal Rights Amendment from their platform.

Back in Seattle, Karen and I decided we would stage a sit in to coincide with Sonia and the women of the DC area who would be scaling the White House fence and taking their protests to the front door of the executive mansion. Today they would have been shot the minute they topped the fence and landed on the other side. Then no one expected women to be so audacious.

Karen and I discovered that no one supporting the ERA had been arrested in a federal building. We'd be the first. To bring attention to the resurrected Congressional Union and let the public know the ERA was not dead as long as the CU was still a force. We held a news conference and symbolically burned promises by politicians. By this time Karen was asking her former church embarrassing questions about why women were treated so horrendously in biblical situations, or why most churches had no women ministers or priests. Or why women were blamed for most everything. No one had ever asked such questions before.

Four or five reporters covered our news conference. We spoke about the Congressional Union. We spoke about how daring the women who had picketed the White House had been during World War I. We said we planned to shake up the present generation. One reporter, a woman, said, "You sound angry." "Yes, angry that women don't have equality of rights," I answered.

A week later we went to the federal building in midtown Seattle. The building loomed over us, new and large. I felt the power of the federal government, remembered the oft-repeated words, "We are the most powerful country in the world." A shaky feeling hit my stomach, but no one ever knew it. I recalled what I'd done and why and immediately got over my jitters. Emulating Sonia, Karen and I, had planned ahead.

Now, we walked in as if we were the sweetest and dearest little housewives about to make a request. We were very upfront; we were coming in to let them know we were going to stage a protest. Dressed in lady-like suits and frilly blouses, our feet in high-heeled shoes, we looked like the traditional suburban housewives we were. We spoke deferentially to people in authority. We looked like we wouldn't say boo to a goose – as Scarlett stereotyped Melanie in the novel *Gone With the Wind*. We assured the very nice man, who was head of Security, we wanted only to rally with a few other women in the plaza in front of the building and make a presence in the lobby afterward. We said nothing about staying put once we were inside, but that was the plan. We'd committed civil disobedience twice, why not a third?

The "action" day was bright and shiny, creating bold shadows on the plaza.. Karen and I wore long white old-fashioned dresses. Theresa Caffrey, a twenty-eight year old woman who had heard about me and had written asking if she could take part with Karen and I in our next demonstration. She came in from the suburbs to join us wearing a brightly-flowered long gown that contrasted brilliantly with our white long dresses and showed up like a dream in photographs.

A half-dozen TV and radio people came to the Federal Building's plaza. I issued a statement and then the media questioned the three of us. Among other things, they asked what we hoped to accomplish. I repeated what I'd said previously, we needed to let authorities know we were serious and let other women know we were on their side. Our supporters and followers were milling around the large piazza, some with signs. Honor thy mother; put her in the Constitution, stood out. We were only too aware that after the Civil War women were successfully written out of our founders' document. For the first time an amendment to the Constitution spelled out the words, "male citizen," making it clear that the franchise and other rights were not for women, only for the newly enfranchised black men.

When the initial excitement, questioning and picture-taking subsided, Karen, Theresa and I sat down in the lobby with a banner spelling out the words of the Equal Rights Amendment on the floor in front of us. We vowed not to leave until the ERA was ratified. Our supporters milled around us. A reporter interviewed me again. A newspaper photographer clicked photos of the three of us, including Theresa's sign that read, "How long must women wait for equality?" After ten or fifteen minutes, Security said we had to leave. Our supporters, and passersby who had stopped to see what was happening, left.

We were alone in that vast lobby, footsteps somewhere behind us echoing. I had time only to think, was Hank watching the news on television? In no time we were surrounded by policemen and arrested and read our rights. They took us by the arms, Karen and I going along, Theresa going limp and being pulled along. We were given a court date and told to go home and behave ourselves. (Like good little girls)

Days passed, and I kept wondering when I'd hear from the government. Women friends were assuring us that if we were jailed or imprisoned, they'd hold 24-hour vigils outside the building or gates or wherever we were held. Our knowledge about the penal system was nil. We hoped they'd give us only jail time. Weeks were speeding by, Hank telling me to relax; it would be months before I heard. It was. But again the charges were dropped.

None of that would be possible today. Sonia would be shot; Karen, Theresa, and I would be in prison, and the others would surely know jail time.

About this same time the religious right began speeding up their crusade against women. Spouting his bible-inspired, anti-woman rhetoric Jerry Falwell came to Washington State. Falwell, the right-wing preacher from Virginia who started Liberty University, had his face and his rhetoric ringing out, not only from his pulpit, but from radio and television shows, and in person throughout the country. For a time I had been getting his literature – "If we are going to save America and evangelize the world, we cannot accommodate secular philosophies." It amused me to have him think I was eating up his words. Actually, I was eating up his postage and printing fees. But when I never responded to his call for money, the guilt-trip literature stopped coming.

During this time Karen and I as well as Betty and others had been a presence in various parades and events in the Seattle area. When we heard Farwell was coming to Olympia, the state capital, Karen and I were there.

Karen wore a Support the ERA shirt. I still was skittish about saying I was an atheist. People invariably frowned when the word was spoken. I had on a T-shirt I'd embroidered with the words "Non-Theist" in letters on the left front shoulder. Falwell and company, his young singers dressed in red, white and blue, were spread out on the capitol steps, singing Amazing Grace and similar songs. When he went to the microphone to speak, Karen and I unfurled a gigantic American flag. At least six foot long it couldn't be missed. I'm sure Falwell saw it and us. At first he was smiling as we stretched out that flag, but then his jaw literally dropped. He had to have seen Karen's T-shirt and possibly mine. We felt our efforts had been rewarded.

As the months went on, Seattle became more and more a focus for speakers extolling the need for equal rights or the need to stop this nonsense and stay home like good women. By this time The Humanists of Seattle, HOS, had gone to San Diego to take part in the American Humanist Association's annual meeting. We were all tremendously excited. We would see people we had only read about before, people like Fred Edwords, the young man who was making a mark in the freethought world by writing about Creationism, even debating some of the foremost proponents of it, others like Gerald LaRue, the biblical scholar who lived in the Los Angeles area.

I had written about my actions at the Mormon Temple to Gina Allen, chair of the Women's Caucus of the American Humanist Association. She had immediately answered and suggested I come to San Diego and talk about the chaining at the national meeting.

I was eager to meet her. She had started the Women's Caucus because none of the women married members of AHA could be located by name. A few short years ago Cleo Kocol was known only as Mrs. Hank Kocol. That women were relegated to this second class status had propelled her into actions. An activist in the larger women's movement in San Francisco, working along with Aileen Hernandez, she had been determined to educate the AHA. I was flattered by her invitation. Indeed, all of us from Seattle were walking on air at the prospect of meeting members of the AHA. And we were absolutely star struck thinking we would see Carl Sagan, the Humanist of the Year. We'd brought copies of his book, Cosmos, with us, hoping to get an autograph, having read the book and watched his television show based on the book.

When I walked into the Women's Caucus meeting and introduced myself, Gina Allen's mouth actually fell open. An attractive woman I estimated was probably fifteen or so years older than me. She told me later, she had expected to see a big, strong woman, and then I walked in. It was a telling moment. Even people who agreed with the need for an ERA had stereotypical views. But Gina, who made a living writing for Dr. Joyce Brothers and who had written a critically acclaimed novel about African Americans when they were still called Negro or colored, agreed with me about most everything. I was soon working closely with her.

After giving my report, excitement ripping through me, I hurried around the corner to the elevators and ran smack into Carl Sagan. We were both thrown off balance. Good gracious, he was like a rock star to most freethinkers, and I was still a neophyte in the organization. I stammered something incoherent, but he recovered before I did. Maintaining his cool, he held me upright and murmured something appropriate. Ann Druyan, who was with him – the woman he later married – appeared to realize my predicament and smiled to reassure me that such things happened. To add to my discomfort, we took the elevator up to our rooms together, me slowly getting over my embarrassment and muttering one or two semi-intelligent sentences before I got off.

Hank and I had cheered when we learned Sagan had been named Humanist of the Year. He was one of us, not a pseudo religionist. No bending of the knee to an invisible god, just a "Hi, Carl." I was so enthralled (and now embarrassed) that I let Hank do the honors and get our copy of Cosmos autographed

The serious side of the convention, however, was that not one newspaper reported upon the national meeting no matter that the AHA had apprised them all that Sagan would be receiving an award and be our main speaker. That is how cowed the nation was by religionist at the time. The media ignored us.

At the same time, the anti-ERA crowd was chortling with satisfaction for time was running out for ratification of the ERA. Gloria Steinem came to Seattle to speak at Shoreline College where I'd also spoken about women's rights and chaining at the LDS Temple. Karen rode with me as I drove down to pick Gloria up at Seatac airport. If Carl Sagan was the star of the freethought world, Gloria was his counterpart in feminism. Very attractive, erudite and knowledgeable, she spoke intelligently about women's dilemma, and she did it often with humor. Her advocates were too large to count. A pied piper, she drew followers as easily as she intrigued the press.

We had her to ourselves for a short while, as the crowd at the college was enormous, but she had us join her in the Green Room before her talk. All of us chatting as well as talking "business", I half-shrugged as I said I was a radical feminist, as if that bore a stigma. Karen and the two or three other women who had joined us said they were, too. Gloria caught my shrug and said we should be proud of being radical. That it meant getting to the bottom of an issue. It was my cue to give her a copy of The Humanist magazine and have her autograph another one for my granddaughter.

I was feeling strong and capable and proud to be with her. She had arranged for us all to sit with her down front before she went to the podium. As we walked through the huge crowd, me smiling at everyone, I didn't see the rope that marked off our reserved seats, and I stumbled. Flailing the air, I would have fallen if Gloria hadn't held me upright!

Later, at a reception at the college, Barbara Dority of HOS arrived while Gloria was circulating. Barbara lived and breathed the Rolling Stones' music. She'd left a Stones' concert early so she could meet Gloria. It's a testament to how women of all ages and temperament were serious about getting equal rights with men and how much Gloria was revered. I was in my early fifties, Karen thirty-seven, and Theresa, who got arrested with us at the federal building, was in her late twenties, and we all practically genuflected hearing Gloria's name.

But all this had little effect on politicians who were threatened by women who wanted passage of the Equal Rights Amendment. While the Illinois legislature continued to vote against ratification, Sonia and other dedicated women, including Catholic Sister Maureen Fiedler, went on a fast in Illinois to bring attention to what was happening to the ERA. In our country, men like Dick Gregory were routinely applauded when they fasted for their causes, but the women who fasted with Sonia were derided, insulted, and treated at times inhumanely. Few people in America now even know the fast happened.

1972

Cleo, Yugoslavia, 1972

Cleo, Seattle

Hank

Hank

Hank, white water rafting

Hank's 1st sky dive

Jerzy & Anna Feiner

HOS, San Diego, Cleo, Dick, Betty, Randy

Humanists of Seattle

Cleo at the White House, WA, D.C.

Karen Beard & Cleo, press conference

Cleo, Federal Building, Seattle

Gina Allen & Cleo, AHA conference

Dolly, Cleo, Sonia, Billie, Joan, WA, D.C.

Cleo & Annie Laurie Gaylor of FFRF>

Mildred McCallister & Cleo, Dallas

Mary Dessein & Cleo, Hawaii

Cleo in performance

Cleo & movie star Dana Andrews

Mynga Futrell & Cleo, AAI conference

Roland Roberge, Cleo, Debbie & Brett>

Hank protesting Iraq war, San Francisco>

Hank in China with Chinese scientists>

Cleo lecturing in Guilin, China>

Cleo & Hank, dancing, Hawaii>

Cleo, Palace of the Legion of Honor, S.F.

Steve & Rhonda, Las Vegas

Terran, age 11

Cleo & Hank, Waikiki after 9-11

Eleven

"It is the business of the scientist to speculate, to hypothesize,
to think of possible explanations – if not in public, then
in the privacy of his own mind...a scientist cannot
help doing so any more than a writer can keep from
thinking of fragments of plot, or snatches of dialogue."

ISAAC ASIMOV (1920-1992) "THE ROVING MIND"

In the meantime Gina Allen and I continued our uphill battle to educate, not only the AHA about the lack of women's rights, but also the larger world. It was certainly an uphill battle because now the Republican Party, with the election of Ronald Reagan began an anti-woman agenda. Feminism became a dirty word.

But Gina implemented without question, my ideas, telling me she liked my style and helping dissipate my anger. My regard for Hank's, Randy's, Dick's and other men's understanding of feminism had me suggesting we call ourselves the Feminist Caucus, a term that included both men and women. I further suggested we give a Humanist Heroine award each year. Gina thought it was a wonderful idea and named Sonia Johnson the first recipient. By this time Sonia had shed all religious connections to any church and was giving lectures at the Freedom From Religion Foundation and other organizations.

(In 1984, at a speech in Madison, Wisconsin, she said, "One of my favorite fantasies is that next Sunday not one single woman in any country in the world will go to church, if women simply stop giving our time and energy to the institutions that oppress, they would cease to be.") Although she was not at that point yet, she minced no words, and we who knew her applauded. Unfortunately for the Feminist Caucus, AHA, when the time came for the award, Sonia and the others were still fasting in Illinois. Gina suggested I accept the award for Sonia. I said I would.

All this was happening while Hank and I were knee deep in work, protests and enjoying our new home and the area, busy with HOS and leading them in marches for women's rights.

We had attended the theater everywhere we lived. But the dramatic event that changed my own life and coincided with Gina's ideas, and had Hank applauding, happened at Seattle's Museum of History and Industry. The museum not only had ongoing and changing exhibits but also a theater where historical plays and shows were presented. We went to see a one-woman show about local history. As I watched the actor perform, a thrill moved through me like a thunder-bolt followed by a thought, *I could do that.* After chaining at the temple, I had emerged a stronger woman, more confident in my own abilities. My mind churned so fast I could hardly contain myself as I watched her move around that stage, as I listened to her speak. Why had she worn shoes that announced every move she made? I wouldn't have. Why didn't she pause before she said a particular word? I would have. I'd never been so picky about a performance before. I had analyzed theater plays and movies in college in an introductory course, but that had been an objective task. This had been subjective. As we left the theater, walking across that parking lot to our car I told Hank I wanted to write a women's history show. Not only would I write it, I would perform it.

He watched me in fascination. "Really? That's fantastic. I'm surprised and yet I'm not surprised. You're very capable."

I almost tripped over my own feet. He'd said I was very capable, and no one, even my parents, had ever said such a thing. "You really think I can do it?"

"I know you can." He chuckled. "Since we were married, you've done everything you said you were going to do."

I could see Hank truly believed I could do it. I felt supremely grateful and confident. Throwing out words, composing as I went along, I said I would portray both characters from history as well as women who would represent a certain era or time. I would use scarves to change from one woman to the next (the woman in the show had used hats.) And I'd have a theme linking them all. The words were brave as well as prophetic. But could I really do it? Again I shot a look at Hank.

He said it sounded great and put his arm around me as we neared our car, hugging me. He was smiling broadly. I still can hear him saying, "Go for it. I'm with you a hundred percent."

My mind whirled. I had no idea how it would happen, but sometime, somewhere, I would perform a play I'd written, if only because Hank so obviously believed in my abilities and I was in awe of his.

Three months later I finished my research and had written the last line of my Heroines show in Vancouver, British Columbia, Canada, where Hank had a meeting. I had gone along, mostly to have a place where there'd be no interruptions and I could finish writing my show. I was so excited when I had that last page in my hand and had rehearsed it, I wrote to Gina about it from our hotel room. A letter was waiting for me when we arrived home.

Gina had put my show on the program for the AHA's conference at the MIT campus in Boston. "It can be a real tribute to Sonia Johnson," she wrote. My heart hit bottom. Sure I wanted to present the show, but not so soon and in front of such a prestigious audience. My stomach growling, I hastily made arrangements to present the show to the Humanists of Seattle first. Their applause still echoed when I was off to Boston.

I'll never forget that show. I was so nervous ahead of time I thought I'd never get through it. In Seattle I hadn't needed a microphone. In Boston, I did. I had seldom used a mic. My voice, which was pitched for the stage, was too loud. It echoed at times. When I finished the presentation, few of the men in the audience were overwhelmed, and I imagined them talking about women's high-pitched voices, a refrain that was often heard in those days. Women were shrill, their voices grated like fingernails on a chalkboard. Oh, yes, I was used to all the clichés. But as the men studiously avoided me, I could see all the women were touched beyond my wildest imagination. Some had cried during my performance, others had tears in their eyes. They had not realized other women felt as they did. Some had only fuzzy facts about the history of women in America. They loved the show and wanted to help the women's movement. If they didn't already belong, they joined the Feminist Caucus.

I began giving the "Heroines" show other places, Pennsylvania, Ohio, Florida. In New Jersey my friends from the Alice Paul Now gave me a standing ovation and feted me during the next few days I stayed in the state. Gradually, other places throughout the country wanted the show. In the beginning, I received an honorarium I gave to the Feminist Caucus. But gradually I got enough nerve to ask for more realistic remuneration to offset traveling expenses. Also to show that what I did was important enough for people to pay to see it.

I wrote two more shows and by that time was being paid as a professional. Women at colleges and universities, in women's groups, women who were Displaced Homemakers, or "girl Fridays" booked performances. Women of all ages and descriptions, amazed at the history, were shocked and energized. By the time I was traveling to New York City to appear at Equal Employment Opportunity venues for the Environmental Protection Agency, I was paid five hundred dollars for an hour's performance. This was in the early 1980's. During the Great Depression, scrounging around for a penny for candy, I had declared people were really rich if they had a hundred dollars. It was the most I could imagine at that time.

I was beginning to hear from women who said seeing my performances had changed their lives. They had been in difficult situations and found confidence hearing about women like Elizabeth Cady Stanton and Susan B. Anthony and the countless women who never made it to the history books but who persevered against odds. Feeling humbled, I usually cried hearing or reading their stories.

My activities in the AHA led to me being elected to the National Board. It was an honor and a time of learning for me. Some of the men were still stuck in the past, others, while supportive of women's rights, were quick not to "rock the boat," but I also found others went all out for women's rights. I was happy that during my time on the board, two women, Faye Wattleton and Margaret Atwood, were named Humanists of the Year, and that I led Humanists in marches for abortion rights and women's rights in Washington, D.C. One of my most ardent supporters, Roy Torcasso, was a celebrity in Humanist circles. He was the man who made it possible for people to be notary publics without swearing allegiance to a god.

My plays were making a difference, but they meant nothing toward passage of the Equal Rights Amendment. And not all women applauded. I had scheduled a few presentations where audiences of conservative women avoided me afterward. It wasn't pleasant standing alone as I waited for my ride to a lonely room. It was as if I had done something wrong by calling attention to the discrepancies between men and women in most all aspects of American life.

I learned quickly that you had to know your audience. If it was a friendly audience, I gave out copies of the Humanist Magazine and brochures listing free-thought organizations. If not, I said nothing. But the rewards were enormous, seeing women who had suffered the indignities of workplace harassment and low pay, women who were in abusive marriages, women who had been denigrated in their own families come up with tears in their eyes afterward to thank me.

Backlashes existed, even in the freethought movement, men who did not understand, thinking that women hated men. Also women who had achieved by being "one of the boys," felt threatened. And, of course both men and women existed who thought we should "move slower." But the denigration of liberal movements and words made popular under the Reagan administrations had young women saying, "I'm not a feminist, but…" before listing their workplace woes. Liberals began to be afraid to use the word, liberal.

As fall segued into winter, most theater weekends we returned home after dark, Seattle's latitude making for short winter days. One day as we entered the dark house, Hank clicked on the downstairs lights, swooped me up, carried me downstairs and set me on my feet, me sputtering the whole way. Immediately, he danced me across the floor to the fireplace. Sometime before we left he had laid a fire, set up a card table, covered it with a tablecloth and set it with my good dishes and silver.

"What in heck?" I said, but he put a finger to his lips and signaled that I should wait for explanations as he lit the fire and made sure I was seated where I could toast my feet while he went upstairs and brought down dinner from the oven. Drinks and nibbles sat on the bar, and he put them at my elbow. Earlier he had taken his special lasagna from the freezer and set the oven controls to go on while we were gone. While the furnace hummed and warmed the corners of the room, we ate while he told me we were going to Egypt and then Berlin. Impressed, I told him he was a keeper.

Not too much later we "did" Egypt, me standing below the only known authentic carving of Cleopatra, Hank snapping photos. Throughout our three weeks in the ancient land, we flew here and there in order not to miss anything. The Egyptians we met or hired, all wanted to stand so close we felt uncomfortable, but seeing that ancient land was like a dream come true. Touring the main Coptic church in Cairo made me think again about all the missing gospels I'd first learned about at HOS.

From the dry, dry desert around Abu Simble, Karnak and all the famous sites, as well as the slums of Cairo, we went to rainy Berlin where the wall between East and West added to the gloomy days. Crossing the wall as tourists to the East was fraught with moments approaching fear. Soviet infused East Germans in uniform took our passports, compared our faces with those on the passports, checked our names against a list, and occasionally went through purses or patted down men. Had our shenanigans in Moscow been recorded? Such thoughts whizzed through my mind. But they gave our passports back and we were free to continue in on the tourist bus to get a glimpse of a city I felt mimicked the grayness of Soviet Russia.

But the high point of Berlin was watching Hank give a speech at an international conference, his words translated into other languages. My pride in him deepened.

But in ways I wished I was back in Egypt. It rained hard most of the time we were in Berlin, and one night we both returned to our room, I from sight-seeing, Hank from the conference, both of us coughing. Mine stopped shortly after I had a hot shower, but his persisted. He went to bed and was too sick the next day to get up. "I can't miss more than a day. You'll have to get me some medicine," he muttered, his voice sounding raw as a hatchet splintering wood.

"How? Where?" I stared at him.

All I needed was to make a couple turns from the Kerfurstandamnn. He'd seen a drugstore in that vicinity.

The people making arrangements for my sight-seeing had spoken English. The docents made a stab at it. But a local pharmacy?

"You'll be okay," Hank assured me. He wrote down all his symptoms. "Take this with you."

The umbrella I'd purchased for sixty-five dollars American, kept me as dry as possible, and I made the walk in less than ten minutes, spotting the pharmacy without difficulty even though night had fallen, street lights reflecting in the wet pavement. The drugstore looked horribly well lit, bright enough I'd show up like a sore thumb. I had taken a conversational German class before leaving home, but none of the words and phrases I'd learned were any help. I didn't want a telephone, taxi, or train station. I wasn't in need of a powder room. All the German that I'd memorized was useless. I could say, "Bitte," but then what? I forced myself through the door.

Two people stood in front of the small counter. I took a place in line behind them. But, incomprehensibly, they waved me forward. I shook my head and motioned them forward. With words that flew past me like confetti, they practically pushed me forward.

I was front and center, on stage without lines. And then it came to me, the phrase I'd never thought I'd use. I blurted out, "Mine man ist krank." My husband is sick."

By now I could actually see the man behind the counter. He was smiling and nodding. The people whose place I'd taken were smiling and nodding. I gathered myself together, pulled out my German phrase book and holding my finger under words like fever and cough, the pharmacist was able with his weak English and my weaker German to gather a formidable bunch of bottles and boxes. I fumbled through a wad of German bills until I got the proper amount and paid him. I still don't know how they all seemed to gather I was a foreigner, I accused Hank of putting a sign on my back. He only said, he knew I could do it. I began to think he was right.

I was still giving my shows (three by now) around the country when we heard from Jerzy and Anna Feiner, the Polish friends we'd met in the Soviet Union. They had been given permission by the Soviet dominated Polish leaders to go to Libya where Jerzy lectured in French at El Fatah University. This time the Soviets let him take his family along.

Immediately, Hank and I made plans to go to Libya to see them, but after a few exchanges of letters, Jerzy wrote that it might not be safe. We cancelled our plans and no more letters arrived from them.   When we had stopped wondering why, we got a letter. On the way home, the Feiners never took the scheduled plane to Poland but defected in Italy. Jerzy used his credentials, a PhD in architectural engineering and a Masters of Art, to take care of his family. To earn money, he painted murals on Italian villas while they applied for American visas. They were coming to America!

A year later, we learned they were in Hollywood, Jerzy teaching portraiture at a college, at times exhibiting his work, meeting American artists and generally getting known. He painted portraits of Michael Landon, of Bonanza fame, as well as the other Bonanza stars. Jerzy, Anna and the children lived in rooms above the art gallery he opened in Hollywood.

Coincidentally, soon after we heard from them, I was due to do a performance in Los Angeles. The Feiners attended my show and afterward we took pictures with movie star and celebrity humanist, Dana Andrews, who was in the audience. It was personally gratifying that someone of his stature congratulated me about my performance. I remember so well seeing him in movies like The Best Years of Our Lives and Laura.

After the audience dwindled away, Jerzy and Anna, Hank and I sat in a booth in all night eatery, and talked. Anna's unhappiness was almost palpable. She had had status in Poland, was important in society. In America she said Polish nobodies claimed titles. Jerzy, who had been feted at Penn State University, and was still an important lecturer, found his architectural credentials didn't reach across international borders. No matter how many buildings and projects bore his name in Poland, Britain, and Italy, he didn't have American credentials. They hoped to go home when the political situation improved.

Their problems seemed remote. I sympathized but my mind was still wrapped around what I'd been doing. I had tried to change society and politics, but no matter how much and how many women spoke, lobbied, wrote, testified in Congress, marched, picketed and committed non-violent civil disobedience, the ERA was not ratified, and I had been in the forefront of activists. For months after its defeat it hit me like a punch to the gut and then gradually it became old news and life went on.

Twelve

"The people never give up their liberties
but under some delusion."

EDMUND BURKE (1729-1797)

By now Hank and I took it for granted that we'd each support the other in their endeavors. Seldom did we disagree, and I felt almost as close to his natal family as he did. His parents had accepted me without question; they accepted our secular ways without comment.

One of my fondest memories was arriving at the annual picnic unannounced. Our surprise had been the high point of the day. My mother-in-law and father-in-law showed genuine happiness at our attendance. Just seeing their delight gave me a great feeling. The food, the games, the conviviality was great, everyone in the Family Club, meaning extended family and friends, participated, and Hank's father ran everything. I facetiously called him The Polish Godfather, for nothing happened without his say-so.

We attempted to go to most family get-togethers, flying to Chicago for a long weekend. Unfortunately, I couldn't get out of a previous obligation when the annual potato bake was scheduled. I hated not going. For years Hank's father had been responsible for various Poles coming to America, helping them navigate governmental regulations, also finding them a place to live and work among the Poles in Chicago. He was a respected figure in the city, and Hank admired his father greatly. He always enjoyed spending time with him. But this time when Hank came home, he wore a long face and his gaze hardly met mine when I ran to meet him, he was that disturbed.

"What's wrong?" I asked, following him to the bedroom where he began unpacking his suitcase. Fall had set in, short days, long nights. I had most of the lights in the house blazing, wanting to give him a bright welcome home.

"I can't talk to Dad," he said, moving abruptly, hanging clothes up, taking others to the dirty clothes hamper.

I followed him. "What do you mean?"

He walked right by me, tossing words over his shoulder. "One day I talk to him, the next day we have the same damn conversation."

"What do you mean?" I repeated, edging by him, forcing him to look at me.

Hank took a deep breath before answering. "He was telling me about his will, about his insurance policies and the deed to the apartment house." Growing up, Hank had helped his father maintain the apartment house. It had multiple renters and sometimes a recalcitrant furnace. "I think he wants me to be executor of his estate. It wasn't clear." He threw up his arms. "Nothing was clear."

"How was your Mom?"

"Same as always."

"So?" I felt as if I were dragging things from him.

"So?" Hank scowled.

"I just wondered if they were having troubles."

He stared at me, his face grim. "They're no different than usual."

"That tells me a hell of a lot."

"Damn it all, he doesn't remember from one day to the next! Literally. I wasn't making a figure of speech I couldn't talk to him." His voice had risen, the sounds harsh, the last words agonizingly slowly spaced one word from the next.

I had never seen him so distraught. "Oh."

He threw a book on his nightstand. "He used to be so blasted smart and now he's just like his mother."

"Your grandmother?"

He straightened the book that had landed sidewise. "The way she was at the last." He turned toward me. "But he's too young to be senile!" Turning abruptly aside, he clicked his suitcase shut and put it away in the hall closet. "But he repeats himself like an idiot." He slammed the closet door shut and took a deep breath. "So let's not talk about it now."

"I really think…" But he appeared so angry, at his father and his own reactions to him that I ended, "If that's what you want."

"I do."

Later he spoke less dispassionately and we both recalled relatives who had not settled into old age gracefully but seemed more like children. It was something society expected. People got old. They couldn't walk, talk or function as well. And then they died of old age. It was a disease, a condition.

Hank's visit to Chicago faded as once again our own life took precedence. I no longer led feminist meetings. They had trickled to an end. NOW meetings seemed dull, were poorly attended. We, who had worked so hard, needed time to digest our disappointment, face the political atmosphere that was evolving. I continued my newsletter, 4 Women, which had evolved into 4 Women and Men at Hank's suggestion. Although not many men subscribed, a few did. In the new political climate, I had fewer and fewer demands for my shows.

Hank began to talk about going to China. Until the American presidential delegation went to China in 1972, the country had been in complete isolation, having fought a civil war that ended with a communist state. We'd been glued to the television watching the photographs of Nixon and Kissinger in China and came away enthralled with the idea of the country. We'd been to Egypt, Europe, Britain, Mexico, Canada, and South America by this time. A few American tour groups were going behind the bamboo curtain, tourists coming back with exotic tales of a people fifty years behind the rest of the world.

Although we'd prefer being on our own, we decided if we had to take a tour to go to China, it would be a new experience. We'd been reading about General Stillwell and the American experience in China during World War II. We'd heard stories about the Cultural Revolution, the chaotic time when the intellectuals had been sent to the farms to work, when young people, given free reign by Chairman Mao, turned on their teachers and sometimes their parents. What was it like now that ping-pong diplomacy and the Nixon administration had opened China to the west? What was it like in a country where god didn't hold sway? Had the Chinese become an ersatz Soviet Union?

One weekend as we walked along the Ave. in the University District of Seattle, that marvelous area overrun with students and small ethnic eateries, we unexpectedly met our friends, Fran and Tyler. Dr. Fran Solomon, a scientist, had worked the phone lines with me for the ERA, she had been among those marching for women's rights, and had been out to the temple several times. Her husband, Dr. Tyler Folsom, had become a computer scientist during its infancy, and the two of them had recently been to China, traveling on their own!

Remembering our experience in Soviet Russia, I stared at them. "I didn't think it was possible to travel on one's own."

Hank repeated my surprise. "We were told you had to go on a tour."

Fran smiled. "You have to jump through a few hoops with the Chinese government to go on your own, but I'm sure they will approve you."

Tyler was sure we could manage getting around once we were there.

If anyone was on the cutting edge of change, Fran and Tyler certainly were. I remember the day she and I were at lunch and she asked me what I thought of planned childlessness in a marriage. I didn't know what to say, for I had desperately wanted a family when married to Bill, but I would have screamed so loud everyone in the world would have heard it if Hank had wanted children. I told her that couples should decide that for themselves, not let society do it for them. Fran and Tyler liked to travel the world, often on bicycle, and both were devoted to their work. They had a full life together as well as alone, each allowing the other space. Although we weren't bicycle enthusiasts like they were, we said going to China on our own was something to consider. We'd get together with them soon to discuss details, but we weren't as sure of our abilities as they were for us.

A few days later I was walking around Green Lake, a favorite place for Seattleites to exercise. Some walked, others biked or skated the three miles, but the paved way always had people coming and going. I was almost back to the starting point where I'd left my car, when I ran into an acquaintance I hadn't seen for a while. It was pure serendipity. She and I were both members of the Older Women's League (OWL) which concentrated on helping find political answers to women's issues in the fifty and above age group.. The Feminist Caucus, AHA had given an award to Trish Sommers who started OWL. Her national motto was "Don't agonize, organize."

Some of the members of the Seattle Chapter of OWL had presented a play on stage at the Seattle Public Library. My Seattle acquaintance had directed it. The story about displaced homemakers, a term used often during the seventies and eighties, referred to women who had been housewives and were suddenly on their own through death or divorce. My character in the play mimed Katharine Hepburn, and at that time I was able to do the Hepburn accent.

My acquaintance asked me what I was doing, and I said Hank and I were planning a trip to China.

Her face lit up. "You won't believe this, but not long ago my husband and I hosted a man from China, a former American who had not been in the States for years. You might enjoy meeting him." A Jew from New York, in China he'd married a Chinese woman, took a Chinese name and became a Chinese citizen.

Talk about serendipity. I was dumbstruck. She gave me his address, and while I was still in a daze, I wrote to him. His response said to call him when Hank and I were in Beijing. He gave a number.

Buoyed by Fran's and Tyler's enthusiasm and this latest information, Hank and I got in touch with the Chinese authorities, received permission to visit certain cities, and set a date in the future for the trip. We would go in October, 1986.

Hank immediately, began a year-long study of Mandarin Chinese, the official language of the nation, studying with a native Chinese teacher, who taught in the University District. He had emigrated from China years before the revolution. Hank's facility with languages (his first language was Polish, English came in kindergarten, and then Spanish, German, and Russian followed), helped tremendously. At the same time I bought Conversational Chinese books and practiced words, phrases, and short sentences, Hank helping me with the pronunciation.

With several hoops to jump, time seemed to drag, but our planned trip began to take on aspects of a real adventure. Hank wrote to his scientific counterpart in China and received an invitation to speak at the Institute of Nuclear Medicine. Then Hank's Chinese teacher told a friend in Guilin, China, that I was a published writer. My writing and acting career hadn't been stagnant, my work published various places including a column in the Humanist magazine.

What cinched it for the Chinese, were my Seattle credentials. I was president of the Seattle-area writing club I'd joined as soon as we'd arrived in the Pacific Northwest. That the club had been founded by a former professor who was well known in the Pacific Northwest gave me status in their eyes. A list of my publications as well as my association with the AHA impressed the Chinese. The head of the Karst Geology Institute in Guilin, spoke to the professors at Gunagxi Teacher's College at the university in Guilin and then wrote to me. Would I give a two-hour lecture about American literature? Two hours! I reeled and then agreed. No matter how educated my Chinese audience, I was the American and I'd research ahead of time to fill in any gaps in my knowledge.

Two weeks before we were to leave, Hank and I were sitting at the kitchen table perusing the Sunday paper and taking our time at it. September had arrived, and once again we'd attended the Bumbershoot Festival at the Seattle Center (bumbershoot referring to Seattle's ubiquitous umbrellas) and been enthralled by the many entertainers, the exhibits, the food, and the wonderful weather.

In fact, unexpectedly, I had been brought on stage in the large theater to stand on the Reverend Chumley's chest. He was lying on a bed of nails! We had followed this magician for years. He called himself a reverend so he could poke fun at religion during his patter. Slowly, he rose in rank in the entertainment world of Bumbershoot. We had been thrilled to find Chumley had become a headliner. And for me, it was an experience I loved sharing. Nothing like being front and center at a magic show!

No matter that July might be gloomy, the early September weekend of the Festival usually had Mount Rainier standing majestically above the city, visible to all in those sun-filled, no-cloud days. Hank and I were reminiscing about Chumley, who shafted religion with a high-class British accent, when I noticed again how blurry the newspaper had gotten lately. I'd noticed it for some time, but I hadn't said anything, realizing that all newspapers were cutting corners. Holding the inner section toward Hank, I said, "They certainly don't use decent ink at the Seattle Times lately."

"What do you mean?"

"It's all blurry."

He shot me a look of disbelief. "It looks all right to me."

"Look," I repeated, pointing to where I had been reading. "It's blurred."

"It's not."

"But it is."

"No, it's not." His serious tone alerted me.

I frowned. "It's not?"

Also frowning, he shook his head and I heard worry in his voice. "I think you better get your eyes checked."

"But when? I don't have time." I began listing all the things I had to do before we left for China in two weeks.

He took my hand, made me look at him. "Just promise me. The first thing we get back, you'll go."

"I will," I said reading the concern in his eyes. I put my head on his shoulder as he put his arm around me. "You think it's serious?" I whispered.

"It could be."

I straightened. "Lets forget it, not even talk about it until we get back. Okay?"

He looked as if he wanted to launch an argument. While he was usually the stubborn one, now I was sticking to my guns. "Against my better judgment, I'll agree, but I really wish you'd go to the doctor now."

"I can see all right," I said. "It's just reading the paper where I have trouble."

We said nothing more about it.

When we left Seattle for San Francisco and then Honolulu, where we'd have a short layover, I was carrying letters from AHA members that I planned to give to middle-aged and elderly people in China, a people to people project I had started through the Feminist Caucus. How naïve I, and the letter-writers, were. When I mentioned the letters in China, I was told they'd be distributed. I expect they ended in the trash. No one in America ever had an answer to their friendly letters.

But that was later, after we arrived on the mainland. First we stopped in Hong Kong for a few days, and my naiveté showed again. I got off the plane and walked into the waiting room and was instantly amazed and a little disconcerted at seeing nothing but oriental faces. Sure, I'd seen people from China, Japan, and Korea in the International Settlement in Seattle. Sure, Margaret Okamoto, one of my best friends, had married a Japanese/American. Sure, I had been to San Francisco's Chinatown, and Vancouver's Chinese center. But this was different.

I had been friends and been acquainted with people of all races and ethnic backgrounds at home. But I had never been anywhere where Hank and I were the only visible members of our race. When I was a child and growing up, all things Chinese were inferior, including the people. The term "yellow horde" was voiced often enough that it both frightened and intrigued me. At home I said that the color of one's skin meant nothing. But, now I had seen the "horde," and the numbers shocked me. Was this the way oriental peoples felt when they landed in America? Was this the way African/ Americans felt? I'd never seen so many people in one place. Americans not accustomed to New York City, routinely bad-mouthed it because of its vast number of people. Too many people for its own good, was said often. But the numbers of people in Hong Kong made New York City look like a small town.

The fatigue of the long trip and culture shock encompassed me, and Hank was not much better. We had no way of knowing that real culture shock awaited in Beijing. Hong Kong was still under British control. Rich Chinese men, afraid of the coming annexation by Mainland China were already looking for a way out, some marrying Australian women who welcomed the money. It was a business affair only.

During our days in Hong Kong, we were thrilled, and a little in awe, soaking up the atmosphere like a sponge. As a child and young person I'd been a voracious reader of Pearl Buck's novels. They were my only in depth look at

Chinese life except for the newsreel theater's "eyes and ears of the world," –
Japan overrunning China, British gunboats in Chinese waters, American mis-
sionaries teaching Chinese children.

Eagerly, we followed the sight-seeing, ferry-riding tourist agenda, smiling
when an educated Chinese spoke English with a British accent, riding the
double-decker British style busses, walking the streets and alleys, and being
thrilled to recognize street names like Nathan Road that I'd read in novels
and seen in movies. But the city, its foreign feel, appeared vastly different
from Europe, but, I realized later, when contrasted with Mainland China was
outstandingly European, the ultra modern buildings familiar as a New York
skyline, only the boat people and those selling goods from a blanket on the
ground were really different.

We flew at night to China's capital, and that first night in Beijing practically nothing registered. Having pushed myself for weeks before leaving
Seattle, having slept little in Hong Kong, not wanting to miss a thing, pure
exhaustion encompassed me. At the Beijing airport, I felt nothing but relief when a government car and two young people, smiling and gracious,
met us. The Friendship Hotel, where they took us as guests of the People's
Republic of China because of Hank's coming talk at the Institute, was not
far from the airport. If I saw anything of the city or the people, nothing registered. The Chinese talked pleasantries, and we responded, me using my
memorized phrases, Hank speaking Chinese to our escorts. They answered
in English, saying young people preferred to use the English they were just
learning.

Very soon Hank and I were deposited in a small room with two single
beds. The room smelled so strong of cleaning fluid that it seared my lungs,
and I had trouble breathing. Sleep eluded me; but every time I tried to sit
up, dizziness struck. Despite the cold Hank managed to get the one window
open. The cold air helped, and we slept a few hours before morning light
woke us.

Shaky, but determined to find a hotel that would be less, "sanitary," we took a taxi to the nearest Cits office, the department that helped foreign travelers. Settling on a hotel where professional Chinese and visitors from European countries stayed, we taxied to it, the city a blur of bicycles and one and two-story buildings interspersed with a handful of western style hotels. Ours was centrally located, and in no way resembled a Hilton. Staying in American style lodgings was something we always tried to avoid. We could stay in Hiltons at home. We wanted to be among the people, not enjoying an ersatz American stay. This hotel with its clean but very modest amenities seemed perfect. I could no longer push myself and welcomed the chance to sleep eleven hours.

In the morning, after that refreshing sleep, I glanced outside, and my mouth fell open. Hong Kong had been like kindergarten. This was like graduate school. The wide, wide street was absolutely filled with people on bicycles, a vast army of men and women filling the street as a far as I could see, jamming the sidewalks, people everywhere. I had never seen so many people dressed alike moving in concert, a never-ending flow or people all on the move. Despite my astonishment, I was anxious to be among that vast army of people.

We hurried downstairs for a rice gruel breakfast that we ate faster than anyone in our vicinity at the long trestle-like tables. Rushing outside, we were immediately enveloped in the ever-moving crowd. Like an ocean tide they kept coming and receding, flowing around us as we stood in rapt amazement. I couldn't see how we'd ever cross the street. The streams of people seemed never ending. I saw no traffic signal, no traffic director. When a small group of people started across, Hank said, "Let's go," and we joined the others, close as shadows.

And yet, by afternoon, we had adapted. It was as if the initial impact had happened long ago. Thrilled by everything we saw, we kept grinning at one another. The people had lived behind the Bamboo Curtain for years, in Mao led isolation, not knowing or acknowledging the Western world. We were the big-footed enemy, the foreign devils

But after President Nixon's visit, the spotlight had shifted, China changed. Students were vying with one another to get to America to study. At home, people said America had opened China up to the world. Now, with Chinese all around me, I realized, China had been ready to join the world again, or the Kissinger diplomacy wouldn't have worked. Now, the Chinese people were eager to know Americans. That first day several teenagers stopped us on the street to try out their English. Everyone was studying our language. College students were intrigued by foreigners, especially Americans.

Hank and I grinned at one another as we navigated the maze of noodle shops and had a meal, bought souvenirs and strolled through a park. At home we had read that "staring squads developed in a moment." American travelers could find themselves in the middle of huge groups of people focused on them. That day we went into a department store where I wanted to buy a padded silk jacket. As I tried jacket after jacket, all too small, I soon had an audience of at least a hundred, all pushing in close, undoubtedly discussing everything about me. The clerks, smiling non-stop, finally brought out the largest size they had in stock before I could find something to fit. At five foot two and a hundred and twenty pounds, I was usually the smallest person in any group. But not in China. Hank thought it tremendously amusing and called me, "One big Mama."

Most of the Chinese surrounding me had never seen a Westerner before. It meant a whole new way of thinking. We represented people whom they'd been taught to treat with derision and suspicion. Now, we were among them. In the subway a toddler, fear stamped on its face, pointed at me and shouted the word for foreigner. Recognizing the term and shocked, I glanced at Hank. Catching my meaning, he nodded, not needing to say anything. Not even in the Soviet Union had children appeared frightened when seeing us. They had been unsmiling and unspeaking, but not fearsome. But most Americans and

Russians had white skin. Among the amber-colored Chinese, we looked like we'd come from an alien civilization.

We found another noodle shop and whipping out the chopsticks we'd brought from home, filled our bellies before going back to the hotel. We knew that the sanitary conditions in food stalls and restaurants in no way resembled ours. It would have been unsafe to use their chopsticks.

Back at the hotel, we each stretched out on a bed and began discussing the day, when Hank suddenly sat bolt upright. "Oh, hell," he said. We had broken an unwritten rule: that is not to leave your hosts with egg on the face. The way we'd left the Friendship Hotel had not been wise. It could be construed that we had spurned Chinese hospitality. Had we unwittingly precipitated an international incident? "I have to offer some explanation, although our actions can never be rectified." The line between his eyes deepened.

Hurriedly, Hank placed a telephone call to the only number he had and hoped his message would reach the right people. At that time very few Chinese had telephones, and cell phones were things of the future even in America. He left his name and a message he hoped sounded diplomatic before giving the name and address of our new hotel.

We were about to lie down again on our single beds – single beds being the norm – as I tried to figure out if I'd be able to read. A fifteen-watt bulb affixed to the ceiling with a pull chain provided the only light except for the 40 watt bulb in the bathroom. I had taken off my shoes and was laying out my pajamas when a knock came at the door. Hank opened it to two middle-aged men, both dressed in the ubiquitous blue Mao suits. They stared from him to me and back to him. I assumed they were involved in the Chinese government's nuclear program, but I couldn't be sure.

But now I felt very aware of being in a communist state. The men looked very official and stern despite polite half smiles. I felt like a country bumpkin gawking at the Empire State Building in New York City. We had shown absolutely poor judgment about the room the Chinese government had provided us. We had not notified our contacts when we left, but had only left a message at the desk that we would not need breakfast as we were moving. That we had acted in a typical do-it-yourself American way would not lessen but could exacerbate the problem. The Chinese had lost face. This could not be an ordinary visit.

Hank seated the two men on the two chairs and perched on the end of the bed closest to them. I pushed my very American pajamas under a pillow and went to where the large thermos of hot water sat, teabags nearby, ready to pour them tea. It was the polite thing to do. As I fussed with the cups, the initial conversation between Hank and the two men sounded like glacial ice breaking up.

"You are comfortable here?" the man who spoke English asked.

"Very much," Hank answered, knowing he'd be the authority in China regarding radiation, China not as knowledgeable as the US at the time.

I nodded affirmation and poured tea in the two cups and handed one to each. The men thanked me and then said to Hank, "But not so much at Friendship Hotel?"

Hank explained we so very much appreciated the facilities at the Friendship Hotel, but we had wanted to be closer to the center of the city. "In order to do justice to your marvelous sight-seeing possibilities. My wife is a great admirer of your art, especially the sculpture."

"Oh, yes," I said, sitting at the end of my bed, desperately trying to remember the name of any of their famous sculptors.

Their nods showed a willingness to gloss over our gaucherie.

Still a small interrogation of Hank's abilities and connections followed. The English speaker had been to the United States. Naming one of the American scientists he'd met, one he'd discussed the future of nuclear power with, he said, "You know him, of course."

I held my breath. That, "of course" had made it clear. Hank would surely lose face if he didn't.

Luckily, Hank had worked with the man, knew him well. He followed with anecdotes to corroborate his words.

The English speaker smiled broadly and exchanged looks with the other man.

After that everything became increasingly relaxed, and we learned that the head of the Department had arranged for us to travel by train to Tianjin in a few days. "Enjoy your sight-seeing," they said when they left, even including me in some chitchat about the Great Wall.

The next few days we immediately set out to see the sights, taking a rick-shaw ride to Tiananmen Square, feeling guilty for having another human pulling us, but I wanted this link to the Pearl Buck era. But it was hard to envision in this "new" China. Awed by the size of the square, larger than any in the world, I tried, instead, to imagine it jammed with people shouting Mao's praise, the words echoing.. Larger than life, his photo still dominated one of the entrances to the square. Although a large amount of people were strolling the perimeter, they seemed like a handful in the vastness. With other tourists, both Chinese and Western on the periphery, we were constantly amazed by the statues, the Great Hall of the People, the immense size of everything. More Pearl Buck like, the Imperial City did take me back to the days when reading opened my mind to the rest of the world.

The following day we boarded a bus to the Great Wall where the wind whipped with fury, and, in order not to shiver unduly – it was that chilly – I had to purchase a T-shirt emblazoned with the words, "I climbed the Great Wall." As I slipped it over my head, Hank pointed out how quickly China had caught on to capitalism. If I had wanted to I could have purchased key chains and one or two other items in the small shop.

On the wall we climbed past a group of Americans and many Chinese on an outing. Children in bright red clothing posed for camera-clicking parents. Often we heard the words, one, two, three in Chinese. While the wall, which rumor says is the only man-made object seen from space, amazed us, incidents involving other people proved as exciting. Several young couples, looking very American, told us they were from Hong Kong. They had concerns about the future, but now they were as wide-eyed as we were at the ancient fortifications.

Everything contained elements of excitement. One day I turned dozens of heads when I entered a large women's rest room where women waited to use stalls that had no doors. My blonde hair seemed suddenly pure platinum among the raven-haired women who all pretended they weren't watching me. Strategically located places for my feet helped me balance over a hole in the floor of my stall.

Before we left Beijing, we had seen all the important sites, rode public transportation, took taxis, eaten in restaurants and, as guests of the government, were treated to a banquet held at a special lodge used only for VIP's and party insiders. A large Russian-type car picked us up, two young men chatting with Hank as we rode through the city, occasionally pointing out edifices they thought would be of interest.

"They act as if we're big shots," I whispered to Hank as we entered the building where we'd dine. Situated in a lovely tree-lined and flowerbed setting near a lake, I got a vicarious thrill over the lengths they were going to entertain us.

"What they don't know can't hurt them," Hank whispered back.

We were both smiling like kids with bagsful of candy at Halloween. That day we'd wandered through the city, surprised to see communal combs hanging on strings before mirrors in one park, thrilled by the chess players, their game even more difficult than the western variety, happy to find groups of people playing instruments and singing. Several young people of university age approached us, wanting to talk. One made the sign of the cross and pointed at me with a questioning look.

I shook my head no. "You?" I asked pointing at him.

His face took on a stern look. "I am Chinese," he said. No one talked about religion, not as if it were a forbidden subject but much like my childhood, something that had no importance.

To this day I'm not sure whether he was merely being careful or had some familial connection to the missionary churches that had inundated China in the twenties and thirties. Like many of the young men, he wore jeans he'd gotten from Western travelers. Kids traded chintzy souvenirs for the jeans.

At the banquet, we sat at a large round table with a Lazy Susan in the center, the older men near Hank, the younger men near me. It seemed they were there to make sure I got the best tidbits of food, while engaging me in "light" conversation. While I was old enough to be their mother, they made me feel much younger. It's important to note, I was the only woman at the feast.

Two days later, we met our escorts at the train station. Our car going to Tianjin had soft seats, one of the better categories of train travel. The average Chinese rode hard seat. We knew about the two categories as Fran and Tyler had briefed us before we left Seattle. Again the two men accompanying us were friendly and semi-knowledgeable about the west. Again, we were put up at a Friendship Hotel, but this one was comfortable, the accommodations better even than our hotel in Beijing. Both places we had comfortable beds, the adjacent bathroom adequate, but now we had a twenty-five watt bulb in the ceiling fixture!

While Hank was busy at the Institute, I'd be escorted on a shopping tour unless I preferred something else. I certainly didn't want to spend my time shopping! I wondered if that was their image of American women. Whatever their reasoning, before we left home Hank wrote that I would appreciate seeing where the average woman worked and what she did with her children while she was so engaged. They had answered I would be accommodated.

The first day while Hank met with his peers before his lecture, an older woman and a young man met me in the hotel lobby and escorted me around the city. They showed me parks and places of note, before taking me to a mill where women sat at sewing machines, small individual lights shining dimly on their work stations. Most of the workers were mothers.

At home women were still struggling to find day care. If they had no relatives or friendly neighbor to baby-sit, it was a big worry, especially since employers modeled their relationships with employees on male workers. The division of labor in America was an unwritten code. Women took care of the house and children. Men were the bread-winners. Although this was always held up as the model, everyone knew there were families where both parents had to work to exist and families where women were the lone bread-winner.

In Tianjin, women running sewing machines brought their babies as well as their pre-school children to work with them.. There were nurseries for the babies and women had time off to nurse little ones or to join their preschoolers at lunch. Grammar school children came to the mill when school let out. No woman had to worry about their children's welfare while they were working. I was flabbergasted.

The staff included doctors in white coats and nurses, all women. Employees got medical care on site. I talked acupuncture and herbal medicine with the doctors. In the classrooms, I was treated to song and dance by the children who seemed eager to perform. None showed the shyness sometimes displayed by like groups in the U.S. during my growing up years. Chinese children are praised and made over, giving them confidence that helps when responsibility is gradually added. Among the adults, who all wore the typical blue Mao suits, the children stood out in bright red or yellow clothing.

With my escorts I also saw collectivized commercial art. The paintings, favored by foreign tourists, were the work of many people. One person did the sky, another added trees, etc. until the whole painting was done. It reminded me of the paint by numbers phase that hit America in the 1950's. I also saw architecture that owed its existence to the days the French dominated the city.

Back in our room at the Friendship Hotel, I waited eagerly to hear about Hank's experiences. He'd surprised the Chinese scientists by giving the first paragraph of his lecture in Chinese. Afterward, his Chinese peers said, "You were understandable." We figured it was high praise. During conversation with the other scientists, Hank learned that pregnant young women were having MRI's and fluoroscopes. If their fetus was female, it was aborted. The population imbalance between the sexes had begun. Although we had done our own sightseeing in Beijing unescorted, the Chinese had arranged our transportation, meals, and sightseeing in Tianjin. The government had hovered over us until we returned to Beijing where the hand-holding ended.

We decided it was a good time to visit the man who had disappeared behind the bamboo curtain after the Chinese civil war, the man my friend from the Older Women's League had drawn to my attention. He had said we should call, but calling anyone was quite an undertaking. We needed the assistance of the desk clerk in the hotel lobby. When after some twenty or so minutes we were connected, he suggested we come see him that evening. We were told we needed to put a taxi driver on the phone so he could be given directions Navigating the narrow streets and narrower alleys of Beijing would not be easy.

The desk clerk hollered for someone in the back room, and the man appeared, ran out into the street and returned with a taxi driver. He talked with the man from America for some time.

Ten minutes later we were on our way. The gray of evening had moved in, and from the back seat of the cab, again I saw little, losing track of the numerous turns and twists. It was clear we had left center city and were in the suburbs traversing alleys so narrow the driver had to inch along, at times scraping against a building.

After more than forty-five minutes, the driver put the car on idle and indicated we should wait while he reconnoitered. We watched him disappear around a bend. Night was closing in fast. We looked at one another and relaxed when he came back smiling. Our friend was waiting up ahead.

Getting out, Hank asked the driver how much we owed him. He shook his head and said. "I wait for you."

I envisioned an enormous bill, but there was no time to worry. The one-time American stood by his gate waiting for us. A tall white man, white hair, tanned skin, he looked like a colonial in India, tan pants and shirt. All he needed were epaulets. Smiling, he embraced us and gestured us through the gate. I remember a yard where roses were growing.

"Not easy in this climate," he said.

I had hardly noticed, but he was undeniably proud of the flowers.

Inside the low, flat roofed house, were the accoutrements of home – television, music player, comfortable living-room furnishings. I felt as if I were visiting at home during the 1950's. Later it became abundantly clear that he lived better than other Chinese we visited. The house was quiet; no one else in evidence.

He said he didn't want to talk about the Cultural Revolution, and that really confused me. What should we talk about? Our conversation grew awkward, stilted. While I was searching for something relevant to say, he suddenly mentioned the subject he said he didn't want to discuss. During the Cultural Revolution the educated, the middle class, the rich, teachers, educators, anyone considered "above the people" were persecuted. His wife and he were both sent to the country to labor in the fields, in different places. They were separated for years

I didn't know what to say, except "That must have been extremely hard."

He nodded.

Hank said nothing.

As the silence deepened, our host questioned us.

We told him our plans.

We indulged in chit-chat about historic sites. I felt extremely frustrated. The only good thing I came away with was his Chinese name.

For a long time I remembered it, now it is like a will-o-the wisp as flimsy as the conversation we had exchanged that night. I had been overwhelmed by the knowledge I had of China, not knowing how much or how little to divulge.

The cab back to our hotel was ridiculously cheap.

The following day we were all set to go to Xian when we were informed that all the hotel rooms had been taken by the Queen of England and her entourage. We had seen the royal yacht in Hong Kong, anchored among the junks that were home to people living on the water. Generations of Chinese had grown up away from the land. The contrast between the spit and polish

British crew and the bent over and prematurely aged boat people had been tremendous. I'd stared. Only the junk people had stared back.

Making a quick decision to go on to Kunming, Hank and I stood in the many lines necessary to buy plane tickets, lines reminiscent of the ones in the Soviet Union. Hank's ability with the language and our own ability to go with the customs helped a lot. There had been a VIP line that people insisted we should be in before we lined up in the others. Everyone in the VIP line had come from a foreign country. At the airport, we were pushed aside by others, everyone racing for the plane. I couldn't understand why when all seats had been assigned.

Of the places we visited, few highlights about Kunming stand out. We arrived there mid-afternoon, found a room for the night, had a wonderful meal and got up with smiling faces in the morning. But no matter that we practically camped out at Cits and twisted as many arms as possible, we could not find accommodations for the following night. We had wanted to spend a few days in the city before going on to the Stone Forest, one of the natural wonders of China.

By questioning several people, Hank found we could get a room at the Stone Forest. The day was overcast and drizzly and we were relieved to have a plan. We booked seats on the local bus and followed a young American couple on. I was struck how both old and young Chinese passengers eyed us as we went down the aisle to the only seats available, at the back of the bus. I had to smile recalling how often that phrase, had been bandied about during our American Civil Rights movement.

The rain came down harder after we started, the drizzle wiping clear the occasional spit spewed by passengers in front. They would hack and then spit out the window. Luckily, in the back the windows did not open. But in Beijing, in a department store, climbing stairs from one floor to another, I'd put my hand on the railing when climbing. It was a mistake. Someone had left a large glob of spit. I never touched a railing after that, even though at night I was finding it increasingly difficult to differentiate objects in the dark. I said nothing to Hank about my difficulty seeing.

After a while the rain stopped and the passing scene was reflected in puddles, the landscape taking on a dewy appearance. The terraced hillsides of rice, the markets in small villages, people jammed together selling produce, the oxen in the fields, all captured our attention. The young Americans said they were on their honeymoon. We offered our good wishes; they smiled and once again turned their attention to one another.

And then suddenly, the bus stopped. Nothing indicated we were near the Stone Forest, although we were approaching noon. We should be close, but nothing indicated a village, a resort, a settlement. Nothing showed why we had stopped. When Hank queried, the driver made it clear: this was the end of the line.

"Now what?" I asked. The bus was turning around, going back to Kunming. Most of the local passengers had departed at villages and crossroads along the way. All that remained were a half-dozen Chinese, the young Americans and Hank and me. Thankfully, the rain had ceased and sun was quickly evaporating water from tiny puddles.

The driver tossed our fancy luggage and shoulder bags in the dirt next to us. The fields surrounding us wore the color of a California desert.

Looking around, I spotted a small stucco building nearby. "Maybe that's a depot."

Hank said, "Or at least someone inside should know something." Other people were going in. He started to follow them when a smiling man approached, calling out to us.

"What is it?' Hank asked in Chinese. The man answered in a spate of rapid-fire Chinese. I could not catch a single word, and Hank shook his head. "Speak slowly, please," he said in Mandarin.

Smiling, the man nodded, and with a mixture of English and Chinese he managed to assure us we would get to the Stone Forest.

While all this was going on, I brushed a fly from my face and watched the local traffic – a man with a stick nudged a pair of oxen by me, two young men pedaled by on creaking bicycles, obviously held together with wire, and several women and children, strolled by, barely glancing at us. I watched with interest but trepidation, too. The bus had been gone at least fifteen minutes. The honeymooners had found a tree to stand under, the woman tapping her foot, the man looking around frowning impatiently.

The Chinese man conversing with Hank spoke in spurts of Chinese and a few words of fractured English. Obviously proud, he showed off a wrinkled American newspaper photo of Reagan, a pen an American had given him. Joe something. Did we know him?

I shook my head, realizing he had gotten the objects from Americans and concluded we had to be in the vicinity of the Stone Forest. I said as much to Hank. He agreed. Obviously the man asking about "Joe" knew what he was talking about.

A few minutes later two donkey carts appeared along the dusty road leading to us. They smelled faintly of fresh manure. With alarm, and feeling queasy, I watched someone hoist our luggage aboard. The man talking to Hank indicated with gestures we should get in also. The young Americans, shrugging and sending a rueful glance our way, jumped into the first cart in line. A small bench spanned the width of the cart in back and formed a seat covered with linoleum. We got in the second cart and were barely seated when the driver smacked the donkey into actions. Away we went down the road, the honeymooners sending us a wave.

We deposited our bags at the tourist hotel desk and found our way to the Stone Forest. I don't know where the honeymooners went. The maze of high cliffs and bluffs of the Forest reminded us of sites in Arizona and Utah. Admiring the red and amber stones, the narrow ways that opened into small courtyards, hidden passages, some with pools of water, others with yellow and beige rock, and boulders where we could rest, it was a true maze. An hour later, the afternoon sun had disappeared, no shadows existed, and our peek-a-boo views of the sky didn't help. Where were we?

Feeling gloomy as well as tired, fatigue set in. The sky at times invisible, I looked at Hank and said what I expected, "We're lost, aren't we?"

"I think so."

"Only think so? I know so."

"If you know so much, get us out of here," Hank said only half teasing.

"I think that way," I said, taking off rapidly. Soon we were back at the pool where we had earlier taken a picture of four giggling girls from a far away province. They had been taking photos of one another with a disposable camera. We offered to take a photo of them all together. Ducking their heads, they thanked us. Now, they were nowhere in sight. "You're turn," I said to Hank

We back-tracked to a split in the trail A few minutes later, we turned a corner and almost ran into a couple from Hong Kong. They were very Chinese in appearance but spoke very British English. "Ah, good, Americans," they said admitting they were as confused by the maze as we were.

We exchanged information about ourselves as we collaborated in an effort to find the way out. "You'd think at least there would be a sign or two," they said sometime later, as we turned another corner. I started to agree, but then they said something that startled me. "But what can you expect from pagan people?"

I must have looked surprised for the woman said, "We're members of the Anglican Church. Are you by any chance?"

I said no. They obviously expected us to be Christian. Weren't all Americans? Hank explained about the melting pot of religions and no religion as we were forced to go single file. Luckily, not much later, we were at the entrance to the Forest and back to the hotel in time for dinner.

I hoped we would see the tourists from Hong Kong in the dining-room, and now, writing this years later, after Hong Kong is no longer British but Chinese, stories are always emerging about the difference between the Hong Kong Chinese and those on the Mainland. While I'd estimate that not many Chinese percentage-wise in Hong Kong or the Mainland cities are Christian, they have all adopted western ideas about living. Except in the countryside of Mainland China.

The glaring difference was apparent recently when visitors to Hong Kong from the Chinese countryside let their child urinate on the street. The citizens of Hong Kong were outraged. They had grown up following Western ways of child rearing, but in the countryside of the mainland, children still wear split underpants and relieve themselves outside whenever they have the urge.

Back in that dining room at the Stone Forest the couple from Hong Kong were not in sight. But a raucous group of tourists had arrived, all speaking American English. Approximately twenty-five Americans were escorted by two Chinese. The Americans were all middle-aged and older, and clearly excited about getting a taste of China. I wanted to exchange a few words with them. We had been in China over two weeks now, and besides the honey-mooners, these were the first Americans we might exchange impressions with. But as Hank and I tried to go to where they were seated at two long tables, two waiters put themselves in front of us. Shaking his head, one pointed to a small table in a bay window. Hank and I tried to explain we just wanted to say hello, but he insisted on seating us at the small table where the honeymooners were already seated.

While the food was good, the dinner was a disaster. The young couple proceeded to belittle everything they heard and saw about China and the Chinese.

After a while Hank stopped talking, and I gave up attempting to carry a balanced conversation.

After we paid our bills, the four of us went to our rooms at the same time. One bedroom opened off the hall, the next room opened off of the first room. Whoever slept in the second room had to pass through the first to get to the traditional toilets down the hall, the usual holes in the floor. Anyone in the inner room would essentially be trapped in their room until morning.

More than a little disgusted with the honeymooners 'Ugly American' at-titude, I threw my overnight bag on one of the beds in the first room. They were forced to go to the second room.

Thirteen

"The applause of a single human being is of great consequence."

SAMUEL JOHNSON (1709-1784)

*I*f the honeymooners showed the worst side of America, we tried our best to make up for it as we flew around China. It wasn't difficult in Guilin. Like Kunming, it lay in the southern regions of China and many consider it the showplace of the country. From the first we were intrigued with the city and its fantastically beautiful surroundings. Karst geology gave the region an other-worldly feel, like an ethereal painting, or the background of a fanciful operetta, the mountains rising to summits rounded smoothly at the top, no sharp points or angles, just nature at its loveliest, all curves.

From the moment of our arrival, we were treated like the crown jewels of America. Our contacts met us at the airport and escorted us to the hotel where we'd made reservations, the same hotel where President Richard Nixon had stayed in Guilin. Every day that followed, someone was with us to translate, to show, to help. We were feted as well as surrounded, treated like visiting royalty and escorted to local sights. After a few days we began to feel smothered, and I began to wonder about the lecture I was to give. Could I live up to what seemed like their expectations? Hank said I'd do great; after all I was the American.

At the college I signed a ledger, and immediately felt humbled. Alan Ginsberg and Toni Morrison had signed immediately ahead of me. How could I compete with that? But I swallowed my jitters as we entered the lecture hall. Because I was speaking to graduate students and faculty only, I'd be speaking without an interpreter.

The small room had no air conditioning, and the afternoon was warm and humid. I faced a podium of rough, unpainted wood. Putting my material in place, I looked out at the sea of faces and began, and any jitters I had felt were gone. I felt thrilled that I was speaking to people who a few short years ago would have reviled me for being an American. The audience seemed attentive, interested. But during a very serious point in my talk, I could not miss seeing two young women giggle and cover their mouths with their hands. Whatever I said had not been understood or possibly misconstrued. I realized how difficult it is to bridge cultures, especially as different as the United States and China were at that time

But I know my talk had been a success. The professor who was a Hemingway scholar approached me immediately afterward to ask if I'd come back in a few months. He was leading a world symposium and would be delighted if I could return. It appeared my remarks and explanations of the Hemingway style had added to my approval.

Another professor presented me with souvenirs and invited Hank and I to a banquet in my honor later that evening. I was thrilled, and Hank was thrilled for me. That they had not asked me until after my talk was not lost upon me. Nevertheless, I felt like a star.

That evening, with professors from the college, we were seated at two round tables and treated to a large collection of dishes running the gamut from shark-fin soup, which came at the end of the meal, and Peking Duck. The conversation, in both English and Chinese, included compliments for our use of chopsticks as well as questions about where we'd been and where we planned on going. I displayed the small snapshot folder I'd brought from home. It showed photos of Seattle and surroundings, including family pictures, our house, the seashore and mountains, all photos properly labeled in Chinese so we didn't have to explain.

Mid-meal, I realized I was the only woman in attendance. It appeared to be a pattern for celebrations during our visit. I knew that the college had women professors. I had seen them, talked to some. A goodly percentage of women taught at the college. "Where are the women?" I asked during a lull in the conversation.

An awkward silence followed as the men looked down at their plates or cast surreptitious looks at one another. The man sitting next to me said, "Ah, yes, they are home baby-sitting." He smiled.

Quickly, without thinking, I blurted, my feminist feelings coming to the fore, "But your Chairman Mao wrote that women hold up half the sky."

Again silence followed, made tolerable with nods and murmured assent. "He did."

My seatmate vowed it would never happen again. Everyone looked contrite.

Two hours later, back at out hotel room, Hank chuckled. "You almost precipitated our second international incident."

I had to smile, my pride coupled with alarm. Only a feisty foreign woman would have been so blunt. "At least you made the first."

"But you quoted from Mao's little red book."

We were both high with all that had happened.

After the banquet, we were treated to a series of entertainments and invited to private homes for dinner. We reciprocated at a hotel banquet room where one of the leading calligraphers in China presented me with a scroll and a poem he had written especially for me. I was touched and deeply impressed. The calligraphy had been executed in both classic characters and modern script. Few Chinese today can read the classic characters and fewer can write them. We were told my friend was famous, selling his work throughout the Asiatic world.

But he wasn't the only one we met who astounded us with his story and his abilities. A young man who seemed to be the nephew of the calligrapher, carved on hair. Neither Hank nor I had ever heard of such a thing. At first I was not sure whether they were putting us on. But they were serious. Later, Hank said he was glad neither of us embarrassed them by showing our doubts. Such art was highly prized in the Asian world and was viewed through a microscope. As a child the artist we met had admired the men who did this, and so began practicing on seeds. Finally, he became good enough to carve on hair. But someone who was envious of his achievements denounced him, and the young man was put in prison. He denied he was a fraud, and, eventually the authorities held a demonstration and the young man proved himself and was freed.

Such a story would be pure fantasy in America. It seemed especially fantastic as the young man we met wore a white shirt, gold cufflinks, a silk tie, and a suit that equaled that of the Italian designers of the day. His girlfriend was equally "modern," wearing a skirt and blouse and high-heeled western shoes. Both, in their early twenties, could have been plucked out of China, set down in New York and no one would have said they didn't belong. He sold his highly prized work at a hotel in Guilin and throughout the Asiatic world.

After these highlights, Hank and I booked a cruise on the Li River, but the day we were to go Hank woke up with a nasty head cold. Immediately our Chinese acquaintances rushed in with cold medication, and Hank took it as prescribed and stayed in bed

The next day, Hank was well enough to go touring. To this day we have no idea what the medications were. They were as mysterious as the names for many of the attractions were poetic, like Reed Flute Cave.

On my own, I enjoyed the wonderful scenery, along the Li River, meeting people from a far northern province who were touring the area, having lunch with one of them plus the only other westerner on the cruise, a woman with a very young child. It was an amazing boat ride, along the river past the fanciful sculptured skyline, watching people fishing using cormorants as bait, seeing occasional women and children along the banks. The river in October was low making it necessary to make part of the trip to a vast outdoor shopping market by bus. Along the way we had lunch below decks, but most of the time I stayed on deck watching the passing scene, taking photographs and at times exchanging words with other passengers.

At the end of the ride, I strolled the open air shops looking for souvenirs, and, at the appointed time hurried back to where the bus had left us. My heart sank. Now, twenty or so busses lined each side of the street. I had no idea how to find the right one. Why hadn't I asked for a number, something to identify it? I'd been too busy talking to the Chinese I'd met on the boat to even think of it. I wandered aimlessly, looking into bus after bus. At the fourth one I struck pay dirt. A Chinese man I recognized smiled and beckoned to me. I got on.

The rest of our stay in China had us equally enthralled and wide-eyed each day,. In varying fashion, we were met with amazing contrasts, bare bones backwardness as well as modern success. It took a while, but we now realized, according to Chinese custom, we were part of the extended family of the man who met us and shepherded us around Guilin.

When we left for Hangzhou our new friends were aghast to learn we knew no one there. They had to rectify that, make sure someone met us. It would have been unthinkable otherwise. One of our contacts in Guilin had gone to high school with a man who had moved to Hangzhou. He called many people before contacting him and making sure we would be met at the airport!

In Hangzhou, two young people, looking very western and assured, escorted to our hotel. They said their fathers had gone to high school with our Guilin associate, and they were thrilled to do this for us. At the hotel, they made sure the accommodations were suitable. We were not displeased when they finally left. Used to the privacy Americans expected, the extreme closeness of the Chinese had been tiring. But we were thrilled that our hotel was near West Lake which Marco Polo had said was one of the most beautiful in the world. It's charm was not to be denied. The young couple assured us, "You will enjoy." It was not the first time we had heard the phrase!

Safely alone at last, we looked at one another and said, "You will enjoy." We did.

Our stay in China was as fabulous as opening a new book and finding treasures on every page. We learned the young couple were exploring the import/export business, just reaching out to the west. I expect by now they are multi-millionaires if not billionaires.

Back in Hong Kong was like returning to the West, the cars, the western dress, the high rise buildings, radio and television blaring, billboards advertising everything and anything one could buy. And, of course, religious books in the bedside tables at our hotel. The Gideon Bible kept company with a Buddhist book. On the Mainland there had been no religious books in bedside tables. On the Mainland, there were no religious symbols, and on the Mainland, no one said like a mantra, "God bless you." Nothing religious was ever heard. The airwaves, filled with communist propaganda, had nothing about religion. No one stood on a street corner exhorting passersby to find

Christ. We saw no churches, only a few Buddhist temples. And most thrilling, no one engaged us in religious debate.

At home we routinely put Freedom From Religion Foundation warning labels in Gideon bibles. The labels spell out the dangers of taking the words of the Bible literally. Once, at home, we had played a game with the maids, putting the bible in the trash each morning and finding it back in the drawer that night. We had begun to ask for Gideon-free rooms. Hong Kong, which had seemed so exotic a month before, now seemed very western.

Back in the USA, not only did we find bibles in hotel rooms but our ears were assaulted by a cacophony of sound I'd paid little attention to before. The babble of radio and television preachers vying for my soul, insulted me. Many advertisements and billboards spoke about faith, people attributed medical care to miracles, some people found the hand of god everywhere, saw statues of Mary weeping. In China we had not once been bombarded by "faith." It took time to get used to the harassment as well as the luxuries we all take for granted in the fast-paced American life.

For a while I felt out of step at home. As Seattle's deciduous trees began losing their scarlet and yellow leaves, I wrote and sent a story about carving on hair to a local Chinese paper. They published it, but nobody but the international community saw it. All the people we met and the sites we'd seen crowded our heads. Today I realize we had seen China during its last gasp as a country living in the past, exceedingly different from America. None of the cities were continental metropolises at that time. Most everyone wore the traditional Mao suit. Only the government and the highly connected owned cars. Everyone rode bicycles.

But all around there were hints China was emerging from its past, waking up rapidly. The young couple we met in Hangzou personified this change. Yet, the people in the hinterlands had only vague ideas what the rest of the world was like. Now young Chinese especially are reaching out to the world, many becoming entrepreneurs living lives they'd never imagined. Those living in the US, Britain, and other places worldwide are returning to China to live the "high" life, owning expensive cars and homes, sometimes fleets of cars and multiple homes. Hank and I had an experience that can never be duplicated in any way again.

With China behind us, Hank reminded me it was time to find out what was happening to my eyes. The optometrist I saw a week or two after our return, looked serious after she finished examining my eyes and gave me the bad news. Something very serious was happening. I had better get to a specialist immediately. I was shocked. I'd thought I only needed a better prescription for my glasses. The words, *serious problem* kept repeating in my mind. It was another drizzly day, my Honda's windshield wipers running intermittently. But half way down to the airport to pick up Hank who had been in Portland, the drizzle turned into a real downpour. I began crying. Hardly able to see, I had to slow down considerably. Was I going blind? I managed to stop blubbering before I pulled into line at Seatac. Hank didn't need a sobbing wife.

"So how was the trip?" I said getting out while he put his bag in the trunk Not trusting myself to get us home safely, I suggested he drive.

He slid into the driver's seat and as soon as we were out of the airport and heading north he said, "So, you getting new glasses?"

I didn't answer for a few seconds, and he shot a quick look my way.

"No glasses." I sighed and then came out with it. "I need to see a specialist."

He gave me a concerned look. "I'm not surprised. Did you make an appointment?"

"Not yet."

As soon as we entered the house Hank went to the telephone and made an appointment for me, but the soonest I could be seen was in two weeks.

That weekend, we went to the Bellevue symphony, Hank asking me now and then could I see the people in the back row of the orchestra. Could I see details about the woman who played third violin?

"I'm okay," I said, wishing he'd stop pushing at it.

Persisting, he told me to close one eye and look. To please him I did and a sense of drowning enveloped me. It looked as if everyone in the orchestra had pieces cut out of them. In shock I whispered about it to Hank.

"It's what I was afraid of," he said softly.

The first appointment was only the beginning. We saw one expert after another in hopes of hearing better news, but each gave the same diagnosis and prognosis. I had Cellophane Retinopathy and there was nothing they could do for it. With Hank ever solicitous, we listened to the specialists at our HMO and at the University. They all said essentially the same thing. I had lost the central vision in one eye and the other eye was seriously impaired. But I still had peripheral vision and could still drive in the daytime. With my usual stoic manner, I downplayed the problem, and many people did not realize the enormity of what had happened. One relative equated my problem with cataract surgery, which was a bit disconcerting.

A few years later, medical science had an operation they hoped might help. The odds were not good, but I said I might as well have the vitreous surgery they advocated. If anything it made my sight worse. I lost the peripheral vision in my right eye, and today I have what is called low vision in my remaining eye. I also have holes that show up like black dots. I have learned not to see them. But one is always present, especially in bright sunlight. Like a little fly it stays with me always, dancing just in front of me. Another dot follows just below a sentence I am reading in a book or paper, like an under-line. These black dots are not floaters, of which I have the largest ever seen by my ophthalmologist in Seattle, but dots that are always in the same place. The outcome is I have not been able to drive since 2001.

Neither Hank nor I made much of our handicaps, he still maintaining great sight in his remaining eye and driving for the two of us. When he was still alive, he liked to say, we had a pair of eyes between us.

Now that it was difficult to read computers in airports, and driving at night was out, I slowly phased out travel on my own. About this same time, I looked for other things to do.

With my friend Mary Dessein, I began Literary Lights. The short story contests we promoted and ran helped fill my hours when I wasn't busy trying to save the world. Mary, who had a career as a substance abuse counselor, including drug court, was also a multi-talented woman I met through the Fictioneers. Today she's a musician, story-teller, singer and sometimes writer. She entertains in various venues playing the harp and amazes everyone when she adds assorted other esoteric instruments to her repertoire, capping all off with song. An MC for a radio show, she interviewed and presented other tal-ented people. Her vocal treatment of the Star Spangled Banner can be heard at local ball games in the Seattle area. Through the years she remained my friend and eventually became part of my family.

I also began teaching creative writing at Nathan Hale High School in Seattle and at Lake Washington Vocational Technical Institute. In the back of my mind was the thought that if I lost all my sight, I needed something I could do with limited or no sight.

The most rewarding moment in my teaching career came when Hank and I were hiking the Cascade Pass. The trail led up and up a pine needle cushioned trail to a spot close to the top where a few boulders provide a place for five or six people to catch their breath or pause to eat their lunch before continuing on. There, by chance, sat one of my former students, recently returned from the Peace Corps. A talented young man, he will never know how good it felt for him to treat me like a guru at a time when losing my sight lingered in the back of my mind.

Before leaving China we had agreed to host graduate students who would study at the university. It was an exciting, wonderful venture. The first to come didn't know how to use the sophisticated faucets in his bathroom, was shocked at a black man hosting a television show and amazed by the vast number of cereals sold in the supermarket. He, and all the others who came, had literally jumped rungs to rise to the top of the intellectual Chinese ladder to come to America. Each of them soaked up American culture and knowledge.

Only one succumbed to the wooing by the "born again" segment of American society. As a minority in China, he had not always gotten the best that China had to offer. But in its rigor to adapt Western ways, the Chinese government had allowed him and his wife to have two children, and gave him permission to come to America with his family. He did not understand our freethinking and we did not attempt to change his thrill over his new "faith-based" friends.

While my repertoire had changed, Hank's did, too. He told me he wanted to take up sky diving as a hobby. By now I knew whatever he did, he did extremely well. So for his fiftieth birthday I gifted him with his initial jump. Not interested in going tandem, he wanted to learn from the bottom up and be in control. He would jump on his own.

To jumpstart his lessons (pun intended) I hosted a picnic for about thirty-five freethinking friends as well as the Chinese students who had stayed with us and now were in university dorm rooms or, in the case of the married student, in an apartment in the university district.

Among our friends were Deems and Margaret Okamoto. As always they helped me with keeping food cold and warm and set the tables. I didn't need to tell them, although I trusted Hank, I was apprehensive. All sorts of things could happen. His parachute wouldn't open, he could run into a power line, or break bones if he landed wrong. But I said nothing and hopefully no one else suspected my worry. We ate, we joked, we laughed, and then we all trooped over to the airport to see Hank off. Unfortunately, the wind had picked up, and the jump school closed for the day. It would have been too dangerous. His first jump had to be scheduled for the following day, a Monday.

It was a pleasant day, the field where he was scheduled to land green with wild grasses, few trees. Watching, I stood alone with a bottle of champagne and stemmed glasses. Finally, I heard a plane somewhere way above. I desperately tried to locate it, but couldn't. When I spotted a tiny orange dot that slowly materialized, I grabbed the binoculars hanging around my neck, but had trouble bringing the dot into focus. Could it be Hank? The image kept jumping around. I let the glasses dangle and scanned the sky until I located what had to be Hank. I stared until I was sure, tracked the large orange canopy and began running toward the spot where he'd land. Rushing up to him, I saw the smile that split his face practically in two. "Hey, sky diver," I said, "How was it?"

"I did it," he called, stepping out of the harness, gathering up the parachute stretched out behind him. He paused to look straight at me and shake his head. "The hardest thing I ever did was leaving that plane."

Holding on he had had to walk out on the airplane's strut, then let his feet dangle and at the jumpmaster's command, let go with his hands.

I let a beat go by before saying, "But you did."

He grinned. "And then it was fantastic, like flying without wings."

My relief, good feelings and admiration for his accomplishment called for another bottle of champagne when we returned home, he more talkative than usual, telling me step by step about his jump, until I felt as if I could do it, too.

It was the beginning of a fifty jump agenda, Hank learning to do tricks in the air similar to the ones I'd seen sky divers do in movies or documentaries. Many times I watched him land, his parachute going from an orange dot high in the atmosphere to a canopy with him hanging from it, maneuvering it so he landed safely. Afterward he was usually exhilarated, becoming almost loquacious. The closeness we shared became even more so after his jumps.

Once, in order to see if I wanted to try sky diving, too, I went up with him, wearing a parachute and given a few instructions by the jump master in case something happened to the plane. My first shock came when we rose to several thousand feet. The plane had been stripped down, no seats except for the pilot's, no weatherproofing, nothing but a vessel for sky divers. A terrific wind-driven noise assaulted me. I asked a question, but no one answered. They hadn't heard.

Soon we were high above the earth, Hank and his fellow divers squatting together. As the plane turned on its side, the jump master opened the door. I gasped. If I moved a foot to the left, I'd fall through the hole that seemed to gap wider and wider as I glimpsed the land so far below.

Suddenly, I couldn't remember what I'd been told. If necessary, did I pull up or down on my rip cord? Or pull the cord to the side? Once more I tried to speak, but my words were spun out and away so fast no one could possibly hear. I had nurtured visions of stepping from the plane and floating peacefully to earth. My ignorance became immediately apparent. Hank and the others literally threw themselves from the plane, some somersaulting into the sky. In seconds they were out of sight. I quickly abandoned any idea of getting photographs of Hank by myself and handed my camera to the jumpmaster. I also abandoned thoughts of taking lessons myself. But that night I told him if he had any other non-jumping plans, I was ready to follow him wherever he wanted to go.

Scheduled to give a paper at the International Atomic Energy Agency in Sydney, Hank said, "What do you think about going to Australia and New Zealand? You can sightsee while I'm in meetings."

We were finishing dinner, the weak sun turning the clouds over the Olympic Mountains a profusion of colors. It was my favorite time of day, but now I had no time for the scene. I jumped up, ran down stairs and grabbed up books about the two countries. Back in the kitchen, I was leafing through a book about Sydney when Hank said, "What do you say we team Australia and New Zealand with Tahiti or Fiji on the way home?"

My eyes, he told me later, got big as saucers. "Tahiti," I said instantly, having grown up with movies about the fabled islands. Even the thought astounded me. Tahiti was true glamour, the tropics at their best. Was this really happening to us, the boy and girl who had grown up in the Midwest? Before it would all evaporate, I said, "Of course, we'll go to Tahiti."

"It is now in the agenda," Hank said reaching for the phone to call our travel agent.

I was putting the last object of clothing in my suitcase when a letter came from the Freedom From Religion Foundation in Madison, Wisconsin. Would I give a talk at their annual meeting being held in St. Louis that year? I agreed and off we went 'down under.'

It was the longest flight we'd ever taken, and it wasn't exactly pleasant sitting in tourist class and being squeezed by a stranger on one side and Hank on the other. But before long we were all on a first name basis and managed to get a little rest on the flight. I had followed the Jet Lag book, eating certain meals ahead of time and was determined to stay awake all day in Cairns, our first stop.

On arrival, feeling the hot, humid weather, we ignored it, deposited our suitcases in our hotel room and went on a tour of the Cypress swamps, me nodding and jerking awake as the guide said one more startling thing about the animals that lived in the swamp. The thought of crocodiles lurking among the green slime kept me partially awake, and that night we "conked off" early and slept the entire night to wake fully refreshed the next day. So, something worked.

We lost no time getting out to the Great Barrier Reef. Transported by boat to the permanent platform, we made a beeline for the underwater glass viewing station and stood transfixed watching exotic, colorful, beautiful fish, blue, green, yellow, and all the colors in the artist's palette. In a submarine we went to the bottom to see the coral formations and the sea life of the deep. We ate ordinary food in the restaurant, but I swam in the sea adjacent to the platform, and that made up for the mundane among the exotic sights. The water felt like silk being poured over my body, warm and soothing, wiping away any remnants of fatigue from the long trip.

I loved Sydney and the Blue Mountains, the Sydney Opera House and all the sights I did on my own as Hank did his thing at the IAEA conference. Sydney's harbor was probably the most beautiful I'd ever seen, the city with its neighborhoods similar to the best the West had to offer. The Aussie English, enchanting if not always immediately clear, enchanted me. To his embarrassment, I began calling Hank "mate." In the evenings we met with other men from the conference and their wives and I loved being introduced to kiwi fruit and all the delicious fruit tarts and pies of Sydney.

After the scientific meetings ended, we flew to the outback, first to Alice Springs, made popular by books and movies, then to see Ayers Rock, that huge orange and tan sandstone monolith in the middle of the country, so sacred to the aborigines. It was the focus of our trip to the outback.

Daylight was pushing the sand from my eyes when we went from our hotel at Yulara, about fifteen miles from the rock. I debated with myself about climbing it; Hank had no such problems. He was set on climbing to the top.

"But it's very steep and a 1000 feet high," I said, hugging myself. My sweater was not quite warm enough, although it would be hot and dry by afternoon.

"One thousand, one hundred and forty-two," Hank said in his instructive voice.

"Oh, come on," I said in my best teasing voice.

He smiled. "You don't want to add your name to the book kept on top?"

"Maybe, but I'm beginning to think I'll let you do the honors." By now I knew he could do anything he wanted to do. He constantly amazed me.

As the sun emerged, it barely took the chill from the air, but later it would be too hot to climb. Mid afternoon temperatures hovered around 100.

From the bus, I got my first relatively close look at the rock. It rose almost perpendicular from the valley floor, the Olga mountains nearby. They appeared red, then orange and beige depending on where rays from the rising sun descended, their rounded tops shaped by winds that swept fiercely at times through the outback.

Leaving the bus, I could see immediately, the Rock was no short rock scrambler's stint, nothing like climbing the slopes or switchback trails of the Pacific Northwest. From the bottom, it looked straight up. Climbers had to find their way up a fourth or so of the distance to the top before a chain attached to the rock offered help of sorts. Taking a long look at that steep rock face, I shook my head. "It looks dangerous. You sure you want to go?" He nodded. Whenever he wanted to do something, he did it, but would this be the one time he didn't make it? Just looking at the rock frightened me.

Hank handed me the camera and binoculars and took off his jacket, his gaze on the route up, plotting the initial climb. "Lots of people have made it to the top. You don't have to be a rock climber. Sure you don't want to give it a try?"

I shook my head vehemently. A few people had started up, including two women who had been on the bus with us. I threw Hank's jacket around my shoulders and watched him go off.

With the binoculars, I followed his progress from a distance. Soon I had a routine. Look through the binoculars, put them down, pick up the camera and record the event. He passed the two women who had ridden in the bus with us, that bottom part evidently no problem for him. For a moment I focused on the two women. They were mid to late thirties, medium build and their expressions were grim. The next time I trained the glasses on them, their backs were pressed against the rock and fear etched their faces.

Momentarily, I lost track of Hank. A short way above the women I located him going hand over hand up the chain. Did he know a man was coming down? For a second they faced one another before Hank let go and did what was expected. Stepping to the side, he flattened himself against the wall, his back, feet and hands pressed against the rock. There was no place to stand.

I had to look away and lowered the binoculars until the women were in the lens again. Clearly petrified, they were unable to move. The man descending from the top, paused near them, and later I heard he talked them down, telling them move for move. I picked up Hank again and stayed fixed on him. A speck on the face of the rock, he barely appeared larger through binoculars. Others were coming down now and several times he had to step aside and press his back against the wall of stone. At those times I had to stop looking. I knew I would have been as petrified as the two women.

When he was beside me again Hank said the view from the top had been worth it, but the wind was ferocious, almost knocking him off balance. Never what is known as a macho man, ironically, he continually achieved in the "macho" world. I always got a kick out of it.

Later I asked him if the women were praying. He said if they were he didn't hear it. Some Christians maintain there are no atheists in a fox hole. The meaning has expanded to mean that people faced with dire circumstances turn to god. That viewpoint has been proven wrong over and over again. I would never call for a god I didn't believe existed. That's why in so many movies and plays, the writers cover themselves with words like, "if there is a god."

After the rock, Alice Springs and a tour of the Olgas, we flew back to Sydney before leaving for New Zealand. That British sounding country showed us glaciers, fiords and a geyser resembling Yellowstone's Old Faithful. We met and talked politics with the native people, finding liberals around the world spoke similar languages. We stayed in two private homes, one a living example of gentile poverty. Hosting the couple at a restaurant, we realized it was the high spot of their year.

In Tahiti we understood why Gauguin spent years there. Lush green islands, surrounded by cerulean colored ocean and blue sky, had me holding my breath in awe. If I closed my eyes, I could imagine the Fletcher Christian story, see the Bounty, see the slow, timeless days of the past. I did see much of that, but I also saw cars spewing out fumes and touristy places where grass huts used to be for living.

Finally we were back in the US, but I felt as if I were still in Tahiti in that hotel room in Papeete that resembled the Flatiron Building on Times Square, New York, except our room faced the ocean with views on each side to converging streets.

Back home, I plopped down at my computer to write a talk for the Freedom From Religion Foundation, FFRF. I managed to pound out a first draft, run our clothes through wash and dry cycles, and read the mail waiting for us before we flew to Missouri. Arriving in St. Louis, my head and body felt as if it were still in the South Seas, walking down streets canopied by foliage, dogs barking at a distance. Too soon I was speaking, reading that first draft out loud and feeling like I wanted to fall into a chasm and hide. My talk was much too long, not properly focused and left no room for questions and answers. I believe I even told an incident that happened in Papeete because it had intrigued Hank and I at the time but had nothing to do with non-theistic topics. But it was amusing.

In Papeete a middle-aged man, learning we were Americans, stopped us on the street one day to ask, "Do you know Madame Rondo?"

The name rang no bells, so we said, no, sorry, we didn't know her. Anyway, we were on our way to Papeete's tiny museum. We'd already learned we could take Le Bus.

"You do," the man insisted and repeated the name. A scowl scarred his pleasant-appearing face.

Once again we took turns saying we didn't know any Madame Rondo. "Sorry."

"You do." He insisted, his voice rising.

We were losing patience. I turned aside, ready to walk away. "No!"

"Madam Rondo!" he insisted. "You know." Looking very disgusted, he made waving motions with a hand and arm.

Hank looked puzzled, and for a moment, I did, too. Then I cried, "Do you mean the sea?" I pointed to the ocean lapping away at the docks, not far from our hotel, waves lapping the shore.

He nodded enthusiastically, repeated Madame Rondo and with both hands made motions that appeared to be a boat riding the sea.

"Ship?" I asked, not quite sure.

"Yes," he shouted. "Madame Rondo ship."

I'd delighted in watching yachts from around the world, all sizes and styles, bobbing at anchor, many licensed in the United States. Some of the smaller yachts had clothes lines on deck, people cleaning up after a long ocean voyage. So this Rondo person had come in a ship.

Hank said, clearly impatient. "Yes, very nice waves, but we don't know Madame Rondo," and tried to move on. We had planned to take LeTruck, to the nearby museum; paying passengers sit in the bed of a real truck. Anyway, it was clouding up, and we had already been caught in one deluge; getting drenched while taking two steps from the hotel's overhang to a taxi. We need-ed to be on our way soon.

By this time our Tahitian friend was becoming angry. "You know," he shouted. "Rondo big shot. Make movie."

I looked at Hank, he at me. Movie. Rondo. The Bounty, I thought.

We grinned at one another and shouted, "Marlon Brando!" simultaneously.

"Yes," the man said, looking proud, looking vindicated, "Madame Rondo."

I have no idea today if I worked the incident into my talk properly. Founders and leaders Anne Gaylor and Annie Laurie Gaylor never let on if they were appalled. In fact no one from FFRF acted disappointed, and I learned, never use the first draft of anything you write.

But as in all my years with Hank, one thrilling event seemed to be followed by an equally exciting one. In 1988 the American Humanist Association's annual meeting took place in Dallas and I was presented the Feminist Caucus Humanist Heroine award. It was an honor I accepted with humility, presented by my friend from the Sacramento chapter of AHA, Mildred McCallister. I felt there had to be others more qualified for the award, but looking back, I realize I had been fully dedicated to both freethought and feminism for years and the award was not unwarranted.

In Dallas, I also got the first glimpse of someone with dementia. Rosemary Matson, who had been an activist member of the Feminist Caucus and also a Humanist Heroine, asked Hank and me if we would keep an eye on her husband, see that he got from the meeting room back to the hotel proper when she was due at another meeting. She said he had Alzheimers.

We agreed and suggested to him that we should walk back together. He said all the proper things during our chitchat on the way. But in the hotel's main lobby, he appeared confused and asked us the direction to the elevators. It was Saturday, and we'd all been there since Thursday, been up and down in the elevators many times. We made sure he got to his room. For some reason, I never connected his disability to Hank's father's problems. If Hank did, he said nothing, but looking back at it, I wonder if he did, for he had been very solicitous of my friend's husband. But neither of us mentioned it the following day as the convention unfolded. We were in Dallas, the place where President Kennedy had been shot. The Alzheimers incident was immediately swallowed up in the sightseeing we did after the conference. Most importantly exciting news came from our Chinese guests.

Students throughout China were embracing democracy. The same year the Berlin Wall came down, Chinese students took over Tiananmen Square in Beijing. Hank and I were thrilled. Jen, one of the young men we had come to feel very close to, kept in computer touch with some of the students in the Square. We were among those cheering for them. And then the government cracked down, and we watched with open-mouthed wonder as a young man stood in front of a Chinese Army tank. I hoped it would make a difference, but knew it wouldn't. Hank said the actions would force the government to escalate their war against the protesters. And it did.

For a while I had trouble ridding myself of images coming from China. Our own visit had provided us with opportunities to, in a small way, know the people. We had fond and strong feelings for the Chinese people and were saddened by all we heard. I began to plan the novel I later wrote and had published under the name, The Good Foreigner.

But in order to stay in Seattle after his federal/state agreement ended, Hank had worked for another branch of the Food and Drug Administration, writing articles and giving talks about food and radiation that were included in a scientific anthology. But he missed doing work that was more closely related to his field. Retiring from the federal government, he put out feelers and found both the states of New Mexico and California were looking for someone with his credentials.

After he and I discussed it, and he interviewed both places, Hank went to work for the state of California. I had always loved the state that offered every climate one wanted and a plethora of grand scenery and a majority of forward thinking people. It had a nationwide reputation for being on the cutting edge. We would stay in California two years and then return to Seattle. But it didn't quite work out that way.

Fourteen

"Not farewell, but fare forward, voyagers."

T. S. ELIOT (1888-1965)

In August Hank rented an apartment in Sacramento, near where he'd have an office. Still teaching creative writing at Lake Washington Vocational, Technical Institute, VoTech, I couldn't leave until the semester ended in December. I had been to national AHA meetings in California and had also given my shows there. I liked Sacramento. The state capital had streets with over-arching trees and maintained a small- town feel while being large enough to have all of the amenities of a big city. We'd keep our house in Seattle and af-ter two years, we'd move back. We couldn't contemplate living anywhere else.

But, nothing seemed right once Hank was gone. Our cedar house that had entranced me, now rattled emptiness. I'd never before experienced "blue" days. Now I did. Getting up each day and seeing no sun ate at me. Even though Hank and I had been apart often, each involved in our various separate activities, I'd seldom lived alone, having throughout my life lived with family, roommates or husbands. The time I stayed in Seattle alone, the city lived up to its gloomy reputation, being rainy or overcast from the day Hank left. If the sun shone, I never saw it. The house seemed inordinately big, the isolation immense. We lived down a long driveway from the road, and I grew nervous about it. I had been stalked.

Coming home from Lake City Way, climbing the hill to 39th Avenue, I became aware of a car pulling out from a parking lot and following me. I thought nothing of it when it passed me, but as I topped the hill and turned left toward our house, I saw the same car approaching me. I began to feel suspicious. During that half mile stretch the car went forward, turned around, and came back. I was really worried. Was the driver waiting for me to veer off into one of those long drives or even key in the code for the locked gates? It would be easy for him to stop, rush me, come in behind me, trap me.

I could see he was youngish, thirty or forty something, blondish, wearing a white shirt. I didn't know what to do. Stoically, I kept walking, options zooming through my mind. The people in the house nearest mine were on vacation. Everyone was at work in the house across the way. The other house had a for sale sign. I could not let him see where I lived.

I waited until he made another u-turn and then I ducked behind a huge row of rhododendron bushes. He could never see me there. When he came down the street again, I waited and then rushing vaulted across the neighbor's yard, jumped the rock wall and hurried down my drive. I ducked out of view a second before his car passed again. Shook, I rushed into the house and called Hank. He said, "Honey, call 911."

With the Green River murders happening during that time, the police patrolled the area for a few days, and that was ostensibly the end of it, although my stalker was never apprehended. Later, I was sure I saw the same man in the doorway of the Pawn Shop and again in the post office. He had to live somewhere in the neighborhood. Although frightened, I wouldn't let him make me a hermit and walked the neighborhood as much as always, but always taking different routes. But with Hank gone, I worried about my isolation, the house set too far from the road for anyone to hear or see if trouble came. Anyone could break in.

A writer's conference at VoTech helped. I gave a workshop and through a new writing group I belonged to, met a comedian and was able to get him for our keynote speaker, learning in the process some of the techniques comedians make when planning their routines. A favorite is the three step buildup. Mention something about the focus of the joke. Later build upon that mention, and then when the third mention comes, the audience has been prepped and laughter is hilarious.

Also, in an effort to keep busy, I tutored a friend's son for his SAT's. I lunched out with friends frequently and walked the trails of the city. But no matter how busy I kept, the nights, mostly alone, loomed large. Time dragged.

By this time our Humanist friends Betty and Randy File, had bought a place in Palm Desert, California, Betty telling me she had had it with Seattle's weather. Randy still had a couple years before he could retire from the railroad, so he agreed to house sit for us after I moved to Sacramento. It seemed like the perfect solution. In December I moved out and Randy moved in.

In California I loved those bright sun mornings, and made the most of the pool at the apartment complex. The strange feelings I'd had those few months in Seattle disappeared faster than ice at the equator. By the time I arrived, Hank was an established member of the local humanist group headed by my friend, Mildred, and soon I was very busy.

The first month in the city, I joined a local writers organization and the Older Women's League, too. Our social life took shape quickly. Every day the California sunshine bathed me in radiance, its brilliance thrilling me and banishing all thoughts of returning to Seattle. In six months, Hank and I agreed, California would be our new home. We bought a new house in a settled neighborhood, and I flew north. I'd put our Seattle house on the market and prepare for movers. At the same time Randy had worked his last days for the railroad and was moving south.

Saying goodbye to friends in Seattle was hard. Our work on Literary Lights had Mary and I together at least once a week. She was also part of a literary critique group I hosted mostly at my house, her astute observations adding greatly to the group.

We also got together with the Okamotos and their two children, the oldest a Navajo girl they'd adopted and their biological daughter, Siri, every Thanksgiving. Sometimes I roasted turkey and Margaret fixed salmon to go with the rest of the feast. One year Hank and I had a Chinese student staying with us, and he became a temporary member of the mix. Another time we all went to the seashore and stayed in cabins, Margaret and I with pies that needed baking. We were shocked to find the rooms had cook tops but no ovens. So we wrapped the pies in foil and heated them slowly on the burners. I was surprised to find it worked. We'd also been with Margaret during Hanukah, and Deems had expressed his gratitude when I included a Japanese/American woman during World War II in my Bus to the White House show.

Because it seldom snowed in Seattle, like Washington, D.C., Seattle was not prepared for a real snowstorm. One Thanksgiving, the city blanketed in snow, we found a few bus routes were still open. Wearing hiking boots and heavy coats, we walked several blocks to a bus line. The Okamotos did the same, and we met in a restaurant half way between for our usual Thanksgiving get together.

Such events did not make leaving Seattle easy. Our humanist and feminist friends were family. In addition we were involved in the politics of the day, lobbying in Olympia and meeting in neighborhood caucuses with like-minded people. Once, because of my out-spoken feminism, Washington being a

Caucus State, I was elected all the way to the state political meeting as our community and then county representative.

The week the moving van would arrive, I kept busy checking in with friends, consulting with realtors, packing what I didn't want to leave for the movers, making sure the yard and house were in shape for viewing, and giving away the bedroom set that had seen better days.

The night after the Salvation Army picked up the bedroom furniture, I shucked my dirty clothes and took a long shower. Water always revived me, and I'd been grubbing around in the yard all day, wanting it to be as "showy" as possible. I came out of the bathroom and came to an abrupt stop, realizing all my clean clothes were in the dresser drawers now owned by the Salvation Army. Too shocked to think straight, I called Hank. "Honey, I don't have any clothes!"

First he laughed, wondering if I was starting some kind of phone sex, he told me later. He continued laughing when I told him the story and in no time I was laughing, too. He said, "You could buy yourself some clothes, you know." Soon, I was pulling on the dirty, wrinkled clothes and rushing to the nearest clothing store. I just made it before closing time and have never done such rapid shopping since.

At the end of the week, Hank joined me. After a few very busy days we watched the movers go off with the furniture that now seemed like trash after they had identified scratches and dents I swore I needed a magnifying glass to see.

Really tired, we started for California with mixed feelings. We had felt at home in Seattle and were a little disconcerted because we hadn't said goodbye to everyone we had on our list. Seattle's beauty had snared us, and the people couldn't have been better, our Humanist friends terrific, my feminist friends fantastic, but time had run out.

The farther we drove from the city, the more I longed for bed and a long sleep. It hadn't been an easy week getting the house ready for realtors and a moving van. We debated spending the night somewhere along the route, but Hank needed to be at work the next day. Better to push on.

It was seven when we arrived at our new house, the sun still up. We grinned at one another. We had made it. Now for showers and bed. But first, a big glass of water and another glimpse of the kitchen. With lots of cupboards, an island with storage space and beauty tile, room for table and chairs, a slider to the back patio, it was the dream kitchen of 1991 and what had sold me on the house.

I took one step inside and let out a shriek. Ants covered the walls, the ceilings, the island, and every conceivable space. We found them on the stove, in the light fixtures and frozen to the ice in the freezer. Three or four hours later we fought the ants to a finish and fell into bed. We did not thank god or blame him. If he existed, which we fervently believed was not so, he was completely irrelevant to our lives.

The next day, Hank went to work full of the story of our "ant fight." His co-workers just smiled. "Welcome to California," they said. Unlike some warm weather climates, no creepy crawlies get in our shoes, no flies buzz around, but ants are a perpetual problem. While the front yard had been planted with grass and flowers and a lone tree, the back was a jungle of wild grasses. We called pest control people and landscapers and began the process of taming the jungle. When we were through, we had two connected patios, a gazebo and a spa plus redwood trees, a magnolia tree, a tulip tree, crepe myrtle bushes, and other semi-tropical flowers I hadn't known existed. With redwood tables and benches and a few comfortable outside chairs, the patios edged with potted plants, were delightful.

And finally, after spotty contact for years, Steve apologized for not contacting me more often. After Rhonda had married again, he had drifted in a fog of self-recriminations and anger at her, at his birth mother and at me, having in some fashion put us all in a box that freaked him out.

The day he told me, I went to Las Vegas to see him. For the first time he told me what stalked him through the years. It was the vision of his mother walking out on him and his sisters and baby brother. He had watched as she threw clothes in a suitcase and then, saying nothing, stood looking at him and his siblings. "Mama?" he had said, making it a question. She never answered. Her latest boyfriend, a man she had taught the children to call, "Daddy," came into the room and said, "You ready?" Again, she said nothing. "It's me or them," he said, and without another glance at Steve or the others, she left. Her desertion had plagued him all those years, buried too deep ever to divulge to anyone, even psychologists and psychiatrists, too deep until he acknowledged it to himself and realized he wasn't at fault. The emotional hurt still dogged him at times.

The next day we stood in that parking lot leading to the casino and coffee shop where he wanted to treat me to a lobster dinner. Putting his arm around me and pushing his face into my neck, he said, "Mama, I'm sorry, so sorry. I love you so much."

I had no tears. He had caused me too many sleepless nights wondering what he possibly could be holding against me. But I was too old to hold anything against him, too sensible to put us into a box of recriminations. "I love you, too, honey," I said, and I meant it, knowing he still had a long road to travel before the past eluded him completely.

Later, enjoying the meal he had ordered, I remarked on his god-less, social conscience. He said, he had listened and observed during those early years with me, and everything he had seen since had only made his non belief stronger.

Now, I had tears in my eyes.

By now, firmly entrenched in California I discovered a few of the members of OWL were also non-theist, although still in the closet. Thoroughly out were our new humanist friends, <u>Drs.</u> Mynga Futrell and Paul Geissert, a couple as dedicated to non-theism as we were, both ex science teachers. Soon after we met them, the American Atheists held a convention in the city and Mynga, Paul and a dozen or so other non-theists in the area attended. Afterward they started a local atheist group, and Hank and I became charter members, fifteen to twenty of us meeting in a room at a fast food restaurant.

The day we discussed and debated, a name for the group, we sat around a long, private table in a room separated from the main restaurant. One after the other, we took turns making clear how we felt.

Some were wary of the word Atheist. For too long, it had been brushed with evil. Most non-theists were just getting to the point of letting others know their beliefs. They contended business and professional people would lose clients and money and others would be ostracized by their family and friends.

Other members were adamant: we had to use the A word. A-theist had a noble ring. For too long we had slunk around as if we had done something wrong, using the word would be a step forward.

I suggested we add "and Other Free Thinkers" to Atheists. It was not immediately adopted, many people finding fault with the words, but eventually, because no one could think of anything else that would please us all, it became the official name, shortened to AOF.

I looked at Hank, he at me. HOS had been the first step, now we were making another large step. We were admitting publicly that we were atheists.

Yet, AOF was different from HOS. The people joining AOF didn't need to read books, discuss religion and/or the lack of it. They had all gone through that before. As a group we concluded AOF had to have both an idealistic and practical agenda, making our presence known in the community and educating society about non-theism as well. We cooked and served meals to homeless men, women, and increasingly, children, too. Hank started, and for several years led, a highway cleanup project.   It has become the longest-running highway cleanup project in the area, now run by Don Knutsen. Highway signs stating the clean-up work is courtesy of local atheists, no longer brings surprise or comment.

One year Hank arranged a debate about the existence of god, using a local religionist versus Dan Barker of the Freedom From Religion Foundation. Dan had progressed from a fundamentalist preacher to a non-theist, in the process marrying Annie Laurie Gaylor of FFRF and being every bit as personable as Annie.

The night of the debate, Hank moderating, and Dan and his opponent following the official rules of debate, people "came out of the woodwork" to be in the audience. People who didn't believe in a god were thrilled to be in attendance. The need to be recognized was great. They were exasperated that people who always led a good, honest life were treated as if hey were worse than murderers. People who did legally reprehensible acts were viewed as better than an atheist. All they had to do was repent fornication, incest, and child abuse, robbery, murder, and thievery, beg forgiveness for their misdeeds and believe in a god. Being good, responsible citizens didn't count as much as believing.

The five years we lived in Sacramento, Hank also started an annual celebration of Charles Darwin, and again the attendance surpassed expectations. With publicity and well-known speakers, Darwin Day is still a vital part of the non-theist community. And now twenty five years later Sacramento is the center of activism for humanists, atheists, skeptics, and the whole panoply of freethinkers in Northern California.

But in those early days we were still establishing ourselves. Mynga, who has an idea a minute, started Freethought Day, an event that has grown exponentially. The first year we received a proclamation from the mayor, met on the plaza adjacent to City Hall and spoke "to the choir." Now, Freethought Day has grown into a large all day event with all aspects of freethought to be explored and applauded, including games and events for children, music and big name speakers from throughout the United States.

Hank and Paul also escorted women going to the Women's Health Clinic. Protesters were making women needing health care walk a gauntlet of men (and a few women) carrying pictures of bloody fetuses, others reading the bible, praying out loud and asking the women to listen to them. While a minority of women were seeking abortions, those who did had to listen to the protesters shouting at them literally outside their examining room. Eventually, the Clinic went to court and got an injunction against the protesters who now had to keep their distance. But it was still nerve-wracking for clinic patients. Throughout the nation clinics were burned, acid thrown on clinic workers, doctors who performed abortions killed. Hank escorted for years, and eventually became a favorite of the young women who worked at the clinic. Again I was proud of his actions.

Although involved in the freethought and feminist activities, from the day I arrived in the area, I looked for writers. One night, less than a month after moving in, at the local writers' club, I announced I was holding weekly critique sessions at my house for people interested in writing novels. About twenty writers showed up. I quickly formed them into smaller groups, passed out guidelines and began to assess those in attendance.

Weeding the wheat from the chaff, I latched on to three people who were dedicated to the art. Naida West, Louise Crawford, and Jay MacLarty became a vital part of my life during the five years we were in the city. Their novels, as well as mine, are listed at the back of this memoir. We met once a week at my house, through my shingles bout, through Jay's back surgery, through Naida's busy life, and through Louise's ups and downs as a young mother, all of us attaining some success in the writing field.

By this time Hank and I were so much alike in our thinking, it was hard to find any difference. Yet, at times he clung to outmoded traditions, and I attributed this to his Catholic upbringing. Because his father had always carried a hundred dollar bill in his watch pocket, Hank did, too. But, unlike his father who drove everywhere, Hank walked to the nearest bus line or, when possible, biked to work. One day hurrying to the bus, he was knocked over a bluff by a man he hadn't seen or heard overtake him. Out of sight of the street, his assailant robbed him at knife-point. Hank stopped carrying a hundred dollar bill. But in all other ways he was the same, and I his firm supporter.

When he could laugh about the experience, he told me, "It was another thing I never questioned. It was part of my daily routine when I changed clothes, change the money from one pair of pants to another. What it takes to wake ex Catholics up! But today I have something else on my mind."

"What's that?"

"I want to fulfill a childhood dream."

I waited for him to expand on his words.

"Go to Africa on safari."

I pictured tents in the wilderness without Clark Gable and the stars of Mogambo. "Really." A woman I knew was making solar cookers she distributed in Africa, but that's as close as I cared to get. I wanted to go back to London, do the theaters. I said so.

He looked at me for perhaps ten seconds before he said. "What do you say we do both?"

His surprises were always superb.

He began to bone up on African safaris and decided we would go to what used to be Rhodesia. Mostly settled by the British, their descendants were still running most of the businesses and farms, hiring indigenous people from the two ethnic groups, the Shona and the Endebele. But after a civil war, the indigenous people, who now ran the country, changed the name to Zimbabwe. Most importantly for him, in Zimbabwe we could ride in open Land Rovers instead of taking turns at a pop-up window like they have to do other places. He showed me a photograph of average safari accommodations. They were a far cry from the tent camping I remembered, so I agreed to give it a try, my focus on the theaters in London.. "When do we leave?" I asked. Life kept getting better and better and it was only 1993.

Fifteen

"And all a wonder..."

ROBERT BROWNING (1812-1889)

*A*fter a long flight across country and the ocean to London, and then a six-hour stopover in London, I thought of nothing but my bed at home. Taking Zimbabwe airlines from London, my fatigue increased, not that there was anything wrong with the flight, the food, the attendants, but I was tired. Yet, when we landed in Harrare, the capital, and I glimpsed the modern city and our hotel with television featuring CNN, I began to perk up.

The next few nights at a game refuge on the outskirts of the city began to prepare us for the wilds and put me completely in safari mode. Drinking champagne at sundown, while viewing wild animals outlined against the sinking sun, was not to be sneezed at. We saw Sable Antelope and other animals we'd eventually encounter in the wild. It was our first taste of roughing in luxury. Out accommodations were far from primitive, our room in an A-frame cabin had all the amenities. We ate at the main lodge in a dining room boasting a mahogany table big enough for a dozen, the servants greeting us each morning with "Mangwanani," meaning good morning in Shona.

Until we'd arrived in Harrare, I'd never seen a truly black African. Vacationing in Jamaica, some of the former slaves we'd seen were almost as dark, but in the United States African Americans were brown or tan or deep brown, or almost white, never really black. Hank's African/American friends at work were tan or near white. My African American poet friend had cream-colored skin. They all were the result of the mixing of races at home. In Zimbabwe, blacks were truly black. But at the safari camps, whites were in charge, the blacks in inferior positions. They were the ones who did the menial chores. The social structure had a familiar ring.

Leaving our suitcases with our London clothes in Harrare, we flew to Kariba in a large jet. We were late getting there, having waited on the tarmac for the King of the Congo and his retinue to arrive, an exotic touch that was not lost on me. In Kariba, a small private plane with a pilot and Victoria Stutchbury, the co-owner of Chikwenya, our first and soon to be favorite safari camp, waited.

The airport was a seething hive of activity. Stutchbury hurried us to the plane, explaining we had to fly over the wilderness. Sitting in front with the pilot, Hank had a panoramic view, but I wasn't complaining. Although still fatigued, I was too excited to nod off.

Flying at treetop heights over the jungle, I glimpsed elephants, cape buffalo, and antelope from the large Eland to the slightly smaller Wildebeest and smaller yet Impala. In back with Mrs. Stutchbury, the view from my window tore all remnants of sleep from my eyes. Blonde and attractive, Stutchbury casually pointed out a pride of lions defending a kill from hyenas. Awake but far from alert, I felt like a rank amateur next to this jungle savvy woman who had seen to the storing of supplies into the plane, shepherded us around at Kariba's airport and generally seemed terribly efficient. At times she spoke what I later found was Shona. At the time I was too tired to do anything but take everything for granted.

But I was not so out of it that I wasn't enthralled with the jungle open-ing up below me, the river she called the Zambesi, the hippos in the mud at river's edge.

"We're almost there," she said shortly afterward and began talking about the camp. Her words brought me to a spine-tingling awareness. While I had trouble putting words to the sights, nothing but amazing, stupendous, and like adjectives coming to mind, I still recall and can paraphrase what she said. We must always remember that the camp is in the wilderness. Wild animals come through at all times. In no way should we attempt to "pet" them, feed them, or ignore them. At night after the evening campfire we could not walk around unescorted. We would be accompanied to our lodging, called a chalet, by a guide with an elephant gun and a flash-light. Once we were inside, we must stay inside until morning. "Wild animals roam through camp at all times."

She told me that each of the thatched roof lodgings had onsite amenities, not luxurious, but ample. If we had clothes to be washed, we put them out in the morning, and they'd be returned clean and ironed that night. We'd have multiple choices of gourmet breakfast and dinner foods and we'd have a boxed lunch at noon, champagne and snacks for sundowners.

And then we were landing on an air-strip that had been hacked out of the jungle, the landing rough, the ground uneven. Waiting for us was a Land Rover with a driver who looked as if he came from Hollywood casting. The owner took off in another direction in a similar vehicle. I learned later the Stutchbury house was at the far end of the camp, invisible from our lodgings. But her words popped into my head as we stopped beneath acacia trees. The first thing I saw were two elephants chomping on the foliage.

It was a great welcome. Our chalet, a few feet from the river and near a huge termite mound, looked welcoming. Still, open from chest high to the roof, it gave me a slight pause. But once I saw the beds with mosquito netting and comforters that would have done any housewife proud, it was nap-time for me. Hank went exploring and came back to wake me up saying it was time to meet the other guests and be taken on a late afternoon game ride. I hurried into my Eddie Bauer safari clothes and followed Hank from the chalet.

Seated in the Land Rover just behind the driver, a couple from Alabama said they were Andy and Lucinda Lee. He named some kind of business he ran, and she explained she usually was more slender, but it was those darned pills she had to take. Sitting next to them Brian, a lawyer from New York, ripped off a string of names identifying his firm, and in the rear, topmost seat, a man from London, Cecil, said he'd just retired. Hank and I explained we were from California, gave our names and joined the Brit in the topmost, back seat. The driver set off on a trail showing previous tire tracks. Late afternoon sun slanted through the trees and cast long shadows.

Like a play running on cue, animals began appearing in the brush, or on the trail in front of us. I took a deep breath and stared bug-eyed as the driver maneuvered through a herd of cape buffalo who gave way only at the last minute. "Just don't lean out," the young blonde driver advised, telling us the cape buffalo was one of the most dangerous animals in Africa. Unpredictable, they could charge at any time. Fortunately, they paid little attention to us. Charles, our driver explained, "Like all the animals here, buffalo see vehicles as part of the landscape. You'll be safe as long as you stay on board."

"I have no desire to go anywhere," Lucinda Lee said. We all chuckled.

I let my breath out as we left the herd behind. The late afternoon sun added warmth to my sudden chill. I undid my many-pocketed safari jacket. A few minutes later I took it off as we parked on a slight knoll and our driver/guide pointed ahead. Beyond us was what appeared to be a well-taken care of park in mainland USA. Light filtering through the large acacia and mahogany trees shimmered, giving a surreal cast to the view. The trees, set a respectable distance from one another, only their canopies touching, covered a hundred or so acres with ground vegetation trimmed to a low height, the underside of leaves silvering in waning sunlight. I pictured myself strolling beneath the trees, taking in long droughts of fresh air, perhaps even singing, like people in Central Park. I wouldn't have been surprised to see a children's carousel on the perimeter. But instead, many of the animals I would see throughout Africa – elephants, wildebeests, impala, waterbuck, klipspringer, steenbok – each "group" grazed almost cheek to jowl with the others, dozens of them. A hushed reverence followed, none of us saying anything. Binoculars were positioned. Whispered ahs of appreciation followed.

As I shook my head in wonder, baboons come down from the trees, hand over hand, swinging one handed and then leaping to the ground, a hundred or so in the troupe. They moved en masse through the park, five or so animals wide. Tears of awe filled my eyes, and I reached out, wanting to share this moment. Hank, sensing my mood, took my hand and squeezed it. We watched silently, grinning at one another every few seconds, he holding my hand like he had when we dated, both of us murmuring, "Did you see that?" Or, "Look over there." In the other seat the southern couple were making similar sounds. But on the whole, we were a quiet group, lost in the majesty of the scene.

"It ever there was a Garden of Eden, this must be it," I said softly.

Cecil, the Brit, looked up from where he'd been jotting notes in a small book "You don't mean a literal garden, of course. If you're speaking symbolically, I cannot agree with you more."

"That's the only way I'd speak about a biblical event." Hank stated in a business-like way.

"Me, too," I murmured. But the two men were nodding at one another, paying no attention to me as the Londoner said, "I must say I tend to agree with you, although I'm Church of England, and all that."

For a while there was no sound except the soft soughing of the wind, the occasional snort of an animal. "I can't get over how peaceful they all are," I whispered.

Cecil was whispering, too "You're looking at a lot of vegetarians. The local lions aren't hungry. They killed an impala yesterday and are still feeding on the carcass. And leopards come out only at night. We saw one on an early morning tour."

He seemed very knowledgeable. I glanced at him. His hair was iron gray, his voice snobbishly high British society, no trace of working class. "You've been here a while?"

"Second trip. Been here a week so far."

"We just got here," I stated the obvious.

"Yes, I heard the plane come in."

Back at camp, we only had time to freshen up before our open-air dinner, a literal feast, three entrees, a variety of vegetables, salads, and desserts, all tastefully prepared and presented on long trestle tables. Afterward with liquor in real glass cocktail glasses, we sat around the campfire in director's chairs and talked. Tropical night had come quickly, and a slight breeze rustled the foliage, and every once in a while I was sure I saw animal eyes reflecting the light from the campfire. I wanted to draw Hank's attention to it, but he and the Brit were deep into talk, the other couple and the attorney talking sports.

"So you're a scientist," Cecil said. to Hank "We have Richard Dawkins, but I can't say I agree with everything he says."

Hank said he wasn't in a league with Dawkins but he admired him tremendously. He explained that the term health physicist had been coined when scientists were perfecting the atomic bomb. "It was to keep a lid on what they were doing. Didn't want to scare people."

"A necessity during World War II. You've impressed me," the Brit acknowledged.

By now the others were listening. "You lost me when you mentioned atoms," Andy, the man from Alabama said, smiling broadly. "I barely got through plane geometry."

Brian nodded in agreement. "They didn't talk about atoms very much at Law School." A short silence followed, no one saying anything. The fire popped, china clicked as the staff gathered together the remains of dinner and disappeared with it into the dark beyond the central area.

Cecil said, "I was always slightly in awe of you scientists. My field was finance. Dealt a lot with you Yanks." His gesture took in the others. "Had to learn how to deal with your freedom and liberty talk. Took quite a go for this loyalist." He chuckled and his hands came together before he turned to Hank again. "So tell me how do scientists who genuflect on Sundays erase that from their mind during the week juggling atoms or whatever?"

"If I ever genuflect again, it would be at the amazing world we live in, the great strides science has made to make our lives easier." Hank stretched out his legs. I could see he was in his element, ready to elucidate.

"Did you use the past tense on genuflect?"

Hank's words exuded confidence. "This cradle Catholic found his way to enlightenment. I'm a religiously dedicated free-thinker now."

"Nice turn of phrase," Brian said.

"And you?" Cecil said to him. "This seems to be general-disclosure-time."

"In court it's very important to use the right words. In my working life, I'm carefully non-committal. But…" He looked around him. "I admit being in the land of claw and fang I must reject the notion of human dominion over the animals." He looked around, a broad smile bending his rather thin lips, "Otherwise my daughter would kill me. She's a flaming environmentalist."

The Brit turned toward me. "Do you agree with your husband? I understand American women don't walk in lockstep with their spouses anymore."

How typical, he'd let the attorney off without digging in like I was sure he would do with me. I debated giving him feminism 101, but before I could speak the woman from Alabama said, "We certainly try walking on our own, don't we?" She caught my gaze for a moment before turning half-way towards her husband. "But my honey keeps me on a short leash." Laughter permeating her speech, she put a mitigating hand on her husband's arm.

I fought back words. It was clear Lucinda Lee didn't understand the first thing about women's rights. Instead I said to Cecil, "Both Hank and I are humanists, meaning non-believers in religious dogma." The whole scene appeared unreal, animals attracted to our light, no doubt circling at a distance, the discussion pushing at the edges of societal norms as if the proximity of wild animals had affected us all.

Mrs. Alabama, leaned toward me, a look of complete confusion on her face. It was clear Lucinda Lee had expected an ally and didn't get it. "You mean you all don't go to church?" She looked from me to Hank and back, her drawl hardly softening her words.

"No, we don't," I said.

Hank shook his head.

"You're, ah…" she paused and then added, "atheists?" making the word sound loathsome even in the romantic African night.

Hank smiled at her. "I envy Cleo, growing up without religion. Once I thought myself out of it, I've never missed it. Religion was like a millstone falling from my shoulders, that guilt trip of Christianity taken away."

"Well, I never. You're the first atheists I ever met, and I gotta say you're freakin' me out." Lucinda Lee fanned herself dramatically.

Cecil leaned toward her. "I'm not a flaming theology advocate, Lucinda, but I'm interested in what you mean."

She sat up straighter, the only one of us who hadn't slouched once, like she'd been instructed by her mother on the proper posture for a young woman and she'd held on to that position as gray took over her sun-blonde hair. She spoke slowly now, looking from one person to the next. "Everyone knows Jesus came to save souls. That God gave his only begotten son so that we might live and prosper." Sometime in the evening the circle had gotten tighter, people pulling their chairs closer as the night had grown darker. I could just make out the outline of our chalet, the others fanned out along the river, far enough from one another never to intrude on the other's privacy, were lost among the trees.

A staff member added wood to the fire; another passed around a tray of snacks and offered to refill glasses. "Fill mine," Lucinda Lee commanded. "I feel a sudden need."

Her husband said a refill seemed in line. "Never drink this much at home, but hell…"

We all opted for another drink. At dinner we'd had our choice of French or Italian wine. Now after dinner drink supplies filled a small table. I spotted Courvosier, Glenlivet, Glenfiddick as well as some American brandies and scotch.

"Tell me, you really don't believe in Jesus?" A line had appeared between Lucinda Lee's brows. Clearly appalled, her gaze went from Hank to me and back. "I admit God's a little hard to get a handle on, but Jesus is pure love. Don't you even feel his grace, his forgiveness?"

I started to ask what she meant by grace. As for forgiveness, what had I done that needed forgiving? Hank spoke before I could marshal my thoughts. A quiet man, when he spoke people listened intently. He always had his facts and he spoke with authority. "Jesus was a popular name at the time. Lots of men with that name. But there's no proof that the one you refer to even lived. If he did, why didn't the historians of his day mention him, record his miracles? They gave us detailed descriptions of everything else that happened in that era." He followed his words with historical details.

The Brit in his objective voice asked Lucinda, "According to my knowledge, Humanists aren't the only ones who don't believe in Jesus. As a matter of reference, neither do the Jews. How do you feel about them?"

"You all but got me there!" She laughed. "But… Jews believe in God." She looked around the circle triumphantly, ending with her gaze on Hank and me. "But our friends don't believe in anything."

"I believe in the ability of people to use science to give us all the miracles you enjoy daily." Hank smiled. At fifty-five, he was in his prime, and as always looked younger than his age. Andy had a paunch that couldn't be missed. Hank had never gained back an ounce after his heart surgery. "As for Jews, many are as non-theist as we are. I'd venture most Jews in America are cultural, not religious."

"Probably the same in the isles. My observation is families tend to follow what their ancestors did." Sounding proud, Cecil added, "My family has been Church of England since the reformation."

"You say many people go to church for social reasons. It's similar in America," I added.

Hank gave statistics that impressed me as well as the others.

The Brit saluted Hank with his drink. "I must say my wife does like to show off a new bonnet in church."

They clicked glasses, and Cecil added, "Live and let live, to each his own, that kind of thing."

"In America the bottom line is separation of church and state."

"Afraid I can't say the same, old chum."

Brian spoke in a judicial sounding voice, "In America, the law is the only thing that lets us all believe whatever we want."

The fire sent fingers of light into the night and a momentary flare lit our faces. Brian held his hand out for a high five and after a while the Brit responded saying, "Is that how you do it?"

"You nailed it." Brian nodded.

The Brit's smile got broader. "Can't say I haven't learned something from you Yanks."

The three men high-fived again, this time adding Andy a split second later. They were all smiling.

For a while I stared as the fire that had burned lower, gleaming red coals predominating.

Lucinda Lee, a plump, shadowy figure, rose abruptly. "Well, if you think it's funny it's not. You'll regret it when you try to enter the pearly gates!" Her drawl had grown pronounced, her voice rose.

"Now, Lucinda Lee," her husband cautioned.

"Don't you Lucinda Lee me. I didn't want to come here in the first place. We could have been in Hawaii lolling on a beach for a month of Sundays with what we're paying for this. But no, you had to go on safari, and I have to hear the lord's name used in vain." She glared at her husband and rushed off, muttering.

"Oh, my god, shut up!" her husband hissed, rushing after her, managing to stop her before she left the area. One of the staff was at their side immediately. We watched him escort them toward their chalet, soon disappearing into darkness.

Cecil took a deep breath. "Well that was something… I didn't hear anyone use the lord's name in vain. Maybe I wasn't erudite, but I don't think I used disparaging language." He paused and then lifted his glass, "What do you say we toast this…" he paused again before adding rapidly, "this wonderful wild place."

"Good idea." The attorney lifted his glass.

Hank held his out, and belatedly, I did, too. When someone offered a way out of a heated conversation, Hank usually took it. Not this time. Later he told me that once free of Catholicism, he hadn't spoken out enough. That night he was eloquent and thorough, taking me and the two men through religious wars and deprivation, through the failure of prayer, through the Big

Bang, through the dark ages, the age of reason, all of it, including witchcraft. If his recitation was not chronological, we were all too tipsy to care.

The hippos were emerging from the river when our guide slammed our chalet door on us. It was past eleven. We literally fell into our beds. But sleep was spotty. All night the hippos foraged up to five miles from the river, lumbered past and around our chalet and at times woke me with their roaring. It was not a reassuring sound.

But in the morning, sunlight slipping through the trees found its way in. Only the insect sounds of the jungle, the wind ruffling the grasses, no other sounds except bird song with the ever present Spoonbill's call, sounding like a person saying, "Work harder, work harder." We were both sleepy but eager to greet the day.

At breakfast no one commented on the discussion of the previous night, and during the days that followed we became a cohesive group enjoying the wild, our differences submerged in the excitement of each day. I sat in a treetop hide with Brian and watched the animals that passed below. Hank spent time in a hide with the Alabama couple near a hippopotami wallow, not exactly the most pleasant experience physically, but it was like the night before hadn't happened. Cecil, and all of us, enjoyed time on the river, identifying bee-eaters, hornbills, rollers, and other birds. Later, as we successfully avoided the hippos, we spotted storks.

Once, a mile or so from camp, we had a flat tire and no spare. By now Hank and Cecil had had a serious discussion about separation of church and state and religion's responsibility to prove the existence of a god, instead of putting it on the atheists. No one else brought it up.

I sat back as the guide called camp on a two way radio system, certain that we'd be helped soon. The staff had taken very good care of so far, not exactly difficult when there were 12 of them and only 6 of us. It was late afternoon, starting to get chilly in the shade. I was grateful we'd stopped in full sun. No one answered the radio. A frustrating half-hour passed as the guide repeatedly tried to contact camp. He finally decided something had gone wrong, and abruptly told us he'd have to hike back to camp. We watched him take off at a jog. I glanced around. Dark would descend soon, but his long, tanned legs would eat up the miles. Or was camp not that far? Even a half-mile could be difficult if he ran into a buffalo herd, or the local pride going out for an evening's hunt.

None of us said anything, all of us lost in our thoughts. Only weeks before Hank and I had seen the movie "Jurassic Park." When the book had come out, we'd stayed up all night reading it. The characters had gotten stuck in a stalled vehicle among the resurrected dinosaurs. The similarities were amazing. Before our young, blonde guide left with rifle in hand, he had instructed us to stay in the Land Rover. "I can't guarantee your safety if you don't."

Not very far back we'd passed elephants, and in the open area we'd spotted a warthog. A short way from us I saw the tail end of a large herd of cape buffalo. Anything could set them off. I stayed seated, getting out once only to stretch my legs, my hand on the Land Rover ready to leap back in if necessary. For a moment the Alabama couple stood beside me and then grabbing their cameras they began inching closer to the cape buffalo. Hank and I exchanged glances.

"Not very prudent," Cecil said.

Thankfully the Alabama couple were back in the Land Rover safely as night crept in around us. We were shifting nervously when someone from the camp zoomed up in another Land Rover. Dark night prevailed by the time we made it back to camp.

Fatigue seemed the natural state of affairs during the days that followed as we mined the properties of three more camps, each with its highlights. At

Fothergill, the island that evolved after the Kariba Dam was built, we left our luxury camp before dawn, before breakfast. Paper cups of coffee and croissants in hand, we bumped along in a Land Rover with other visitors.

I spotted the lions just as the sun peeped above the horizon. My scalp tingled and I poked Hank, but he had already spotted them. As everyone became aware of the advancing pride, coffee and rolls were set down and conversation trickled off.

A pride emerged from our right, tawny females, sleek, beautiful and deadly. With their offspring, almost grown males and small female cubs, they kept emerging from the dim regions. I held my breath. At the same time a herd of impala silhouetted against the rising sun got wind of the lions, halted momentarily before leaping and bounding as they raced off. The lions paused watching the impalas disappear into the shadows, and then they began moving again, soft-footing as they split into two groups and passed around our vehicle, utterly surrounding it. I wanted to say something, share my fear, my admiration, my astonishment, but I remained in respectfully-frightened silence. I could have reached out and touched a female, she was that close, almost brushing the side of the vehicle with her powerful shoulders. I smelled her breath bathing me, hot and foul, saw her muscles sliding one into another as she passed. She was so close that after she passed, I expended my breath with a whoosh, not realizing I had been holding it.

No one made a sound, and I breathed shallowly as the lions continued pacing by, one then another. As the last one crossed in front of the Land Rover, belatedly I grabbed my camera and began snapping photographs, catching two looking sidewise at the Land Rover, their eyes reflecting the flash as I snapped several times.

When the pride was safely out of sight, a man sitting in the seat behind me said, "My god, that was something." Awe, and tamped down fear, filled his voice.

"She had nothing to do with it," Hank said, easing the tension. A woman laughed.

Her laugh set us off. All seven of us talked at once, interrupting one another as we told how we'd felt, what we'd seen, laughing and repeating ourselves. One man said he was sure there were fifty lions. A woman said it looked like a hundred to her. "At least it will be a hundred when I tell it back home." We all giggled. I finished eating my croissant. I felt overpoweringly hungry.

Hank said, "Actually there were thirty lions. I counted."

A fearsome roar caught me mid-bite. Talk ceased. In the new silence I heard the driver chuckle. "Look," he said when the roar subsided. In the bush, beyond where the pride had emerged, a huge male sporting a black-mane rose from his bed and looked right at us. We said nothing as we inched by. I called that morning our second Jurassic Park moment.

The third came when we followed elephant spoor down a dry creek bed at a camp with A-frame chalets and a large open-sided, centrally located lodge. The first night checking in, we met two women from Washington, D.C. one fairly high in one of the government agencies. I was delighted to find women who had made it in what was still a work world dominated by men. We seemed to get along well at dinner, exchanging chit chat about where we'd been, where we were going as we indulged ourselves eating the usual gourmet selections while relating stories about zebras and giraffes as well as all the other animals we'd already seen.

Afterward, at the gleaming bar, sipping tropical drinks, we got into a discussion about women's rights, me the quintessential feminist, and the women as anti-feminist as one can get, saying ridiculous and irrelevant things such as "why do you hate men so?" I was glad when Hank, who had been consulting with one of the guides about our agenda the next day, joined us. While I conferred with him, the two women left. I concluded they were old enough to be "one of the boys," women who never rocked the boat and as a consequence had become tokens in the government bureaucracy.

The bartender, who had told us earlier he had grown up in Zimbabwe, had observed from a polite distance. Now, he said to me, nodding his head in the direction the women had gone, "You and the ladies, you all come from the United States of America, don't you?" I said we did. He shook his head. "I don't understand. You seemed...different. Not like you're from the same country." I said we came from different areas of the country but we were all Americans. "We differ on how we see things." It wasn't the best explanation and only served to confuse him further. He shook his head. "Strange."

I'm sure he was even more surprised in the morning when we were all slated to follow elephant tracks together. When we entered the lodge that morning, the guide rushed over to Hank. "Are you and your wife okay having the ladies going along this morning?" We assured him it was fine. But I could see he wasn't quite sure until he saw the ladies greet us politely and all of us laugh at our enthusiasm defending our beliefs the night before. "Americans," I imagined the Africans thinking

My apprehension later was almost as large as the elephant's spoor. A bull elephant had passed by camp earlier, his prints in the dry riverbed were less than a half-hour old. He was probably foraging as he went. Male elephants sometimes join in small bands of young males, sometimes with older bulls, but the adult bulls almost always were alone. And this time of the year they were in must. If frightened, they would charge. Again, silence predominated. Flies buzzed. The "work harder." cries of the spoonbill carried on the warm breeze.

The tops of the Umbrella trees, set sparsely along the bank, swayed slightly. Through them I glimpsed a meadow above. Because we were into the dry season, the guide with the lethal looking gun cautioned us not to step on twigs that would snap and alert the animal we tracked. He pointed out where the elephant had stopped, where he'd moved faster. As the gully got deeper, twice as high as our heads, silver terminalia trees formed an almost impenetrable hedge for a quarter of a mile or so until a natural rock formation created an abrupt change. Mahogany trees predominated, deep roots bridging the gap between the meadow and the stream, creating nooks and crannies behind roots as large as small trees. When the guide whispered the elephant wasn't far ahead, I looked around for a place to hide if necessary. If he charged, I'd need to scoot under one of those caves created by a large tangle of roots and the bank.

We turned an abrupt corner in time to glimpse the elephant topping the bank and disappearing from view. I exhaled with relief. He'd been larger than I'd ever imagined.

The guide took a step up the bank. "Or we can call it a day?" In unison, the DC ladies, Hank and I said we weren't eager to follow. "We are now in absolute agreement," the high government lady said. We all laughed and talked about what we would have done if the elephant had charged. I told my plan. Hank said that was his also. The guide said it was an excellent idea. "If you could get there before me." We all laughed again.

The bartender's apparent naiveté was matched by another guide we got to know in subsequent days. A nice-looking white man who had grown up in Zimbabwe, he told us he was married and his wife and two children were with him living in one of the chalet's. Our A-frame had a toilet, a shower and two beds, the other chalets the same. I was too shocked to ask if his family got their meals at the lodge, or what. They had to be on a very small income. He had not passed his test yet to be a senior guide and was studying every chance he got. Not only did guides have to know how to protect safari clients, they had to know everything about the flora and fauna of the area. One day he drove us to a remote water hole where we observed a bull elephant in must, making me realize fully how dangerous our tracking could have been.

Snorting and running toward the females at the water hole, the bull made all lesser animals scurry out of the way.

We had driven on a two-lane paved road most of the way to the watering hole. The guide explained the road was a gift from the American government. It was evident he was very proud of it when he asked, "Do you have roads this good in America?" I could not say we had huge super highways, with clover-leaves and pedestrian walks, on and off ramps and so many cars it was often gridlock. He couldn't have pictured it. I just said, "Yes, we did."

That night before we went to sleep, I asked Hank, "Know what I'm think-ing of?" It was chilly, and the down comforter felt wonderful. Fresh flowers in a ceramic vase appeared in the bathroom when we returned from dinner. Large, fluffy, clean towels hung on the heated towel racks. The native carpets were strategically placed so we never had to step on the flagstone floor.

He was amused as he always was when I wanted him to guess something. "I haven't learned to read your mind yet."

"The guide's words made me remember growing up. I must have been six or seven years old. During the Great Depression, my mother baked all our bread. But one day she ran out and sent me to the store with a dime. She told me bread cost eight cents, and not to lose the two pennies change.

It was a warm day. I remember coming home from the store, clutching the change and the loaf of bread so tight the wrapper broke in the middle. I had a hard time keeping the slices from falling to the sidewalk. I started to cry. A lady in one of the houses I was passing came out. All the houses had base-ments, and you went up steps to the front porch where the richer people had swings and porch furniture. It was late afternoon so she was probably sitting outside. I'm not sure but I think women listened to fifteen-minute soap operas in those days. Maybe that came later. Anyway, long story short she came out with a paper bag and I went home with the bread intact, and I had the change. Sometimes, today, I have to pinch myself. I can hardly believe I'm really here."

A moonbeam was streaming through the high window above the door, highlighting the bedside tables, the upholstered chair. I felt as if I might simultaneously laugh and cry. I'd experienced the Great Depression and now had seen poverty throughout the world.

Hank's voice went soft with remembrance. "When my father was at war, after school I helped my mother in the Mom and Pop store she was running on a shoestring. People charged groceries, and she had me write their names and the amounts they charged on a lined tablet she put in a ledger later. Sometimes she let me run the cash register, too."

"How old were you?"

"Same age as you when you almost dropped the bread – six or seven."

"Were you good at it?"

"She said I was."

"You were, I'm sure." I reached across the narrow aisle between our beds and touched his hand.

"Once. I came home from kindergarten crying because the nuns accused me of something I didn't do. I know I said this before. I tried to tell her, but she just said, the good sisters don't make mistakes. I didn't either after that."

"What a lesson."

"The joys of religion."

We were silent for a while, and again I grew aware of the hippos rooting around nearby. "Do you hear that? Probably Pink Floyd." I reminded him of the hippo who stayed near our first camp, wallowing in mud so that he usually had a pink tinge.

"We're lucky."

"I know I am."

Neither of us said anything for a while and by the time Hank murmured good night, I was nodding off. I expect animals growled, snorted, and roared like they had previous nights, but by now I was too tired to hear them.

At Great Zimbabwe, the high point historically of the ancient country, the stone-work was so "developed" that early European explorers thought it had to be the work of Arabs, not the Africans. As we settled into our hotel room, vervet monkeys living in the trees nearby tried to get into our room. We learned to slam the door quickly when we entered or left.

At the ancient site we met an African woman as black as an unlit spelunker cave. She told us her daughter studied at the University of California, Fresno. She, herself, traveled the country talking to women about their rights, seeing that their daughters went to school; it was a government position. I wanted to hug her after the bad taste left by the D.C. women, but she seemed too dignified for that.

That night we had our first taste of sadza, the meal that tasted much like American grits. Hank liked it so well the waiter always gave him an extra portion

We ended our safari in real luxury at the Victoria Falls Hotel, that beautiful green and white colonial structure a mile or so from the falls. Even in the dry season the mist could be seen from the hotel grounds. The falls were impressive, the hotel with its traditional British touches, dining on impala, and dancing in a jeans skirt (the dressiest thing in my safari wardrobe) was relaxing and fun. Watching a British woman bungee jump from the bridge leading to Zambia, eating outside in the lovely gardens, walking to the nearby village – it was the perfect place to relax. Now Mugabe, the leader who had such promise when the people got their freedom from Britain, has driven most of the white citizens out and made others, like that woman we met at Great Zimbabwe, fight enormous poverty.

Sixteen

*"The bible has noble poetry in it, and some clever
fables, and some blood-drenched history, and a wealth
of obscenity, and upwards of a thousand lies."*

SAMUEL CLEMENS, MARK TWAIN (1835-1910)

From Zimbabwe we went to London, me coming down with a cold that I fought all during a week of theater, seeing Stash and Louise, a couple we'd originally met in Poland, going shopping and to the museums again, and eating in restaurants that had become much more sophisticated since our first visit years before.

In London, bringing my mind to the subway system, sorting out streets that were like a maze, climbing up double-decker busses seemed impossible. In my foggy, virus-infused head, civilization intruded, jet travel too fast, me still in Africa. Thankfully, Hank never got lost, or fumbled his way. I relied on him extensively. "You're fantastic," I said one day.

He shook his head. "I work at it." He maintained that all his life he'd had trouble with his memory. That in college he could never remember the short-cuts for equations, that while everyone else was utilizing the shortcuts, he was doing problems from step number one, but that he was so fast, no one ever knew. He also kept notes in his pockets about his everyday life. I remember once on a dance floor, a couple we hadn't seen for a few weeks were suddenly dancing next to us. Hank whipped out an address he had promised to give them. He told me now that he would have forgotten what it was they wanted if he hadn't made a note.

"But we all forget things like that," I protested.

"Not like I do."

Not long after we were married I realized he needed quiet to read or study. He told me that at work it took all his concentration to overcome the noise I never put this together with the dementia that assailed him later, but now I often wonder if dementia, isn't a lifelong disability that is overcome by youth and extreme intelligence. In any gathering he continually impressed me, knowing a great deal about many topics outside his field and being an expert within.

And then we were home, immersing ourselves in our real life again – my writing chums meeting at our house the first week we were back, a meeting of The Older Women's League, the Humanists needing help to get a charitable status – what Hank had confided got buried beneath the many pressing events of our life.

He usually left for work early, but one winter morning in 1995, I got up to find him wearing a bathrobe with a jacket over it, standing in the kitchen breathing steam from a teakettle. "What's going on?

"I think I'm coming down with a cold. I can't breathe properly."

He hardly ever wore a bathrobe and certainly not with a jacket over it. He was very pale and seemed far off somewhere, far from normal.

I called our medical provider and got him to our family physician. In no time the doctor discovered he was having a heart attack, and he was rushed off in an ambulance. On hindsight, what is remarkable is that he never had any of the classic symptoms, no pain in the jaw or radiating down the arm. No pain in the chest as if someone were beating on him, just the difficulty breathing, the fatigue.

It began a period of observation culminating in open-heart surgery to replace four faulty valves. After quadruple bypass surgery Hank stayed the requisite time in a Catholic Hospital where, in a diplomatic way, he made it clear he had no need for visits from priests or nuns. They respected his wishes and he ignored the ubiquitous crosses on all the walls, friends taking them down while they visited and replacing them before they left. Every day I drove in to visit him, leaving my car on one of the streets in what is called Sacramento's Fabulous Forties, a succession of streets with beautiful mansions in a variety of styles. That way I avoided the dark parking garage and could walk two or three blocks to the hospital. It was so reminiscent of that time in Philadelphia, but with such a different outcome. Each day Hank looked better and soon was home again. Six weeks of rehabilitation followed and started him on an exercise regimen he followed the rest of his life. I attribute that to his continuing good health afterward. He had gone in twenty pounds overweight and came out with the twenty pounds gone. He never gained them back

No matter how much Hank enjoyed his work, traveling throughout the state and working with congenial people, he set a retirement date. "You've followed me and my career around the states. It's only fair, you choose where we'll live when I retire."

For a year I kept temperatures for a variety of warm weather locations, recorded the average, the median, the highs and lows and made graphs to show each. At the end of the year, I had made my decision. We would remain in northern California. It had the best year around temperatures of all the places I'd studied – southern California, extreme southern California, Arizona, and Nevada. .

In late 1995 we went to Belize, the highlight of our trip Tikal, the ancient Mayan site in Guatamela. It was one of the largest archeological sites of pre Colombian Mayan civilization. We had already visited the sites in Mexico and were fascinated by the history and the grandeur of the architecture. But touring Mexican archeological sites was easy compared to going to Tikal from Belize. Civil unrest within Guatamela had penetrated its most remote regions.

To get to Tikal we bumped over a dirt road at fifteen miles an hour, our driver stopping every twenty or so miles of the one hundred plus miles, to confer with men, sometimes masked, all carrying rifles at the ready. It wasn't exactly a relaxing trip. I had left home with a cold and now was pumped full of aspirin in an effort to make the trip less stressful. My head felt as if it were in a vise. But passing through tiny Mayan villages, seeing peacock's nesting in trees nearby, and finding archeological sites everywhere, was worth it.

Tikal's peaks literally rose above the treetops. Once again I watched Hank climb so high he was a tiny figure in my binoculars. I went up the lesser ruins, my imagination working full time imagining the sounds and sights of the ancient past.

After recuperating, literally baking under the sun of Caye Calker, an island off the coast of Belize, we had agreed about the future. We were moving to Sun City, Roseville, a retirement community that was being planned fifteen miles from Sacramento, one advertised as a place for active adults.

By this time we'd been married twenty-five adventure-filled years. We were moving into a community of 3200 privately owned homes. The centrally located lodge contained all the amenities. While neither of us was interested in the 18 or nine hole golf courses, we liked that there were swimming pools, a fitness center and just about anything one could wish for. What cinched it for us was the feeling of security. As an adult, it had always been Hank's goal to spend winter months in places even warmer than Northern California. We would go each year to where palm trees swayed and tropical breezes were a given and not have to worry about the safety of our house.

About the same time we settled into another new home, the inside done to my specifications, we grew increasingly aware of the growing fundamentalist Christian movement in the United States. I had been on the national board of the Atheist Alliance, International as well as the national board of the AHA. In addition to receiving literature from AHA and FFRF, we subscribed to Americans United for Separation of Church and State and freethought newsletters such as Margaret Downey's from Philadelphia. The news wasn't good, and I was getting very concerned.

Hank's concern equaled mine He had discovered local school boards in Roseville were dangerously close to having fundamentalist believers in charge. He and I testified regarding evolution at a school board meeting, interviewed people running for various school boards in the county, and gave the results to the local Democratic Club. Hank also contacted the National Center for Science Education in Berkeley and got them involved. They in turn got local science teachers to take on the cause. The fundamentalists lost their fight.

But creationists had started talking intelligent design and using it in stealth attacks on school boards. It was time to start a freethought group in our community. Hank asked if I was I ready for tomatoes thrown at our house, people snubbing me at the lodge? I knew we had to tread lightly. We now lived in the most conservative county in California, second only to Orange County.

With hope and fear pressing on me, I put an advertisement in our onsite magazine and newspaper. In our church going community, the word atheist was still anathema. People were even afraid to say they were Democrats. I wrote: Wanted: Non-theists to start a club, and I added my telephone number.

We needed twenty-five people backing our suggestion to start an official orga-nization.. With the help of other non-theists we'd already unearthed, we began collecting signatures for the Activities Department.

The first month after my announcement was published, twelve people met at our house. Twenty showed at the next meeting, and after that I pre-sented the list of signers – now thirty-five – to the Activities Department. Our Humanist Club now had use of a meeting room. No one threw tomatoes, although our flyers kept disappearing in bulk from the kiosk in the lodge. Hank talked to the head of the Activities Department, and it never happened again. Unfortunately, because of community rules, we weren't able to ally with local or national non-theist organizations. Few outsiders were aware of our existence. Through the years we hosted a variety of speakers on social and religious issues and I routinely published quotes and sayings by famous non-theists in our in-house publications.

It was a busy time for both of us. I had started a community club with many facets under its umbrella. Hank and I also served as jurors at McGeorge School of Law in Sacramento. Students ready to graduate tried pared-down cases in their "courtroom of the future." The one day trial took place in front of real judges. The judgeship was so popular judges throughout California and Nevada vied for the position. The courtroom was state of the art at the time, TV screens between every two jurors and the jury room on camera so our deliberations could be filmed.

We also attended California State University's Renaissance Society, a learning-in-retirement organization with a difference. Retired judges, police-men, secretaries, teachers, dancers, singers, academics, housewives, firemen, you name it, can be found among the membership and anyone with an exper-tise can teach a seminar. We loved the seminars, taking part and also teaching.

In no time Hank became one of the most popular speakers for the Renaissance Society's 1500 members. He talked about science and the scientific method, about nuclear power and power plants, he talked about Humanism, he talked about Carl Sagan and other well-known non-theists. Quickly, he drew a following.

One time he was to give a talk that he mistakenly thought started at ten-thirty in the morning while it was actually scheduled for ten. One half hour late, I trailed Hank into the lecture room, and the audience was still in their seats waiting. Seeing him, everyone applauded. They not only loved his expertise, they liked his modesty and his integrity. They knew he would be late only if it were necessary; he would never be a no-show. Talking about non-theism, he didn't deride or argue with nay-sayers, just quietly presented facts. And people listened.

His question and answer periods always amazed me. He usually knew the answers to even the most esoteric or outrageous questions. Completely at ease during q and a, he had my deepest admiration. When I first started giving talks, Q and A made me anxious. Now, I feel little discomfort. While most of the time I know the answers, if I don't, I don't mind saying I don't know. If anything, Hank shone during the follow-up to his talks.

Having a clever wit, he loved playing with words and playing pranks. In elevators throughout our married life, he often said something that made it sound as if we weren't married and he was hitting on me. The other riders usually betrayed their shock in some way. One time, At McGeorge, he told a prospective juror that I had been a showgirl and he a pit boss in Vegas. It led to a fun time at lunch before he revealed the truth. I loved this playful side of him for I often thought he had sprung from the womb fully grown.

Most always we thought alike and came to the same conclusions about the trials, but many years after we first served, we differed. A criminal trial had me sitting on the edge of my seat as witnesses (student volunteers or friends or family members of the student attorneys) described scenes and actions that made the trial result seem very clear. The other jurors and I all voted for a lenient sentence. Hank declared emphatically that the man was guilty. I couldn't understand his reasoning, and we squabbled a bit on the way home. I eventually concluded his extreme "law and order" decision had been a hold-over from his black and white Catholic upbringing. Much later I attributed it to an early sign of dementia.

About this time Turkey had become the "in" place to travel. We'd both paid attention to the muttering coming from Moslem countries. Turkey was being billed as the "Arabic" country most like the west. Neighbors talked about their trip, spoke about the great exchange rate. Other residents of our community praised a tour group. Having always traveled on our own, we were leery about taking a tour. We were afraid we'd be riding busses for hours, told to shop for hours, none of which appealed to us. Hank talked to the tour headquarters and was assured nothing like that would happen. We decided to give it a try. It was time to sit back and relax a bit. Hank was 60, I was 70. Although neither of us looked our age, we were far from "spring chickens." We signed for a three week tour and began to read about the country that was at the end of the Silk Route from China. We would be somewhat knowledge-able, but we could also relax and let others take over the day-to-day planning. No problem. Of course all the things we feared happened. And worse.

Seventeen

"Murphy's Law. If anything can go wrong it will."

Anonymous

The tour started out pleasantly in Istanbul. We admired the old town with its palace and mosques piercing the sky with turrets, the golden horn joining Asia and Europe, the river trip where old houses of wood cost more than the mansions of marble. It had all been a delight – until now. Half way through our travels throughout Turkey, Hank's stomach upset suddenly found release. In a barely adequate hotel in the middle of Turkey's vast spaces, he had the worst diarrhea either of us had ever encountered. Nothing helped. One whole night, we got no sleep. I had to roust hotel staff in that remote village so we could have clean bedding, could get water and medicine. As morning crept in I was blurry eyed, Hank, weak and trembling. I couldn't see how we could continue

Before breakfast, I talked to the tour guide, my voice pitched for his ears although only a dirty looking man wielded a mop, and I assumed he didn't understand my English. None of the people on our tour were up. I explained Hank needed rest and we both needed sleep. I suggested we could stay over, catch a local bus and catch up with the tour in the next town. Our tour guide said it would be impossible. We might and might not get a local bus. Their schedules weren't predictable, and it would be very uncomfortable and slow. In addition, we might run into trouble-makers. I translated that to mean we wouldn't be safe. The guide stressed we were riding in a Mercedes bus, the best there was. We pulled ourselves together as well as possible and got on the bus.

Two hours later Hank, pale as a ghost, said he needed facilities – fast. None were available. I alerted the tour guide. He spoke in Arabic to the driver, and the bus came to a rubber-burning stop. The guide pointed to the side of the road, and Hank stumbled off the bus. Everyone averted their eyes as Hank traipsed into the meager brush. He wasn't the first to be so afflicted. Two or three others had suffered the same indignities previously. We hadn't realized the severity of the disease until it hit Hank. Luckily by that night his problems were under control

In the meantime, during the second week of our trip, I was feeling sick, each day a little worse. But not in the same way. I had a horrible feeling I needed to vomit. But nothing happened except I kept feeling worse. The man in the seat behind me complained when I reclined my seat as far as possible to ease my aching head, my roiling stomach.

Hank said, "Can you cut my wife some slack. She's not feeling well."

"Well, I'm not feeling well with my knees up to my chin," the man retorted.

Hank replied and the two men exchanged polite but stern words, neither giving an inch.

Outside a blur of open land was brushed with an occasional desert plant. Although I'd seen more desolate places, it seemed like the worst. My head spun and I thought I might faint. Suddenly, I upchucked, all over myself and the floor.

While I dabbed at myself with tissues, the bus came to another screeching stop. Mustapha, the good-looking, young tour guide raced down the aisle to the back where we were sitting. He spoke good English and had enjoyed talking languages with Hank. Now he looked fierce, practically dragging me outside. In the gravel at the side of the road he gave me moist tissues and I dabbed at myself.

Then without warning the young man slapped me on one cheek and before I could protest, he slapped me on the other cheek. Did he think this would stun me into sensibility or what? I felt like a little girl who had been reprimanded. I just stared at him. The old-fashioned response to my illness did nothing to make me feel better. But at least when I got back on the bus, the man behind me did not berate me anymore.

It seemed like forever before we arrived at a hotel on the coast in the city of Izmir. Not long after I fell into bed, a Turkish doctor arrived, looking officious and hovering over me. Before leaving home I'd read that under no circumstances should a foreigner go to a Turkish hospital, that the conditions were far from sanitary, that patients picked up diseases and some died. I needed to see a physician, but I needed to hedge my bets. I asked Hank to make sure the pediatrician from America who shared our tour was in the room when the Turkish doctor examined me. He at least could see if they were using sterile techniques.

Soon, my bed was the center of a group of people, the tour leader, the American doctor, Hank, the Turkish doctor and nurse.

They listened to my heart, took my pulse, looked in my throat, my ears, and thumped my belly. Soon I was hooked up to an IV, a blood test taken and Hank was told to keep me on bland food. They would report back on the blood test soon.

A few hours later they were back, and we were told I had a tapeworm. We were aghast. At home tapeworm was something American doctors never see anymore. Somewhere along the line, eating the delicious buffets, the seafood, the wonderful Mediterranean dishes, I had been infected.

The Turkish doctor wanted to hospitalize me, but I steadfastly refused. Turning to Hank, they said they'd be back the next day and demanded American cash for their visit.

A flash of concern crossed Hank's face as he practically emptied his wallet of money. As they pocketed the cash, they turned back to me and smiled before leaving. The American pediatrician who had been with us said they had used sterile techniques. At least one thing was alright.

The next day the tour went on without us, someone leaving me their paperback books so I'd have something to read, the tour guide telling us to get a plane at the end of the week and join the tour again in Istanbul.

That day Hank left me in bed hooked up to the IV and went to find a bank to begin the lengthy task of contacting banks at home. We were flat out of cash. He had no luck, but said he had only tried nearby.

The following day he went further, leaving our hotel about nine in the morning. Weak sun wasn't reaching my window and the room was utilitarian only, nothing to brighten the leaden walls, the bare floor. I felt very much alone. I attempted to read one of the books someone in the tour had left, but still hooked up to the IV and a little worried, I couldn't concentrate. Our building sat on a corner, hard against the narrow sidewalk separating it from the street. I was very aware of everything happening outside. Traffic honked and backfired and men shouted at one another sixteen hours a day, only slightly muted because we were on the seventh floor. The Turkish drivers seemed to go out of the way to call one another names.

I tried reading a novel, but its story was simplistic, its style non-existent. Soon bored, I looked at the blank walls, the thin crack in the ceiling and finally clicked on the television. The only channel I could remotely follow was one coming from Berlin. I heard President Clinton's name and was sure they were talking about his impeachment trial. But the channel kept fading out.

At eleven-thirty a man knocked at my door.

I called out, "Who's there?"

A key was inserted in the lock, and the man, who spoke no English, backed in with my lunch.

I almost vomited again looking at the mounds of mashed potatoes bolstered with mounds of rice and a pot of tea. I longed for fruit and vegetables. Besides, I was getting antsy. I'd not heard from Hank all morning. In all our married life, in precarious or strange circumstances, he never left me long without keeping me updated on what was happening. This was unusual, but I comforted myself with reasons. Before the days of universal cell phones, it was not always easy to find a public telephone. Or if he was talking through an interpreter and stuck in a bank officer's office, he would not be able to let me know.

That kind of thinking didn't soothe me for long. I was becoming more and more nervous. He was always so open and trusting. Had someone hit him in the head and dragged him into an alley to rob him? I had always been more suspicious of people's motives than he. Despite his ever-growing cosmopolitan ways, he at times retained some of his Polish/American upbringing. People are friends until proven otherwise. Americans are instantly recognized everywhere in the world. Anyone on the noisy, busy street could see him as a target.

Startled by my thinking, I inched over in bed and tried to figure out the telephone on the nightstand between the twin beds. Finally after several tries, I got the desk.

Someone answered in Arabic. Earlier Hank had determined that only one man in the hotel could speak and understand English. All his other languages flew by them as foreign as English. While the Arabic words swirled by me, I kept repeating, "I'm the American woman on the seventh floor. Please let me speak to someone who understands English."

Finally, the English speaker came on. I repeated my worry about Hank. I thought we should alert the police. The man I never saw, but who sounded kind and sympathetic, persuaded me in his broken and far from grammatical English to wait at least a half hour before alerting the police. I finally agreed.

In exactly a half hour, the door opened and Hank appeared, looking sweaty and tired but satisfied. He had endured almost a classic American comedy episode. He had had to go to three banks before he got one who would be able to contact America. They had directed him to a line, but when he got to the front of the line, the clerk had left for the day. Another line proved to be the wrong one. Another one had a clerk who shrugged and left, probably for lunch. At the final bank and line he had to tell his story to several people before he found one who understood that his credit was good, but that he needed cash. Of course the time difference between our two countries didn't help, but he finally got everything straightened out.

I almost cried on the fourth day when the doctor took the IV away. I could hardly stand being bedridden. Shakily, I got up and dressed. No more mounds of mashed potatoes. I went with Hank to the hotel restaurant for dinner. Tourists from the hinterlands sat at tables around us, all middle-east-erners. Like so many times before in places we traveled, we were the only ones with light-complexions. Still queasy, but eager to eat "real" food, I or-dered a dinner and picked at it while a Turkish piano player serenaded us with tunes from the nineteen thirties and forties, "Night and Day," "Blue Moon," "Red Sails in the Sunset," and "Satin Doll." When we thanked him and put some money in his tip box, I asked, "Where did you learn those songs?" He only shrugged and said, "No English." We decided he must have heard old recordings. At times his renditions were far from accurate, but they gave the touch of home I needed.

We finally started the trip from Izmir to Istanbul, spent another night in a hotel and left for the US in the morning. Back in the states my doctor had to contact the Center for Disease Control to know how to treat me.

A tour in the United States where so many people got sick would have been investigated and probably stopped. Nothing of that sort happened in Turkey. While our ordeal was far from pleasant, I still look back at the sights in Turkey as spectacular. The tour guide and Hank had more than one discussion about religion, too. The young man told us he admired Ataturk, the country's first president. He had brought secularism to Turkey in 1923. But while secular thought and actions and western dress had taken sway in the large cities and among the educated, in the countryside traditional customs and religion predominated and apparently has gained a very strong hold today.

Eighteen

"There is only one happiness in life, that is to love and be loved."

GEORGE SAND (1804-1876)

After the difficulties in Turkey, spending the months of January and February in Honolulu had a wonderful sound. We had vacationed on Hawaii (the Big Island), Maui, Oahu, and Kauai, but Oahu had the most to offer for an extended stay. Capital of the Hawaiian state, it had beauty as well as many cultural and social possibilities

In a vacation mood, we flew United Airlines across the Pacific. Years earlier, on our honeymoon trip, I had won the game United plays, passengers judging when the plane gets to the halfway point. Now over twenty-five years later, I won again. It put Hank and I in a grand mood to enjoy our stay.

Coming in from the airport in a taxi, I loved each tropical tree I glimpsed, basked in each breeze. The first day, while I was unpacking, Hank memorized a dozen bus schedules and told me which bus to take to go wherever I wanted to go. Before leaving home he had arranged with various companies to have our bills, our magazines sent to our Honolulu address. The postal service forwards for thirty days only. In the following days in the city he found the location of the best grocery stores, told me where to find a farmer's market and how to get to theaters, restaurants, and all the cultural events we'd enjoy each year. It was the same wherever we went, he guiding me, whether it was Moscow, Beijing, or Cairo. It wasn't until later, after his dementia became evident that I realized how much I depended upon him. Because of his love of numbers, he dealt with all financial matters, kept detailed budget books, and made sure we never were late with payments when we traveled.

That year in the islands, we felt like a couple of kids stocking a first apartment. We'd grab the number 2 or 13 bus to the Safeway store. We'd return to the apartment with backpacks and fanny packs loaded with staples, just like everyone who lived on the island. On Safeway shopping days lunching at Auntie Pasto's on the corner of Beretania and Pensacola became a habit. A few blocks past Auntie Pasto's we discovered the Honolulu Academy of Arts. It's design, consisting of several courtyards separating galleries devoted to various Asian arts, as well as changing local artists' exhibits and paintings from around the world, coincided with our idea of a great art museum. In addition it's restaurant, open on one side to the Trade Winds, faced water tumbling over a wall and served scrumptious continental lunches, including at times the fabulous lilikoi (passion fruit) chiffon pie.

We bought Hawaiian language books and did some cursory study. Hawaiian sounded easy to learn, having only 12 letters, and we found certain words had been incorporated into everyday English on Oahu, and probably used on the other islands as well. Makai means toward the sea, mauka means toward the mountains. We heard these and other Hawaiian words in conversation and they appeared in newspaper stories. But Hawaii was much too inviting to spend all our time studying.

Quickly, we established an island routine, going to the North Shore when the surf thundered in, picnicking on Magic Island when it wasn't, patronizing the symphony at the Blaisdell Center, attending Humanist meetings, going to the Manoa Valley and the Diamond Head theaters as well as the smaller theater companies, some with only Hawaiian actors or directors. We attended ballet performances and when January chills struck at home, we got a kick out of sipping mai-tais on the terrace at intermission.

Theatrical events from the Mainland often debuted in the islands. The Vagina Monologues was one. Almost daily we saw free concerts or dances at the Ala Moana Mall, the International Center or on a street corner. Walking on the beach in the morning, eating where the locals ate, riding The Bus with them, admiring their solicitous way with the elderly, all that made us feel like haoles with a special dispensation to pretend we were locals. We even attended movies, which at home was never high on Hank's list.

I absolutely floated from one amazing scene to another – banyan trees high on my "tree list." One banyan could cover a whole block if its aerial roots weren't cut back. The branches of monkey pod trees spread yards beyond the trunks and reminded me of Longfellow's "Under a spreading chestnut tree, the village smithy stands." But my favorite, and seldom glimpsed Mindanao gum trees have trunks covered with streaks of color like a watercolor painting, rose bleeding into yellow or blue, green and white. But no tropical place is without palm trees. In the iconic picture, the extinct volcano Diamond Head in the background, date palms give dimension to the photo, but royal palms, coconut palms and fan palms were everywhere. Gilding the lily, hotels and the city sometimes wrapped palms in small winking lights. It was a fairytale sight.

Located a half block from Beretania, the street that gained importance because President Obama had once lived there with his grandparents, we discovered Kaiser Permanente. Being members of the HMO on the mainland, we were assigned doctors in Honolulu. But our most interesting discovery was linking up with the Humanists of Hawaii. They were few in number, but the members were fervent, holding monthly meetings, putting out a newsletter, and having social events. One year a party was held at Queen Emma's Condominiums, in a gazebo in the garden. Among a treasure trove of tropical foliage and koi ponds, we were unaware that more than one gazebo existed. Although we didn't recognize the man who handed us a drink, and we saw no familiar face among the people milling around, we were not alarmed. Too new to know everyone in the organization, we suspected many members showed up only for social events. The trade winds were blowing softly, flower fragrance drifted, and I felt truly as if I were in paradise. As I sipped White Zinfandel, Hank introduced us and explained how to pronounce our last name.

The man smiled and made out a name-tag for each of us. A few minutes later, our comments made it clear we had recently joined the Humanists of Hawaii. The man, who had been welcoming us so nicely, suddenly scowled and named his church group. Abruptly, he pointed out the turns on the flag-stone paths, and a few minutes later we arrived where we should have been.

It wasn't our biggest blunder.

In one of the freebie papers, we learned about a dance to be held in the public rooms of a condo not far from us on Kalakaua Avenue. Thrilled by the idea of an extended stay in Honolulu, we made plans to attend. I bought a long Polynesian dress, white with green and violet flowers. My sandals were violet. Hank let me talk him into getting a silk multi-hued Hawaiian shirt and white pants. That night he came into the apartment carrying a florist box. Inside was an orchid lei. I kissed him a couple times before I applied lipstick. We would be elegant, twirling around with locals similarly dressed. You can see my thinking was still tourist inspired. The Poinciana trees were showing their winter blooms, and life was perking in ways I loved.

The night was perfect, a soft breeze, the air cool but not cold, the wind gentle enough it didn't snarl my hair. We walked arm in arm to the condo. The dance was in progress when we arrived, a band playing, fifty or so couples of all ethnicities on the floor. We joined the dancers. This was going to be fun. We had already learned that the largest ethnic groups on the islands were Filipino. The Japanese came next and then all the rest. I glimpsed a table be-ing set with pineapple and tropical fruits and probably punch. People smiled at us, and we smiled back, although I had begun to notice, no other women wore leis and few wore Hawaiian dresses.

When the music ended, we took two of the seats set at intervals around the room. Almost immediately the music started again, playing a waltz, and a man and a woman, approximately our age, approached us. He wore khaki pants and an aloha shirt with a tan and yellow flower pattern. She had on some kind of white pants suit. She was pretty, he good looking. We smiled, ready to make friends, but the man pulled me onto the floor, saying we can talk later. The woman took Hank's hand and led him out, too. He looked disturbed as the man waltzed me away. I sent an encouraging look his way, but the man was whirling me fast. I had never danced as well before or since. With his strong lead, the man had me doing dips and twirls that amazed me. After several fancy steps, he led me in the traditional box steps and asked where I was from.

"Originally Ohio," I said, looking up. He was taller than Hank.

"A buckeye," he said, adding that he had originally come from Pennsylvania. "But I mean now, where do you live now?"

Later, I realized he meant in what part of the city, but I said truthfully, "California, but my husband and I are here for two months." I looked around for Hank, but could not spot him.

My partner looked puzzled. "How did you happen to come to this dance?" His voice had lost its honeyed edge.

"We saw the notice in the paper."

He danced me in place for a few beats. "Oh, great. Somebody goofed. Do you know this is a dance club for singles?"

It was my turn to look puzzled and getting a little defensive I said, "It should have said that in the paper. It didn't." My indignation came through. I pulled away. "Sorry," I said. "We didn't mean to crash the party."

"Not your fault. We might as well finish the dance."

I had no desire to keep dancing, but I did, not wanting to create more of a flub than we already had.

Looking dazed, Hank was off the floor before me. "I don't like feeling really stupid," he said in a grim soft voice, "and I think I did." It was a position that bothered him tremendously. To ever say he was acting dumb was an insult he didn't like.

As the music started again, he said, "I was so damned shocked, I couldn't remember how to waltz. I stumbled through the situation. Let's get the hell out of here."

I agreed. I looked like a tourist for sure. Thank goodness my lei wasn't one of those paper things. I glanced behind us. Through sliding doors I made out a patio and a shadowy yard. I didn't relish going through the dance floor again. "Let's go out this way."

"Good idea."

But a path between bird of paradise and fan palms led to a wall. We had no choice. We had to go back inside and walk across that dance floor. After that Hank got me leis only on special occasions, my birthday or Valentine's Day when everyone made much of the sweetheart theme, husbands taking their wives to dine, bringing them candy and flowers, sometimes a lei. But the biggest change after our snafu was the dance club notices made clear it was for single residents only.

In a short time, we were feeling very much at home in Hawaii. We attended events at the University of Hawaii. We heard lectures and panel discussions by US Supreme Court justices and attorneys whose names routinely made the news. We spent Fridays on the grounds at the Iolani Palace listening to concerts by the Royal Hawaiian Band. What could be better than sitting under a Monkey Pod tree and enjoying hula dancers and singers. Invariably the band began with the official state song, sung in Hawaiian, and ended with Queen Liliuokalani's Aloha O'e. The last official royal ruler of the islands, the Queen had been deposed and put under house arrest in one of the palace's rooms. A friend told me, "She did her best against Dole Pineapple and the American Marines, but they were stronger." The official state song starts most all events on Oahu.

Oh, yes, it was paradise, and Hank and I felt like honeymooners again milking each moment of its intellectual, sensual, and adventurous components.

Each year I looked forward to our Hawaiian hiatus, never realizing it would in some way be the place where our life together would begin to tear apart.

Nineteen

"Do not shorten the morning by getting up late."

Arthur Schopenhauer (1788-1860)

At home again, we settled back into a normal routine, Hank going to the fitness center early each morning, me having breakfast while he was gone, he eating when he returned.   One morning while I was perusing the Sacramento Bee newspaper, the telephone rang.   I couldn't understand why my friend, Dorothy Cysewski, was calling so early.   Dorothy and her husband Richard had been friends since 1996.   They were both non-theists having thought through their Catholic upbringing late in life, and they both had Polish/American backgrounds. We had a lot in common.

"Do you have your television on?" she asked.

"No." We seldom turned it on until dinnertime.

"You better turn it on.   We've had a terrorist attack."

In a daze, I clicked on the TV and got hit with all that happened on September 11, 2001.   Shocked, frightened and full of questions, I called Debbie Roberge, who flew for United.   When she answered the phone, I felt instantly relieved. She was safe, not one of the pilots the terrorists had subdued with box cutters. She assured me she was all right and filled me in on details about the United Airlines planes, her own shock as great as ours. She knew some of the flight attendants and perhaps one of the pilots on the hijacked planes. She had more of an emotional stake than we did.

I just looked at Hank when he came in. He said, "I saw it." We'd been scheduled to fly to Spain and Portugal for a vacation trip. Not knowing how safe we'd be once America's grounded airlines were in the sky again, we canceled. We needed to be home, among Americans.

All day we sat glued to the television screen. We witnessed the second plane slam into the South Tower of the World Trade Center, saw Americans run before clouds of smoke and debris, saw people leap or were pushed from the towers, falling like traumatized birds to the ground. "I can't believe this. I can't!" I cried. Was this a dream, was I hallucinating? I had trouble believing what I saw. Our country, so powerful, so dependable, had showed its vulnerability. I wanted to cry.

"What can we do?" I faced Hank over the Chinese takeout he had brought in that afternoon.

"Nothing. Continue our own life as we always have."

Of course, it was something I knew, but Hank was my rock, my intellectual giant, my wonderful dancing and traveling partner. No matter what, we'd be fine.

Returning the next year for our winter hiatus in Honolulu, we found the beaches were almost deserted. Restaurants were ready to seat you when you walked in, few tourists anywhere. Yet, despite having to practically undress at the airport, our life was minimally changed by what happened. Instead, it changed in a way I hadn't expected.

Approximately the fourth year we wintered on the islands, we had been to the movies at the theater closest to the university where foreign films and Hollywood films out of the mainstream were shown. While Hank never talked in a movie and was always visibly annoyed if I whispered something about what we were seeing, this time after a flashback, he said, "Who in the heck is that?" In the dark of the theater, I stared at him. It was too dark to see his features, but he sounded angry. This makes no sense," he said.

After the movie was over and we were outside the theater, he said, "Movie making is going downhill. There was no introduction for that new character, nothing."

"Do you mean that kid?"

"Yes, of course. It was the only new character." Not hiding his irritation he also managed to convey his impatience with me for not immediately understanding his position.

"Hank, it was the main character as a child," I said as we hurried to catch our bus.

He shook his head. "No, you're mistaken." He took my arm as we started across a side street.

"No, you are," I said as we began to run before the light changed. We could see the bus coming behind us and didn't want to miss it.

He didn't say any more, and I attributed his words to his not really liking movies. By the time we were home again, I was too busy to even think of it. In the chilly days of March, life took on its usual rhythm.

A few years after moving into Sun City, I lost my driver's license, unable to see street signs until I was under or next to them. Hank drove for the two of us, whether it was locally or into Sacramento. It was also a time I added poetry to my writing repertoire. Since living in Seattle, I had written a poem or two each year, but I had never considered myself a poet. I had poets from Sacramento speak at the Scribes' Club I'd founded in Sun City. One of the accomplished poets looked at my early efforts and declared them poetry and invited me to come to a California state poet's convention being held in Sacramento that year.

Being among people talking about metaphor and simile, line breaks and enjambment, I was instantly hooked. The next year Hank accompanied me to the convention held in southern California where I won the first of many awards. Tremendously proud of my achievements, he told everyone I was responsible for his interest in the literary and visual arts, although he had always been a big fan of Shakespeare, having studied the plays during his college years. Early in life his love of mathematics and science, had translated into a love of music, but going with me to see an exhibit of the impressionists had whetted his appetite for painting. We seldom passed up a chance to visit an art museum or cultural and/or historical show.

One day at home, wind whipping at our backyard fence, he was working on our monthly budget, and I was writing a poem about what was happening in the world. Excited with the first draft, I showed it to him, and we spoke briefly about the wars. We had protested the war in Iraq, attended "do not go to war" rallies and marches in San Francisco. Both of us, through the years, had published articles on the internet about freethought, world politics, and feminism. I was incensed about what had happened to women in Afghanistan before the attack on the World Trade Center. The Taliban, who were running the country, didn't let women and girls attend school, get medical treatment, or appear on the street unless accompanied by a male family member. Women were punished for not covering themselves completely, a mesh slit for the eyes the only opening allowed. They were beaten for a glimpse of white sock, stoned to death for other infringements of Taliban rule.

Eager to show Hank my poetic efforts, I waited for his comments. He seldom had anything but praise, but sometimes he said he didn't understand, and I had to check to see if I had made my point sufficiently clear. This day I definitely had. We were both nodding.

We discussed the Taliban. I said interest about women's issues wasn't very high in the United States. After a few minutes of conversation, I returned to my computer and left him hunched over his books. Then thinking of something that I should have added to our discussion, I ran out to get his reaction. Only five minutes had gone by, but Hank didn't know what I was talking about.

He said, "You should announce your topic. Too many people get to a certain age and do the same. It's a disservice to listeners. You might say it's not the kindest thing to do."

That didn't really sound like him, but I recalled a couple old ladies I had known in my youth and saw his point. "Sorry, I didn't mean to be impolite and certainly not unkind." I conceded to myself that I had not explained what I was talking about. But back in the other room, away from his considerable powers of persuasion, I rethought the incident. Normally, people remember topics for more than five minutes, especially if nothing else is said in the interim. I mentioned the happening to no one, but it began to bother me, especially as it happened with alarming frequency.

Another incident bothered me. He began to complain about having a cough; yet I had not heard him cough. He cleared his throat and said, "Hear that?"

"That's not a cough. It sounded as if you were clearing your throat."

The next day he complained about the cough again. I repeated myself. So did he.

Was it part of his ethnic background, calling throat clearing a cough? Eventually, I quit saying anything.

We had been going to Hawaii several years by now, having started in 1998. About the same time, cell phones were taking over the lives of almost everyone we knew. Family members began calling on cell phones. People in the street walked around with a phone held to their ear. Hank bought one that came with a booklet of instructions. I saw him reading the book and fiddling with the phone.

"What's the matter?"

With disgust permeating his voice, he said, "It's impossible to understand the directions. They must have hired an intellectually challenged child to write them."

I was sure that was the problem. Various times I'd run into problems with directions that were far from clear. He used to laugh when I said, "Read the directions only if you can't figure it out for yourself. You'll be right fifty percent of the time." He'd never had trouble understanding anything. He did the New York Times crossword puzzles in ink, understood subtleties, loved Shakespeare's most obscure plays, and loved solving problems involving algebraic equations. I was sure he'd contact the manufacturer about the phone. That one was probably a lemon.

I was wrong. He continued giving out his cell phone number. He had figured out how to initiate calls, but he didn't know how to answer if someone called. I was flabbergasted. "You should have left our land line number," I said the first time I heard him leave his cell phone number.

"Why should I?" He looked puzzled.

"Because you don't know how to answer."

He said, "I just pick it up and answer. Why are you picking on me?"

I'm sure I looked perplexed, but he never noticed. Luckily, he got no important incoming calls on his cell phone during this time, and I put the occurrence out of my mind. I had never been much of a telephone person, having grown up when telephones in the home weren't standard. Most of my young life, business involving a telephone took place in a phone booth. Hank's difficulty with his cell phone made me think I didn't want one. I'd never known anyone who knew so much; he couldn't be wrong.

Following the cell phone incident, the next winter when we returned to Oahu, the owner of the apartment we'd liked so well was no longer renting it, but moving in permanently herself. We felt lucky to find another apartment in the same building. At the end of Nahua near the Ali Wai canal, our location gave us a great place to hike each morning. A sidewalk parallels the canal from the bridge at Kalakaua Avenue all the way to the library on Kapahulu. In the early evening, we loved watching the Hawaiian outriggers practice for the Hawaiian games. University students as well as other residents rowed. Held once a year in February, we made a point to attend the ancient Hawaiian games and watch the outrigger races.

We also weren't far from the ocean. Some mornings we'd hurry along the paved walkway that stretched to the Hilton Hotel. As the years passed, more and more sand covered the walkway, more of the beach disappeared. The hotels began hauling in sand, adding to breakwaters. As we strolled, waves often lapped just a few feet away. Climate change couldn't be disputed, the ocean gulped more beach annually.

But Waikiki Beach broadened as we approached the wide expanse of green grass, trees, flowers, and paths at Fort DeRussy Park. Each morning, in the shade of monkey pod trees, a local man led exercises. We enjoyed moving in concert with residents and tourists following his directions. Not far from us, the younger crowd played volley ball as we stretched, bent, kicked, danced on the grass. Behind us, and to the right, the tall distinctive white-barked Royal Palms swayed slightly in the always welcome Trade Winds.

We looked forward to a day or two of catching up on mainland news when Debbie, our United Airlines pilot friend bid the Honolulu run. Our condo wasn't far from Cha Cha Cha, the Jamaican/Mexican restaurant adjacent to the hotel where United Airline crews stayed. Getting together with Debbie brought a change of pace from our island routine. Sometimes, we took her to the rooftop of our condo, drank wine and watched the lights of Wakiki wink against the velvet sky. Or we sat outside in the Tiki Torch light of Cha, Cha, Cha and laughed a lot. Because she needed to be alcohol free before her flight back to the mainland, after that first day, we did "touristy" things. She was with us on our trek to see the Doris Duke mansion, Duke one of the richest women in the world in her day. One wall of her house is reputed to be worth a million dollars because of the expensive Middle Eastern decor.

So the apartment had a lot going for it in addition to being adequately furnished and the whole building being on a security system showing entrances and exits on a television screen playing in everyone's apartment. We felt very safe. Like all vacation rentals, the place had an adequate supply of towels, bedding, dishes, pots and pans – everything needed to keep house on a vacation basis, including a washer and dryer.

I had the comforts of home, but increasingly I felt as if I didn't quite have the man I'd married. I made some passing references about Hank to Debbie, but I could see she didn't understand what I was trying to convey. She saw nothing untoward, knowing him only as the witty scientist who knew east from west while her husband Roland and I spoke in terms of right and left and "that brick house across from the gas station."

After moving into the new condo, Hank discovered our mail wouldn't be delivered in the building. That was highly irregular. Our mail had always been delivered to any building where we stayed. It made no difference if the building was on the ocean or a half-mile away, or if it was a residential hotel or a condominium. Everyone in the building had a mailbox and received mail daily.

Hank called the owner and was told we had to rent a box at the local post office. I was as shocked as Hank was. Suspecting the owner was flouting the law, Hank spent innumerable hours finding out what laws the man had broken (and he'd broken many) and calling, not only the owner, but also every law authority who could help fix the problem. Unfortunately, many times Hank was put on hold. One day I returned from a morning walk to find him shouting at the telephone. At first I thought someone was on the other end of the line, and I said in a startled voice, "What's going on? What are you doing?" He had always been nothing but diplomatic with people who were belligerent or ignorant or who just liked to give people a hard time. He told me without hesitation, that being put on hold was reprehensible. That it was like someone giving him the finger, and he wasn't going to take that kind of treatment any more.

I agreed that no one likes to be on hold; it's a waste of time to sit with a phone spewing out music you don't want to hear. But most people didn't react as he was doing, and, as the weeks passed, I was appalled to find him repeating the routine often.

Once, my own patience cracking, I said, "You don't need to go ballistic."

"Then you handle it." He tossed down the receiver and stalked from the room.

I certainly didn't want to make all those calls; it was enough walking a mile or so out of our way, to pick up mail forwarded from home. "Sorry," I said, realizing I needed to placate him, that something unusual was happening. That weekend we had planned to go to Kailua for the sand castle competition, and I didn't want to miss it. He enjoyed it almost as much as I did. Yet, as the days passed, it seemed as if a cloud hung over him, no matter how delightful the days. It was hard to describe the difference in him, even to myself. Sometimes I thought a gauze curtain hung between him and the world.

He continued to make the telephone calls, and like a detective, he ferreted out information. After we returned to the mainland the owner was forced to make restitution. But being on hold still bothered him to proportions that were ridiculous. Angrily, he changed our television provider when he was put on hold for a TV problem I didn't believe warranted a change. When the new provider put Hank on hold for some minor problem, I interceded. "Please, Hank, take it easy.

Scowling, he said, "You take care of it from now on," and stalked from the room.

Fixing the problem wasn't easy as someone had ripped off our credit card number and had run up large bills charged to us. In the process of getting the problem straightened out, our credit card company was late getting the payment to our television provider. There were calls and e-mails from the provider excoriating us. I had to sit on hold many times before I got it all sorted out. So I tended to give Hank some slack for his tirades when put on hold.

But I also began to suspect his actions could be the beginnings of de-mentia. The very thought disturbed me, for everything else in our life was great. We still went to the theater, to dinner, took part in freethought and political organizations, and saw friends, who for the most part, saw nothing amiss. And for the most part I said nothing about my growing concern. He still made sense in debate and used language in a superior way. I realized other men and women, in the privacy of their own homes, had aberrations of behavior, and they didn't inflate the problem by telling everyone about their worries. I mostly kept mine to myself. Sometimes they came out in a poem.

Spousal Adjustment

Dark words, taken from some deep realm
he cannot know, whiz by me. Denying
them a target, I pretend not to hear.

In memory, words of light pile higher than
spindrift on sand. Once we frolicked in surf,
made love instinctually, our leitmotif assured.

His eyes now filled with emptiness, remembrance
comes in waves bathing a reluctant shore.
Shrugging off the encroaching darkness of
his mind, I smile reassurance and offer a salve jar of
conjugal living and open a door we both can enter.

Twenty

"Abide with me: fast falls the eventide."

HENRY FRANCIS LYTE (1793-1647)

The next year I decided we should winter in Miami Beach instead of Hawaii. Putting time between the frustrations Hank had encountered there might be advantageous for both of us. Maybe in a different location, such things wouldn't happen and he'd be calm by the time we returned to Hawaii again.

It appeared to work. During the whole time we were in Florida, Hank showed few symptoms, gave me no problems, and we both enjoyed what Florida had to offer. But I also realized I had taken over and was planning our every move.

Neither of us had realized that South Beach was "the" place to be. The rich and famous showed up as well as others getting away from the snow and cold. We visited the everglades, Key West, and friends in Tampa. It was fun. When we took an Elderhostel trip centered in St. Augustine we learned that Florida and Hawaii can differ widely. That year Florida orchard growers had to get out the smudge pots it got so cold. I wasn't prepared to ride around in an open-air trolley in St. Augustine, but one of the men in our group had come from Montana or Minnesota and had two heavy jackets with him. One kept me warm for the few days it was colder than usual.

Back in Miami Beach the usual seventy-something days followed. All winter photographers' models posed on the wide sand beach on the Atlantic Ocean. Hank and I would take beach chairs and watch the models emerge from a travel trailer and pose where the photographers had set up their equipment. Sometimes on a walk, I watched models strike a pose in front of one of the art deco buildings that gives the area much of its charm.

Our condo, while small, had lovely touches – mica imbedded in the black stone countertops in the kitchen, white as well as violet rugs and pillows that complimented both in the tiny living room. But we had to explain to the owner that we needed more than one set of sheets and pillowcases for the bed. Still, the whole works was cheaper than Hawaii, and Hank seemed like the man I'd married.

During our South Florida days, we went to the symphony every time the program changed. We'd long been fans of Michael Tilson Thomas, the orchestra's conductor. During the rest of the season he led the San Francisco symphony. Once we took the train to Orlando to see friends from Sun City who had moved to Florida, all possible in one day on the high-speed train. We also flew to Puerto Rico for a week.

In all our years of travel, we'd seldom encountered life-threatening problems. Now, we did. Approximately half way to the island, the pilot announced we had to return to Miami because of electrical malfunctioning. Surprisingly, no one shrieked or cried out. Instead silence prevailed.

Hank said, "If it happens, it may be for the best."

Did he understand, for him, it might be a blessing? As the thought fought for purchase in my mind, he took my hand. I looked at him and another thought came: we'd had a marvelous life, seen exotic sights, had grand adventures and hopefully had done our share for humanity. "Yes," I said. I'd had a good life. If it happens, it happens.

We sat quietly, talking of the past until Florida's coastline appeared like a smudge below. As we landed in Miami I gripped Hank's hand and breathed a sigh of relief when the fire trucks waiting weren't needed. Soon we were in another plane and headed out again.

On the island, we hung around Old Town San Juan, loving the up and down streets and the colorful houses and great restaurants. We visited El Morro, the largest, most complex fort following the Christopher Columbus era. But the high point for Hank was going to Aricebo, where Carl Sagan had set up his search for Extraterrestrial Intelligence. I loved his enthusiasm. Yet, he had also done something he'd never done before. Formality in most things suited him. All his life he'd worn his shirts tucked in, no matter how casual the situation or how casual the clothing. In Florida, he wore his shirts out, began conversations with strangers and did other small things that were unusual. More than once my father-in-law's dementia entered my dreams. Walking along Biscayne Bay, past the huge yachts at dock, I knew a loneliness that I'd never quite experienced before. I had no one I could talk to about Hank.

As soon as we were home again, I spoke to my doctor. He suggested Hank accompany me the next time I came in. It was a great solution; I was sure he wouldn't go if the appointment were for him alone. But if he thought he was helping me...

Before the appointment day, as I fixed dinner, Hank came to me shaking his head and frowning. He looked as if something drastic had happened.

I turned from the stove, my own face going grim. "What's wrong?"

He confessed, for the first time in his life he'd made a mistake in his checkbook. It absolutely devastated him. Here was the man who said numbers were his friend, who looked as if he might cry over that one mistake.

He went to the doctor's appointment without an argument.

Our young, pony-tailed primary physician listened, nodded appropriately and then sent him to a psychologist.

I sat with Hank in her office and listened as she asked him asinine questions like, "Who is the president?" Didn't she realize he'd always know that. His disdain and impatience with her was apparent, and like a mother hen, I interceded. I know I said too much in an attempt to try to get her to understand the problem.

"I'd prefer to talk to your husband alone."

I wanted to protest, cry, explain that he was the most intelligent man I'd ever met. That, of course, he would know who was president, that it was not that simple. Instead, I left.

After that meeting, the psychologist reported it was too soon to make a diagnosis or prognosis.

In the meantime other things happened that frightened Hank immensely. For a long time he and I had been part of a philosophical discussion group that had started in Sacramento. Facilitated by a professor from California State University, Sacramento, it had run smoothly for years. When the professor died, attendance dwindled, other members moved, and it looked as if we would be forced to disband. Hank and I took it over, and the people we invited were faithful for years. When one of the members had trouble starting a sentence and stopped speaking mid-sentence, we all noticed, but no one said anything. It was apparent that he suffered from memory loss. One day he told us he had Alzheimers and would no longer attend.

Afterward, Hank kept saying, "Am I like that?" and went out of his way to do everything he had done before. He became so tired trying to stay on top of things, that one night he slept twelve hours. He had never slept more than seven in the years I'd known him. He was becoming exhausted mentally.

Our primary physician sent Hank to a neurologist who gave him a battery of tests and affirmed that he was experiencing mild cognitive impairment, early dementia. A six-hour test procedure with a psychologist specializing in neurology followed. The test usually takes six hours. Hank finished in four. The results showed nothing conclusive. We went on as usual, but little things kept happening, although nothing that seriously intruded on our lives.

At this time I had a landmark, 80th birthday, and planned two events, a week apart, one a party for friends and another for family. I worked hard planning a program and putting together a display of photographs and written commentary that read like a book covering my life in seven large framed pictures on easels. But, unlike celebrations in the past, Hank let me arrange everything. Various friends gave tributes, made jokes, read poetry or sang, and Hank spoke lovingly about me. It was gratifying, but not as gratifying as it would have been even ten years earlier. Although he helped coordinate the scrumptious buffet and made sure the catered food arrived on time, Hank had taken a minimum role in getting the party together. I was both proud of him and worried. Would I be able to help him when the time came?

For the family luncheon, we rented the solarium at Timbercreek Lodge, and with no little excitement picked up Steve at the airport, and my talented friend, Mary, from Seattle. At the same time Melanie, my dear niece and all her California family, drove up from the Modesto area. Hank helped with logistics and gave a lovely tribute to me at the lunch. If he was having problems, they didn't show, but again, all the planning was mine.

Some family members weren't able to make it, but Henry and his wife Chris flew out from Chicago, got a rental car and drove to the house. They made up for the absent members, and he and Chris, Steve and Mary spent a week with us. Although Henry's politics were diametrically opposite those of the rest of us, he seemed to enjoy every minute we were all together. During that week, Hank and I shared time with him and his wife alone. We also shared alone time with Steve who seemed more like the boy who had so enchanted me years ago. It was a most congenial and warm time. Mary began calling both Henry and Steve, "bro." I loved having all of us together, all of us seemingly interested in one another's welfare, and Hank basking in the moment, none of them aware of his problem.

After everyone was gone, Hank and I went to the Alzheimer's organization in Sacramento and came home with tons of literature and read it all. Although he'd never been a heavy drinker, Hank had liked a martini or highball of some kind after dinner and two or three times a week, wine with his meal. But liquor kills off brain cells. Reading that, Hank never again drank even a glass of wine. He was scared, although he never said so. In dementia tangles develop, synapses between cells get destroyed, and he didn't want that to happen prematurely. We learned there were many different types of dementia, but his symptoms, primarily memory problems, put him in the Alzheimer's category. Although nothing could stop the progression to complete senility, to the complete loss of any comprehension, to what Hank called a vegetative state, luckily, the disease moved slowly, and we could plan on several years of a relatively normal life.

But he had other ideas. He began to push himself, as if he could still accomplish anything if he worked harder. He took a power-point class, but never did anything with it. When I asked him why not, he said the teacher was not very good. With a sinking feeling I realized he hadn't understood what the teacher had said. A photography class followed with the same results. He crammed before getting together with his Spanish speaking group, and I never learned how he'd done during those years his mind deteriorated. He insisted on accomplishing tasks that had come easily to him before. Forgetting how to use various computer programs, he would work all day trying to figure out what he wanted to do. Sometimes after six or eight hours of frustration, he'd achieve success, but he could never remember how he did it, so he repeated himself often. If I tried to get him to leave whatever he was doing, forget it, read a book, watch television, go for a walk, he became stubborn. If I tried too hard to get him to relax, he got angry. I resorted to bribery at times, and sometimes that worked.

The doctor prescribed a medication that had proved helpful for some people, and for six months he was upbeat and seemed very much like his old self. Our mornings together were almost like they had been for years, both of us reading the local paper, and one of us, intrigued or exasperated by an article, calling out to the other, "Did you see this?" And then we'd talk, dissect the article, give our take on whatever it was, sometime one or the other of us changing our minds in the process. I adored those six months and could, for that time, forget he had dementia. We took short hiking trips, went to the theater, saw friends, went to Bend, Oregon, to visit our friends Marv and Kay. They had been early members of AOF. The four of us had much in common, and while we were in Bend, I told Kay about Hank's dementia, happy that it was not evident during our visit.

At home again, Hank's memory problems increased, but he continued giving talks at Sac State and in Sun City. Only I could see that his talks had gone from excellent to good, but good was fine with every audience he spoke to. Decline showed again six months after taking the new medication, little things happening frequently. He had to be "right" about everything. If he said the earth was blue and the sky brown, and I unwittingly said it had always been the opposite, he'd be angry. If I smiled at something laughable that he didn't consider funny, he'd wax sarcastic. I could see at some time in the ensuing years life was going to change drastically for me. I began to reach out more. We had always done things together, almost as if we were joined at the hip. Looking toward the future, I knew I had to find hobbies and events I could do alone.

With the backing of the Activities Department, I began giving talks at the lodge in Sun City, researching historical figures I felt would be interesting to most people. I had long attended and admired Peter Lorenzo's Speak Out Sun City talks. The ex political science professor spoke about world problems and then opened the floor to questions and comments. I would concentrate on fascinating folks in history, like Thomas Jefferson, John F. Kennedy.

I started with Maximilian and Carlotta and branched out from there, scheduling four talks a year, alternating months with Peter. I spoke about a host of people, events and happenings in America from colonial days till the present. The talks proved popular and propelled me into giving a poetry workshop that first year. Years earlier I had given talks at assisted living venues. Now, I contacted the nearest one, upped my fee, and again was scheduled to speak. That boded well for the future.

Joining a scrabble group, I loved the challenge presented by the game, and meeting new people I liked. At times, at home, Hank played the game with me. Once he learned the rules, he had no problem, except that he insisted IQ was a word. I tried to explain that it was an abbreviation standing for two words. With an insouciance that he might have smiled at in his earlier life, he maintained that the abbreviation was used all the time and thus had attained the status of a word. Admiring his quick wit, and rather than argue with him, upsetting him needlessly, when we played, we followed his rationalization. IQ became a word.

Twenty-One

"Not in the clamor of the crowded street, not in the shouts and plaudits of the throng, but in ourselves are triumph and defeat."

HENRY WADSWORTH LONGFELLOW (1807-1882)

In 2010 or possibly 2011, Hank promised to speak in September at the Mini-Forum at the Renaissance Society at California State University. All summer he worked at putting a talk together. As the air conditioner hummed during two weeks of over 100 degree F. weather, I saw the piles of paper on the floor next to his computer grow. One day I asked, "How's it going?" The nights were getting cooler; fall wasn't far off, and the fall semester would begin. He admitted he was having trouble.

"Can I see what you have?"

He had nothing. He couldn't remember what he'd done the day before and which paper was which. As August heat began to wane, with trepidation I suggested he cancel the talk. Reluctantly, but without arguing, he consented. The coordinator, who had no idea he had a problem, wasn't happy about it, making it plain she'd have a hard time finding anyone else at such a late date.

Hank didn't seem as bothered by the aborted talk as I was. Had he already forgotten it? He began talking about spending three months in Hawaii during the coming winter. We had done it once, but I had found it too long to be away. People we had enjoyed the previous year were gone. Members of the Humanists of Hawaii could not fill every segment of our social life. We had seen every tourist attraction, gone everywhere, knew where to go to attend local events and the only new events were visits from mainland friends.

Once Debbie, our pilot friend, had brought her husband Roland, and son Brett to Oahu with her. All of us went to Kauai for three or four days. But there was no guarantee that anyone would visit now. Marv and Kay had spent a week. Mary had come out twice, Melanie once. I talked against going for three months. Hank finally conceded. We'd go for two months instead, he announced, making it sound like his idea.

For our 12th winter trip, we rented a condo in the same building we stayed in the first year. But now life was grossly different. That first trip Hank had gone out the first night with twenty dollars cash and returned with cereal, milk and bread from the closest tourist store. After that, as I pointed out earlier, the next day Hank had all the bus lines memorized and knew the location of all the "regular" grocery stores. Now, during our last trip, when we started down the elevator to go grocery shopping, Hank didn't know what bus we had to catch. My heart thumped against my chest. In the dim light he appeared unconcerned. By now all my siblings were dead. I had no one to lean on except Hank and in small ways he kept going down that slow spiral that ended in complete senility. "The 2 or 13," I said and silently thanked my own memory for coming up with the right numbers. Although I had been making most plans for our life since the onset of his dementia, I suddenly realized I had to be responsible, not only for myself, but for him, too. It shouldn't have been that way. I had always seen him taking care of me toward the end of our lives; and he had, too.

It was the strangest two months we'd ever spent in Honolulu. One day half way into our stay, I went shopping at the Ala Moana mall. Hank didn't want to go, so I left him in the apartment. While most of the shops bore upscale designer names, a few, like Sears carried clothes tailored for Hawaii, tropical, sometimes with an Asian flare, well-crafted and more reasonably priced than Chanel or Dior. I found a few things I wanted and caught the bus home. I found Hank distraught. He had taken our laptop computer to be repaired.

"What happened to it? It was okay this morning."

"It's just no good."

"I used it this morning."

"Well, it's not okay now."

I tried a few more pointed questions, but he never made clear why he'd taken the computer in to be fixed. He said he'd left the computer at a geek shop on Beretania somewhere on the route to the university, but wasn't sure of the address.

I managed to say quietly, "Could you recognize the name in the phone book?"

"No but I can find it if we just walk up toward the university."

I put chicken from the freezer and vegetables from the farmer's market in a baking dish and stuck it in the microwave while I prepared a salad. Hank set the table on the lanai. Rush hour had begun below.

We ate in silence, the murmur of traffic lessening as the sun made its daily disappearance. I could almost set my watch on the appearance and disappearance of the sun – six-thirty to six-thirty. After dinner, the lights of Waikiki beginning to wink on, Hank began to speak, his voice bearing traces of bewilderment and embarrassment.

He told me he had been looking at pornography before the computer started acting up, and he worried that the police would be after him. He looked like a little lost boy caught with a Playboy magazine under his mattress.

As bewildered as he, I stared at him while I managed to say quietly, "Were you watching child porn?"

His head jerked in shock. "Oh, no, not that. I was looking at adults. After you left, I was lonely. Then the computer went haywire, and I took it in to the shop. Then I thought what if they find out what I was watching and they call the cops."

I wanted to cry. His innocent confusion shone as brightly as his disturbed thinking. "It's all right, honey. You won't be in any trouble." I reached out, took his hand.

"You sure?"

"I'm sure."

But trouble hit him anyway. He didn't drink enough water, became dehydrated and had trouble breathing. I had to take him to Kaiser.

It was far from an enjoyable two months. So often he sounded like the old Hank, and then there would be the aberrations. Whatever he thought was wrong with the laptop cost us two hundred dollars. We could have bought a new one for that. I was careful not to even suggest such a thing.

We went to the movies, but he was restless, again having trouble following the rapid sequences. He didn't want to walk along the beach with me. He no longer wanted to go to the rooftop to watch the Hilton's fireworks display. The look of worry on his face didn't go away.

Despiet that I contacted them repeatedly, the people working on the laptop didn't deliver it until the day before we left. I began to feel, but managed to conceal it.

At the airport, leaving the islands, I went through security ahead of Hank. Finding a chair, I sat down and was putting on my shoes when I realized he wasn't right behind me. I glanced back, and couldn't see him. People were everywhere. I got up and went back toward the gate and spotted him. He'd had some sort of trouble, losing his pricey belt buckle in the confusion. Seeing his semi-belligerent but little boy lost countenance made me want to cry out loud. I felt so sorry for him.

I returned home with an aching heart. But back in familiar surroundings again, life went on in an easier vein. Hank still went each morning to the fitness center. He still drove, seemingly without difficulty, forgetting routes now and then but able to correct himself. I told our friends Peter and Marilyn Lorenzo about Hank's condition. She has forgotten more about art than I ever knew, and in addition we had a lot in common. Keeping the confidence, they treated Hank the same as always, Peter using Hank to explain the science that occasionally popped up in Peter's talks. Although I feared Hank would someday look blankly when called upon, he acquitted himself well.

At the Renaissance Society, I was the only one who realized he wasn't as sharp as ever. It gave me a sick feeling. I got a sicker one when we visited friends we'd known since our days in Sacramento. I shouldn't have accepted the dinner invitation. A few weeks before I'd told her about Hank's dementia and she'd said, "Oh, I've never witnessed dementia from the beginning," as if it were a game she was eager to observe. I'd forgotten that when the invitation came, my own mind filled with all the things I had to do.

That evening, after we had admired her splendid garden, she passed around a tray of appetizers, and asked if we'd like some wine. She'd opened a new bottle of Bordeaux, but she had some white chilled if we preferred.

Through the living room windows I could see her yard, the flowers, trees, pool, spa, statues, potted plants, all enclosed in a "fence" of bamboo, the yard large enough to have mini climates. I said the red was fine. She turned to Hank.

He said, "I'd prefer a soft drink if you have one."

A look of amusement crossed her face. "Really, Hank, you always liked wine. What happened, get a bad bottle?"

"Nothing happened, I just don't want any."

"But why?"

"No reason," he said.

"Everything has a reason," she said in her best professorial voice. She taught at a local college, and our friendship had been full of intellectual discussions. "You scientists know that, I'm sure, one thing leads to another. So what is it?" she persisted. "What brings about this change?"

Hank looked confused and glanced at me.

"Do you have seven up?" I asked quickly. "It really goes well at times."

She looked from Hank to me and said in a dull monotone. "I suppose I can make lemonade. We seldom drink colas or things like that."

"Water will do," I said.

I blamed myself for putting him in such an untenable position. When we left, he said, "I don't want to go there again." We didn't. She was the only person I told who reacted in such a hurtful way.

I mentioned something about her a few days later, but Hank apparently had forgotten for he said, "Are we going there? I like to be on time." Throughout our married life, Hank liked to arrive at destinations early, I always wanted to be on time. We had learned to compromise. No longer did he arrive for social appointments a half hour early and I learned to enter a class, a get-together or party fifteen minutes early.

One day after we left a Renaissance symposium and were on the way home, he accused me of making him late to the meeting. That he couldn't hear a thing the speaker said. I was shocked. The seating was in the round and he was in a front row seat. I pointed out that no one sat in front of him and that we had arrived fifteen minutes early. Not really listening to me he pounded the steering wheel and accused me of making him late, that I had made it difficult for him to hear the speaker. "Well, didn't you?"

"No, I didn't," I said in a perfectly calm voice while my heart thudded. As he said a few more things, I managed not to argue with him, and after ten minutes or so, he quieted down and then a half hour or so later he turned to me and said "You never do anything wrong." His words were tinged with an element I couldn't describe, as if realizing he had erred and it saddened him. I can only conjecture, but I believe he had trouble following the speaker and this bothered him tremendously.

That night he admitted he was getting worried about the future. We were sitting in the family room, dinner over, the dishes, which he always cleared, rinsed and put in the dishwasher out of sight. Both of us sat on the couch. Having watched the News Hour, we were deciding whether to watch television or read. Suddenly, he talked about euthanasia, the Good Death.

I realized he was backing into another discussion about what he called The Ultimate Plan. Although I agreed with the concept, I couldn't agree with his plan. Early that day he had casually stated, as he started out the door on his way to the fitness center, that when the time came he'd stop taking his heart medication. "I'd have a heart attack and that would be it."

I had been aghast and stared at his back as if he'd lost his mind, which was exactly what was happening, but I couldn't comprehend it fully. Had he thought I was going to watch him die a horrible death, he clutching at his chest, me not calling for help? I was so shocked, I shouted, "Just a minute. You expect me to stand by while you fall to the floor and lie there moaning in pain? Haven't you got one damn thought for me?"

He swirled around, his face a study in confusion. "What?"

"Promise me you won't do any such thing."

For a few seconds, he looked as if he were going to argue, pout or get very angry. Then he swallowed and looking at me with the saddest eyes I'd ever seen, he muttered, "I'm sorry."

A few more seconds went by. I heard my bird clock sing the hour.

He looked down at the floor. "I just want to be in charge, be able to do some damn something."

"Oh, darling, of course, I understand."

He faced me. "You've got to know I love you."

He looked so sad and so serious I nodded and murmured that I loved him, too. If I hadn't I wouldn't have agreed with his plan to take his own life. But I could not contemplate seeing this highly intelligent man become a gibbering idiot. The thought of it bothered me as much as it did him.

After that he quit talking about nonsensical solutions, and life went on more or less as it had. If he thought about The Ultimate Solution, he didn't talk about it to me. I noticed, however, he was reading books about death. I said nothing to him; his whole demeanor said he wouldn't take kindly to any interference. By this time he never did anything without consulting his calendar. Occasionally, he forgot to enter something he was scheduled to do, but for the most part the calendar kept him on track. Occasionally, he checked for mail on Sunday. I always pretended not to notice.

I began going to a discussion group at the Roseville Martha Riley Library with the woman who had started the scrabble activities. One day Hank said he'd enjoy going, too. I was thrilled. He'd make an excellent addition to the group that had more women than men. He drove us over, made one or two cogent remarks during the discussion. Afterwards, as we left the library, he said, "It was good to get back there."

"You mean the library?" We'd gone only occasionally, checking out novels and DVD's, but it was not a place for research, nor did it carry the kind of books Hank usually read.

"No, the discussion."

"But this was the first time you were there."

"Oh, no. I remember everything about the man leading the talk, the type of discussion, everything."

I tried not to stare at him or say something I'd regret. Had his faulty brain merged two or three events? Did he mix up our home-based discussion group with the new one at the library? He looked so happy; it was I who wanted to cry. I said nothing more that day and let him elaborate about how thrilled he was to be back with the discussion group. I couldn't help thinking, with Alzheimers, care givers often died before their ill spouses

A few days later, fall firmly in place, the neighbor's leaves piling up in our yard, Hank asked me to check out whether the organization, Final Exit (FE), could help him. A member of the Humanists of Hawaii had brought our attention to the problem of attaining a Good Death. A member of the Hemlock Society, she explained that people with terminal cancer or other physical problems could control their own death and avert long-time suffering. The Hemlock Society had changed its name to Final Exit. We had belonged to the organization for years, not because we thought we would ever need their counsel, but because we felt one's final days should be one's own decision, not societies. While we had never attended any Final Exit (FE) meetings, either locally or nationally, we paid our annual dues and had no idea if there was a local chapter.

I sent a hand-written note to the national office. "What about someone with terminal dementia? Can you counsel them?" They answered in the affirmative.

We read their literature, and any other we could get our hands on. FE made clear that a person had to be in charge of his or her own death, that no one, neither a family member nor Final Exit volunteer could help. Anyone who helped could be charged with murder or homicide. Taking one's own life was not against the law, and it could be accomplished by breathing helium. Hank went to the local toy store and bought a bottle and put it in the garage. "For when I need it," he said. After a while, we hardly noticed it for life went on in satisfying ways as I ignored small abnormalities, let each day speak for itself.

Each Monday Hank got together for lunch with other scientists who were retired also, all men except one. One Monday they met in Sacramento, the next in Davis, the third in Roseville, and then the cycle started again. It was a congenial group. Not only did they speak the same scientific language, their belief systems were similar. None were theistic; none were Republican, but all were vastly interested in learning. New findings, new ways of looking at an object or subject was always fuel for discussion.

Occasionally spouses attended, and we all got to know one another. Twice Hank made his special Lasagna and had the group over to our place. Often we went to Galt to Jack's house for a picnic lunch.

One day when it was Hank's turn to host at a restaurant in Roseville, he never queried the loose membership about who was coming. He never reminded anyone about the date, and worst of all to him, he never showed up. He'd forgotten all about it until one person queried him by e-mail wondering if he was well. Hank said nothing more about it to me, but silently he brooded.

During that same month, we were on the way to a medical appointment, Hank driving. He'd always been an excellent driver, even managing to drive through Britain and Scotland on the "wrong" side of the road. He taught Steve and Mary how to back into a parking space and was proud when they backed expertly into our garage. He'd never had a ticket and never an accident or close call. Now, he attempted to merge into a right hand lane. But it wasn't empty. Luckily, the other driver swerved to the outside lane in time to avoid a collision. His quick action averted what could have been a lethal accident to me or to all of us. The car in the extreme outside lane also swerved to the shoulder so that none of us collided. Someone leaned on their horn as if to say watch what you're doing. The sound played in my ears long after it stopped. "Hank!" I cried. "Watch where you're going."

"I am,' he said. He didn't seem to comprehend what had happened. It was like he wasn't there.

Nothing else untoward happened during the following weeks. Thanksgiving came and went, Steve sharing it with us, Mary coming for a few days. We played games and took turns cooking and going out for dinner. Hank enjoyed that time as much as anyone. It was a fun family time, and we had had so few we had loved it immensely. Hank, too, had lost his natal family to death. We both enjoyed the "family" we had created.

Then, after years of being part of the group that went to the fitness center early each morning, Hank stopped going. I never knew why. Was it because he had trouble running the machines? Was it because he could no longer go as fast on the treadmill as he used to? All he said was it was easier getting his exercise walking.

I worried about his getting lost. All of the houses have attached garages in front and the many tiled roofs and Spanish style exteriors gave them an outward similarity. It could be confusing for anyone. I timed how long he was gone, and invariably began to worry when he was longer than an hour, looking at him closely when he returned for clues. Nothing was clear. If he got lost, he never mentioned it, walking for miles daily.

Throughout his life he had read the paper from front to back, in order. Gradually, he quit reading all the articles. Then he abandoned the New York Times crossword puzzle and had trouble finishing the local puzzle. The latter he used to say was for kindergarten kids.

He started spending hours playing Sudoku on the computer. In the past his bedside was filled with books on science, philosophy, religion, and travel. He also read scientific journals and popular magazines like Science, Scientific American, the Smithsonian, and the National Geographic. Now, he read only at bedtime and then only briefly. I think he read the same article over and over. My worries grew.

Twenty-Two

"We cannot tear out a single page of our life."

GEORGE SAND (1804-1876)

December 2012 began with obligations for me as well as parties. While I had always been the program chair, Hank had taken care of chairing meetings of our Humanists of Sun City group. Usually we had a holiday luncheon in December, and I hoped someone would volunteer to take over the event. No one did. I had to come up with a program for the luncheon,. Close to the day of the scheduled event, I finally decided to recycle some Mark Twain I had used years ago. I expected Hank to MC the get together as he had done in the past and he said he would.

When the day arrived, I said casually, "Do you have your announcements ready for the luncheon?" We would be meeting in the Solarium, and twenty some people had indicated they were coming.

Hank said, "I don't want to do anything."

"Okay," I said after a slight pause, knowing I had to take over. It added to the stress I was already feeling. If anyone noticed I was chairing instead of Hank, no one said anything, and if they remembered the program was a retread, no one said so. I learned that Twain can be enjoyed over and over. I also realized Hank could not be relied upon to do anything anymore. I had already conscripted friends to drive us places and told him they suggested driving us to medical appointments and other places I was afraid were beyond Hank's abilities. He still drove in Sun City and close to it, never suspecting that I was slowly taking away his driving.

From then on Hank did nothing for the Humanists of Sun City, and I added that to my already full plate.

At a Democratic Club board meeting I had suggested we hold our holiday party at the lodge. All organizations could use the ballroom facilities gratis once a year and we never had. Because I spoke out, I was put in charge. I arranged for a program, and with a committee, consulted and worked with the catering department months ahead of time.

That party was a task I didn't want. It was not a good time for me. My hip and back were giving me problems and my doctor had sent me for physical therapy, which I finally concluded was making the pain worse. He arranged for an MRI, but it wouldn't be until after the first of the year. To have a physical problem added to my worries about Hank and my obligations to the club became a bit daunting. I tried to back out of leading the Democratic party, but the president said she knew I had my ducks in line and wanted me to continue. I suppose I was the only one who wasn't looking forward to the celebration.

In December, 2012, the day of the party, when I woke, Hank was already up, fully dressed and sitting at the kitchen table, and he wore what I called his angrily stubborn face.

"What's the matter?" I asked, a frown developing on my own. The room was chilly; the furnace hadn't been turned up. Wind beat against the side of the house.

"I've been making too many mistakes," Hank announced.

I looked past him to the bird clock on the wall. It was 6:32. I'd slept in. My usual getting up time was 5 or 5:30. "What do you mean?"

"I mean it's time. I'm not waiting any longer." He glanced down.

That's when I noticed the canister of helium at his feet. The room began to swim, and I shook my head to clear it. "Hank, what are you saying?"

"I'm taking the helium today."

"Oh, my god," I cried. "You can't."

"Yes, I can. I can't keep doing the things I've been doing to my friends, to you, to myself."

"What are you talking about?" I stepped slowly toward him, hugging myself to stop the shaking that began inside. It didn't help that he hadn't turned on the kitchen light and only a dim light from the family room out-lined him.

"You know," he shouted. "They sat there and I never showed up! I never called, I never did anything."

Showing nothing of what I felt – my god, how could this be happening to-day of all days? I stood near the end of the table. "I know," I said, realizing he had probably been brooding for weeks over letting down his friends, repeating the words over and over again so they were foremost in his mind. "So you're going to take helium?"

"Yes, I can't wait any longer."

I took a deep breath. "Please listen to me."

"I'm listening." He tapped his foot on the floor, the sound reverberating in my head.

"I think you better rethink that helium business." My voice was even, betraying nothing of what I felt. How could I ever get through this day? "If you make a mistake, you may end brain dead but alive." I repeated what was in the literature. "It's necessary to have volunteers here who can watch to see that you do everything properly."

"I'm not stupid. I won't mess up."

"Anyone can. You forgot your friends, you could forget something now," I said, hoping he would see the logic. "You could forget some detail, goof, and then where would I be?"

"I have to do it now." He banged his fist against the table.

"And if you goof, you could be a vegetable."

He frowned.

"And I have to be up at the lodge no later than nine. Have you forgotten it's the Democratic party today?" Of course he'd forgotten. I wanted to cry. We'd been married now over 41 years; I was not young anymore. Always we'd thought I'd die first, that he would hold my hand at the end. It was still dark outside, our reflections showed in the bay window.

"I won't stop you."

"But you will if you insist on this. You don't even have all the equipment." I pointed to the canister as realization rose above the extreme stress I was feeling. Hank's thinking had disintegrated greatly. Although he had the canister, he didn't have the connections or the plastic hood that were necessary. "And stop giving me a hard time."

For the first time that morning he looked as if I had gotten through to him. "I never want to give you a hard time," he said, for the first time really looking at me.

I sat down near him and blinked back my tears. "Honey, I have to be there for the Democrats; so much depends on me. Or should I call and say I can't come because I have to be here with you?"

For a few seconds he looked startled. Then he shook his head. "No."

I waited a few seconds and then I asked if he had eaten. He said he wasn't hungry. I suggested he take his shower and get ready for the party while I had some breakfast. I was taking a lot for granted. I held my breath, but after a beat, he reluctantly said he would, but he had made up his mind. The end would come soon.

I watched him leave the room, waited until I heard the shower running. The shaking had started again. I wanted to roll up into a fetal position and just cry. But I had to be adult, capable, understanding. I drank a cup of tea and forced down a piece of toast. What to wear? Where was my folder with notes and times for this and that, names of people to laud? I couldn't think of anything but Hank's desire to end his life.

He had dressed and was sitting on the end of the bed just staring at the floor when I came in.

I pretended nothing was amiss and forced myself into the shower and into some kind of holiday clothing. To this day I don't remember what I wore.

Lorraine Talbot, who had taken on the chore of getting table decorations, was already in the ballroom when we arrived. I seated Hank at our reserved table and helped put the decorations around. The tables looked festive with red and green napkins at alternate places, creamy tablecloths. I wanted to scream, holler, but there was nothing I could say.

People came. People said hello. People placed their packages for homeless children under the tree with the winking lights, packages Lorraine would distribute later. I whispered what had happened to Marilyn Lorenzo who knew Hank was having problems. I don't think she really comprehended what I said or what I was going through. I had not elaborated, not stayed to hear her comment, just said, "Don't say anything to anyone." I had to get through the day.

Somehow I managed to stand in front of all those people, smile at the camera when my photo was taken and say something appropriate most of the time. The ballroom seemed to stretch to eternity, the stage behind me, decked out for the holiday season, a mockery of what should have been. No one ever caught on that I was at my nerve's end. But I knew. I kept seeing Hank and that canister. I realized all that had been was really coming to an end. The life we had made together was unraveling faster than I could think. When it was time to introduce the president of the club, do you think I could remember her name? No way. Among the other things I uttered, I finally said, "Let's all give our number one lady a big welcome."

It was an endurance test I never want to repeat. Fortunately, the veil hanging over Hank partially lifted during lunch. He went through the buffet line twice and even talked a little with the man who sat next to him. Had he already forgotten?

A few days before the New Year, I talked to Hank about what had happened. He showed little response, speaking only when directly asked a question.

He finally told me, "I'll let you know when to contact Final Exit."

A shiver of doubt ran through me. Would he remember? Would he be able to ascertain when the ultimate moment came or would he wait until it was too late? I wanted him to remain forever, but I knew it was impossible. He didn't want to degrade in front of me, and I didn't want him to. He had aged lately, worry showing on his face, but his hair still had no gray, and his body was lean.

At the same time my back, hip, and leg were hurting me tremendously. An MRI showed my spine was out of whack. The doctor put me on medication that didn't work. One night I ended up at the emergency room where they pumped me full of high-powered medication to bring the pain down to where I could handle it. While I routinely walked two miles a day for exercise, now I could barely hobble across the room. The doctor talked about a walker. On a scale of one to ten, the pain was now an eight. Melanie came to help take care of me. An epidural a few weeks later took the pain away before a walker became necessary. Soon I was back to walking my usual two miles a day.

We began a time when Hank and I talked about the past, when we went through old photographs, reminisced about trips we had taken, people we had known. I fixed all his favorite foods. We were very close, but it was the closeness of a mother and her child, or two very good friends, one the leader, the other the follower. He was exceedingly sweet. He had always had pet names for me, "Pretty" was one. During our stay in Seattle, he'd come in from work and call out, "Hey, Pretty, where are you?" In Sacramento he used the term "Precious," and that morphed into "Sweetie," in Sun City. Now, he began to tell me I was the best thing that had ever happened in his life, that he had become a better man because of me. I said it went both ways. We both had grown during our marriage. His words were heady stuff, but a month later, I mentioned a personal incident we'd shared, and he looked at me with a blank face. He'd forgotten. The early years that had meant so much to both of us had faded away.

During this time he liked going to the movies, a complete turn-around. Together we chose three he said he'd like to see. Two of them showed at the nearest theater complex to home, and we went and enjoyed, Anna Karenina and another film related to the classics. The third movie was at another venue, one we hadn't gone to for years. In the stadium seating, we sat half way to the top, getting seated before the lights went out and I'd have difficulty seeing.

The film had barely started when Hank said he needed to go to the rest room. Off he went, and I didn't think anything of his absence until more than ten minutes had gone by. I debated what to do. Should I attempt to leave in the dark? But what if I went out one way and he came in the other? He knew I was in this movie. A half hour and then an hour passed. My heart began to race. Was he out there on the street somewhere? I would have to contact the police, but like always, I had forgotten to bring my cell phone. The theater manager would have to assist me. I barely saw what was happening on the screen. Luckily it wasn't a long movie. When the lights went on, I hurried over to the wall and, went down holding on to the railing.

I found him sitting in the hall. "Oh, my darling, what happened to you?" I cried running to him.

He had forgotten the name of the movie, he had forgotten where it was playing. Looking for me, he had gone in and out of all the movies in the complex. "I didn't see you," he said. "I would never leave without you."

Again, it was one of those times when I wanted to cry. Like a good child he had waited for Mama. And yet no one would have recognized his deterioration, he still could converse intelligently, could bathe and dress himself and knew who everyone in his circle of friends and family were.

After that episode, he asked me to contact Final Exit. Without argument, I wrote to the main office and received a perfunctory letter in return. I felt let down, having expected some hand-holding reassurances. Didn't they realize what we were going through? Of course, they did, and it only took me a few minutes to come to that conclusion. But they weren't nursemaids. Their letter said they would refer me to someone in California.

A week or two of waiting followed. Then one day I got a call from a woman who listened with seeming sympathy to all I said. She told me everyone working in the Final Exit network was a volunteer. Most had had a family member die in extreme pain or conversely had sought out help. She explained she was an intermediary in the organization; that she would get me in touch with the proper people, but first Hank and I had several things we had to do. Hank had to see his doctor again, get the latest assessment. We had to send a copy of the doctor's examination record to her.

We made the earliest appointment available. It was three weeks away.

After the close call in the car earlier, I didn't want Hank to drive. Peter and Marilyn drove us. Hank thought it was nice of our friends to offer. He never suspected I had any part in it. We went out to lunch after the doctor's appointment and talked politics, Hank more adamant about his beliefs than usual, his choice of words left no room for compromise. All his life he had used compromise as a favorite tool. Now he was fervent in his beliefs.

It took a few days for the doctor's report to go through the proper channels. I sent a copy to my Final Exit contact.

Three days later she telephoned saying she had received the letter. Now Hank and I needed to write letters stating what was troubling in his life. I related the facts. Hank's letter was pure poetry. He said he couldn't conceive of putting me through what could happen if he hung around. He couldn't conceive of possibly impoverishing me if he needed to be put in a home. And finally he said he would rather be dead than ending up in the state that Alzheimer's sufferers finally achieved.

My contact said she'd never had such a beautiful letter from someone facing death. Too choked up by what she said, I could not reply. She said we would be hearing from another contact, and this would be for a telephone evaluation of Hank. They had to hear in his own words that he was capable of doing what he said he wanted to do. Our letters and the doctor's report made it clear what was necessary, but could he really do it?

A man called, and asked Hank a series of questions, and Hank answered in the affirmative to them all. The FE volunteer said we'd be hearing from another person, but it might be a week or so. There were not that many guides available. This one lived several hours away and, in addition to his volunteer work, had a responsible job and family. But he would be getting in touch with us.

I contacted Steve, Melanie, and Mary about what was ahead of us all, and they were all supportive, but like so many people, all of them voiced things they had heard. Wouldn't suicide be breaking the law? Wouldn't I be held accountable? I soothed all their fears, and they all said they definitely would be with him and me that final day.

Hank forbade me to get in touch with Henry. Since my 80th birthday party, he and Henry had exchanged E-mails. To see him, we had gone to Illinois, outside of Chicago where he and Chris lived, had seen their house, went to the Fermi lab with them and out to dinner several times. It had been a rewarding time. Once they asked us about religion, and we said we didn't care what religion they believed in as long as they believed in separation of church and state and allowed us our non-theist beliefs. They didn't really answer, just nodded and said, "Okay."

After that Henry's E-mails showed his Tea Party and religious bent. He had logic of a sort; if you believed his first premise, the rest followed. Hank responded with true logic, and suggested he and Henry not discuss politics in the future. The problem was Hank forgot what they'd agreed to do, and Henry, always eager to expound on his thoughts, gave Tea Party references and religious thinking.

As the years passed, the two repeated arguments they'd essentially thrashed out earlier, neither one believing the other and Hank not remembering what he'd written. As his memory faded more and more, unbeknown to him I read his and Henry's correspondence. I had never done this before. Hank never read or opened my E-mails and I never opened or read his, just as we had never opened the other's snail mail, sharing the news afterward, but giving each a sense of privacy. Now, I realized I had to intercede. I wrote to Henry that his father's memory was shot, and I'd appreciate it if he didn't write to him for a while. Henry agreed, although he asked nothing about what was wrong or how his father was feeling, what it meant for the future, nothing.

Neither Hank nor I heard from Henry again during those difficult days.

By now Hank had purchased and was reading Derek Humphrey's book about death and dying. We knew a great deal when the guide called and went over with us all the things the other FE people had said earlier. Hank had to do the whole thing himself, purchasing the helium and other connections and attaching the hose, putting the hood in place, turning on the helium and breathing it in.

What had sounded strange began to sound familiar. The FE contact said we'd need two meetings with him, one a sort of rehearsal, the next carrying out the plans. Because of his own schedule, it would be several weeks before he could come for the first meeting. Then it would be another week before he could come again for the final event.

I felt as if a stone had hit me in the chest. Would that be too late? Hank was obviously concerned, shaking his head. My heart beat faster, although I had never had any heart trouble, it seemed to be responding to my rapidly racing mind. It was already March, and for the most part Hank seemed oblivious to what he had planned, never speaking of it, indeed acting as if our life together would go on forever.

I called the initial contact and told her my concerns. She said she had another guide she'd get in touch with. A week later that one called. Her home was closer and she could arrange her life so that we could have the initial meeting one day and the final one the following day. She gave us four dates that she was available. I asked Hank which he would prefer. He chose the earliest date in April.

All those days were so damn hard. I loved Hank with a fierceness that comes only between most mothers and their children. He was the man I most admired, but he had become a sweet, trusting, adorable, exasperating child. I had trouble not crying every time I thought about it.

Steve arrived a week ahead of the day. He was quiet, more subdued that usual. Mary arrived later, her ebullient personality also subdued, and Melanie who hid her feelings behind accomplishments, arrived the night before Hank's ultra brave moment.

With Steve, Hank and I talked current events and spent those seven days going places, doing things, making Hank's last days as sweet as possible. One day we went to an expensive restaurant and blew the budget. Another time when we were out for dinner Hank ordered something omitted from his heart-healthy diet for years. Until Alzheimer's made it difficult, he had watched his diet "religiously." We both smiled when he told the waiter, "I'll have the Liver and Onions." We enjoyed one another's company, although I couldn't help thinking each time: this will be the last time we can do this.

Twenty-Three

*"Death always releases something like an aura of stupefication,
so difficult is it to grasp this interruption of nothingness
and to believe that it has actually taken place."*

GUSTAVE FLAUBERT (1821-1880)

The guide and her assistant came the afternoon of Friday, April 19. One, a professional dancer, had helped her mother during her final illness, the other, a former district attorney, had been with her husband when he took the Final Exit way out.

We talked and talked and talked, and never once did they spout religious platitudes. The women were sympathetic but businesslike, friendly but focused. Many times they asked Hank if this was really what he wanted to do. Each time he answered in the affirmative. He had purchased most of the supplies, leaving only a few to still get after the women left. They had told us the whole procedure would keep the family occupied all day; police had to be notified. They would come en masse. The family would be questioned, reports made out. It would take time It was best that Hank do what he had to do in the morning. "What time do you want us to return tomorrow?" they asked Hank as they moved toward the outside door.

The sun was shining but not overpoweringly, the temperature within the proper range for spring.

Without hesitation, he said, "Nine."

"We'll be here on time," they said.

I don't remember if Hank, Steve, Mary, and I went out to eat, whether we brought in take out. I know none of us cooked. I know that Melanie arrived before we went to bed. We – Steve, Mary and I – filled her in on what role we all would play the following day. Nothing else of that evening remains in my mind. I know I felt very tired and thought I would not sleep, my mind so full. But I did, and to my knowledge, so did Hank. I would have known if he were tossing and turning. I do know I woke up early and sensed that Hank was awake. "Honey?" I whispered.

"I'm awake."

"Did you sleep?"

"Yes. I'm going to take my shower now."

"Leave the shower running. I'll get in after you."

"Okay."

It could have been any morning, only earlier than usual.

We were in the family room and kitchen by four, when Melanie joined us. I started the water for coffee and tea, set out cups. Melanie got down the coffee. Hank shut off the house alarm and went out and brought in the paper. I could hear someone else stirring, and when I turned around, Steve had joined us. We had exchanged "Good Mornings," when Hank got his jacket. Mornings were always chilly, but not in the house.

"What are you doing?" I asked.

"Going for my walk." He seemed surprised I had asked.

I couldn't help worrying. Had he forgotten what day it was? Would he get lost? Should I stop him?

I whispered my concern to Steve.

"It's okay," he replied. "He's following his normal routine."

An hour later Mary was up and we were all fixing our own breakfasts, mostly cereal, toast, and fruit, when Hank returned after his customary three and a half mile walk. A week later, I found the slip of paper with street names and directions in his coat pocket.

After he ate, we all went to the family room. Hank and I sat hip to hip on the sofa, holding hands. Dawn had barely grazed the horizon as we talked about the news. We were all sipping coffee or tea, laughing occasionally, making lame jokes when Hank spoke of the distances everyone had traveled to join us, saying he appreciated it. It was our only reference to what lie ahead, but I'm sure it was uppermost in everyone's mind.

Mary was talking about her latest gig, playing the harp and telling stories at the Thumbnail Theater when Hank got up to put empty cups into the dishwasher.

I said, "You don't have to do that."

He answered, "I want this day to be as normal as possible."

I pressed my lips together hard. We were with him because he did not want to die alone, and this was the day my husband of forty-two years had chosen to take his life, April 20, 2013. His bravery was never disputed and the years we had spent together whirled through my mind like a kaleidoscope focusing on ever-changing events. As a scientist, a health physicist who loved to educate about radiation safety, a world traveler, a sky-diver, a hiker, a reader, a man who never passed a museum without going in, that he would succumb to a debilitating brain disease had never occurred to us until it happened. I'm sure genetics played a large role. As if he were explaining the stigma he'd first felt when he realized he had a problem, he had stressed to the FE guides that his father, his grandmother, and his uncle all had had dementia.

That last morning he seemed so normal I had to remind myself the disease could eventually lead to loss of speech, an inability to eat or walk, a complete oblivion of the man he had been. That in time he would not even recognize me.

Lately, I had been putting out feelers to selected friends. What did they think of suicide as an eventual answer to our problem? Some could not believe there was a problem. Hank was far too intelligent and logical for that. Others talked vaguely of getting in trouble with the law. Few knew anything about death with dignity. They had seen news and television shows about Jack Kevorkian who helped terminally ill people die. We certainly didn't want anything to do with Dr. Death, did we? Wasn't it sort of sleazy, and didn't Kevorkian go to jail? They talked about doctors in Oregon giving cancer-ridden patients drugs. Was that what Hank was thinking of doing? Taking an overdose of something? I wasn't sure I had gotten through to them

Again I reminded myself it was time for the end. In Alzheimer's a small Window of Opportunity exists. A patient who admits his problem, although memory-impaired, can still understand his or her difficulties. A month or two later, the same person might not understand. He or she might even think there was nothing wrong. Catching the proper time is a fragile balancing act.

During this sort of no man's land, I had to remind Hank of things he had to do. He kept forgetting to write the necessary personal letter to FE. After several days, feeling as if I were treading thin ice, I had couched my words carefully so as not to make him feel derelict but manage to show him the necessity of not delaying another minute. It was not easy and gave me temporary feelings of guilt. Reading a copy of his letter later, I cried, the wonder of our well-lived life encapsulated in his words. That week I also suggested Hank leave a suicide note. I wanted it clear that I wasn't in any way coercing or giving him the kind of assistance that would be against the law. Again, he kept forgetting, but mid-way in the week, he typed and signed a short, concise and perfectly lucid note.

Now, I watched him put the cups in the dishwasher before coming back to sit near me. A lull came in the conversation. I heard people on the street, their voices a murmur.   I glanced at Steve, he at me. The guides had asked, "Did we have neighbors who would suddenly "drop in?" It was imperative we would not be interrupted. Could this be the religious zealots who occasionally showed at our door, inviting us to services? Jumping up, I went to the front room to look out. Two people, on a morning walk, were passing.

"Come sit down," Hank said, setting the tone. He appeared so relaxed, I felt sorry I had showed my broiling inner self. His demeanor buoyed us all up. No one was maudlin; no one was angry, there was only a quiet acceptance. This is the deal that life had dealt us, and we would face it squarely. I felt incredibly close to Hank, and I believe he felt close to me.

At nine the guide and her assistant arrived. Once again we went through the procedure we would all follow. Once again they asked if this was what Hank really wanted to do. Once again Hank's voice rang without hesitation, "It is." They looked at me and then at the others. I nodded my agreement. The others followed suit.

The Guide proposed we all go into the bedroom where Hank chose to recline on the bed, fully dressed. Ahead of time he had placed two helium

tanks, connected by a hose, at bedside. Two tanks were necessary because
of the possibility one might be empty. It had never happened, but we could
not take any chances. On his bedside table he had placed Derek Humphrey's
book as well as his suicide note.

Hank said goodbye to everyone individually and then to all of us as a
whole. No face was dry as hugs were exchanged, but no one cried, no one
protested. The guides suggested we bring chairs for everyone. Steve hurried
to comply. I sat next to Hank on one side of the bed, Steve on the other. The
others sat at the foot of the bed. We all exchanged a few words with Hank
before he followed the routine he had practiced.

Pulling down the clear plastic hood, he made sure it was securely in
place before he reached down and turned on the valve. I felt myself wanting
to shout, not yet, not yet, but I said nothing. The hood in place, he turned
to me and said, "I love you." All he years of our lives together were encompassed in those words. I told him I loved him. We exchanged a look that
said it all and within seconds his eyes closed and he was unconscious. There
was no pain, no problems. He would never suffer the indignities that he so
abhorred. I would never have to see my very intelligent husband become a
non-person, a thing.

We sat quietly, watching. Within twenty minutes or perhaps a half hour,
Hank breathed his last. Steve, who had been monitoring him said. "I get no
pulse."

I don't remember the exact time, but the Final Exit team said a half hour
is average. With Steve's pronouncement, they left the room. My family saw
them out and Hank and I were together alone for the last time. I wanted to
say how grateful I had been for our years together. I was holding his hand,
and now I leaned forward, closer to him. I needed him to know how precious
those years together had been. "You will never be forgotten," I said, enunciat-
ing clearly, the words coming from somewhere deep within me.

His right eyelid fluttered at least three times as if he were trying to open his good eye and see me one more time. I was sure he heard me. I said that to the others when I forced myself to leave him and went out of the room. They said it had to be a reflex action, and reluctantly, I agreed. But a few weeks later I read an article about the brain during dying, that the very outside of the brain deals with emotions and can be cognizant after other parts of the brain have died. I believe now that he heard me, was trying to open his good eye, and my sharing our story is a way of keeping my word to him. He will not be forgotten.

Fifteen years before, for his 60th birthday celebration, I had invited friends and family to attend. Two of his now long dead sisters attended as well as two nephews. Various friends sang and gave tributes. I also wrote and read the following poem to him. On July 16th each year afterwards, I read it to him again, sometimes alone, sometimes with others around. He was 75 when he died.

What A Dance We've Had

Splendid tunes vibrate
the air, whisper the wind,
while a siren song of experience
dangles a promise of ever-
lasting, loving care.

Seldom faltering, we
shuffled through a
promenade before we
found the beat—two steps,

break, repeat—Cinderella
at the ball, the prince in
mufti, a concert we taped.

Seldom gliding to authoritative
rhythms, we whirled when others
dipped, free-moving, feet tapping,
minds soaring, thrilled with life's
essence, we waltzed into the future.

Oh, yes, what a dance we've had,
And the music's still playing.

After Hank died, I wrote the following:

Second Sight

You walked and foliage
crackled as you passed.
You swam and water parted.
Your vision stirred the air.
Once I was certain only
you could find footprints
in shifting desert sand.
But morning comes
again without your head
upon the pillow of our
marriage. I count waves

battering the shore. Will
you rise like Poseidon
from the sea? The sun
sketches a path through
cloud cover. How long
before I see without
the veil of the past

Addendum:

I wrote this memoir because I wanted the world to know how much I admired Hank's courage and selflessness and I wanted people to know there are alternatives to suffering and pain during one's final days. I had no idea when I started writing that to do justice to our story I had to reveal more of my own life than I had contemplated. But to make the story read more like a novel than a "telling of facts" it was necessary. I also found that while one can take charge of one's own life at the end, one can also take charge of it throughout one's life.

As the Final Exit Network website states: there were times when civil rights, women's rights and disabled rights were causes everyone was talking about. While we still must safeguard those rights, it is time to spotlight another. That is the right to control one's own death. We, not society, should decide when the pain and suffering is no longer bearable. I have never forgotten the title of a Jane Fonda movie, "They Shoot Horses, Don't They?" Why is it that animals are put out of their misery, but humanity is left to suffer?

Too many people have bought into the God myth, that the Lord giveth and the Lord taketh away. If there were a father-like god, like most fathers, he wouldn't want his children to suffer. The opposite type of father is the aberration. Today more and more people dismiss that biblical kind of thinking, but nevertheless a cultural bias exists. Unless we speak up, more and more of our loved ones will endure needless mental and physical suffering. Everyone should be entitled to a peaceful, dignified death. Concerned Americans need to speak out. At this writing the California legislature is considering a death with dignity bill. I was among the attendees at the first committee meeting and one of those who testified.

In the writing of this memoir, I realized once again I had shared a wonderful life with Hank and I wanted to share some of the highlights. In many different ways we had worked through the years to further secular thinking. Writing about our life, I realized we were very committed and very busy. We also shared adventures that I would never have experienced without Hank, and he without me. We complemented one another, he the scientist, me the creative "artsy" one. Although saddened by happenings that could not be helped, we lived the good life and felt lucky every step of the way.

Now, getting this memoir, ready for publication, I have to smile at some of my early attitudes. In 1970 the difference in Hank's and my age was of concern. What "the neighbors" would think was still taken seriously. Life has changed, not only for me but also for all Americans. My life has been good, and as I have said time after time…life is what you make it. I like what Hank and I made of our time together.

My historically based fiction can be found on Amazon. com under the name Cleo Fellers Kocol. The novels are: Fitzhugh's Woman, Cleopatra, Immortal Queen, The Good Foreigner, and the romance novel, Midnight Skies, written under the name, Crystal Barouche. In addition my work is found in the following anthologies: Riffing on Strings, string theory wedded to literary art, When Last on the Mountain, by women age fifty and older, The Women Who Walk Through Fire, science fiction and fantasy and Tahoe Blues short, short stories based on life near Lake Tahoe. Some of my stories and poems can also be found on various sites on the Internet. I also have several poetry chapbooks.

My poetry won various local, regional and national prizes. I recall particularly when my poem won the Artists Embassy International Dancing Poetry Contest. My poem was set to music and danced at the Palace of the Legion of Honor in San Francisco. In the audience were several fellow poets from Sacramento as well as our friends Debbie and Roland Roberge and Hank's cousins Bill and Virginia Gibson. After the presentation I was called on stage to take a bow, which I did dramatically, showing the elation I felt.

My Sacramento writing groups' books include those of :

Naida West. Her rich historical fiction about California is also available on Amazon.com: Eye of the Bear, River of Red Gold, Rest for the Wicked

Louise Crawford was the most prolific of my Sacramento writing buddies. She writes under the names Louise Crawford and L F Crawford. Her mystery, romance, fantasy, and dark fantasy novels are also available on Amazon. com: Blaize of Glory, Blaize of Trouble, Hat Trick, Fortune Cookie Karma, 12 Jagged Steps, Born in Blood, Memories in Blood, Dark Angel, Beverly Hills Voodoo, Bad Moon Rising, High Flying Love, Power of Love, Rhianon, A Witch for Good Luck, Trouble in 3-D, Jarad's Return, and written with Ramona Butler: Sabrina Says, and Jaded Hearts

Jay MacLarty, 1943-2010, Jay's thrillers followed the same protagonist. His novels are still available on Amazon.com: The Courier, Bagman, Live Wire, Choke Point

Made in the USA
Las Vegas, NV
19 September 2023

77837779R00203